THE PEOPLE'S WAR
Moray Memories of World War II

THE PEOPLE'S WAR

Moray Memories of World War II

Compiled and edited by
Pauline Taylor

Foreword by Air Vice-Marshal
George Chesworth, CB, OBE, DFC

Librario

Published by

Librario Publishing Ltd.

ISBN No: 1-9044406-49-0

Copies can be ordered from retail
or via the internet at:
www.librario.com

or from:

Brough House
Milton Brodie
Kinloss
Moray
IV36 2UA
Tel / Fax: 01343 850617

Printed in Times.

Cover design and layout by Steven James
www.chimeracreations.co.uk

Printed and bound by
DigiSource (GB) Ltd.

Cover pictures courtesy of John Rennie,
Peter Bruce and Ken Tuckwell.

Dedicated to all those who served at the Front,
and on the Home Front, during World War II.

Profits from the sale of this book will be donated to appropriate charities.

Contents

FOREWORD

PAULINE TAYLOR'S INITIATIVE in compiling the wartime memoirs of Moray folk, and those now living in the area, provides an insight into the experiences of people of all ages, from all walks of life, in and out of uniform, at home and abroad. This book is essential reading for younger generations who will have formed their impression of war from films and television and have little, or no, real idea of how the war impacted on their forebears. It demonstrates that World War II affected, in some way, the whole population in every corner of the land.

Some of these stories are amusing, others tell of horrific experiences of battle, wounds and captivity - all tell of disrupted lives and never to be forgotten memories. Pauline Taylor provides the reader with the opportunity to share, and reflect on those memories.

Air Vice-Marshal George Chesworth, CB, OBE, DFC.

Lest We Forget...

IT IS 60 years since the end of World War II: a significant milestone. The number of people who remember those dark days is dwindling.

I do not subscribe to the view that we should forget what happened in 1939-45; that the memories of war should be allowed to die with those who experienced them. We have a responsibility to keep alive the memory of the agony of war and its causes, so that we can ensure that it never happens again.

Many books have been written about battles, but few about the lives of those who took part, or who waited back home for the outcome. That is the purpose of this book: to record for future generations what war was like for ordinary people, whether at the Front, or on the Home Front.

Without the support of Air Vice Marshal George Chesworth, former Lord Lieutenant of Moray, this book could not have been compiled. I am grateful to him, for his encouragement and enthusiasm when I first suggested a book of Moray war memories; and for his wisdom and advice.

Thanks are also due to RAF historian Jim Hughes for his valuable contribution; to my colleagues at The Northern Scot for their tolerance – in particular Graeme Bravin, Bob Bruce, Mike Collins, Ian Gill, Chris Saunderson, Jan Scott and Daveena Thomson for their help.

But most of all, thank you to all the readers of The Northern Scot who answered the question "What did you do in the war?" so splendidly, contacting me with personal, occasionally funny, but often painful memories of World War II.

It has been a privilege and, in many cases, a humbling experience to listen to your stories.

Pauline Taylor, June 2005.

Ian McConachie

THE BIG PICTURE

Although it was the men who went off to fight in 1939, the people left behind at home also had a part to play in the war. On the Home Front they faced the threat of invasion; rationing and shortages; were entreated to 'Make Do and Mend' and 'Dig for Victory'...for one young boy, the world was about to change. Ian McConachie (b. 1927 d. 2005) was just 12 when the war started. He grew up to be a popular local performer, remembered in particular for his splendid pantomime dames. Ian had the talent and the opportunity to become a professional actor, he chose instead to remain in his home town of Elgin, but in addition to his performances in amateur dramatics, he also worked in the entertainment business as a cinema projectionist. His memories are reproduced with the kind permission of his family.

WHEN WAR BROKE out we were living in a part of Elgin which, unfortunately, has been completely eradicated. Situated between Roddie Gordon's close and the Elgin Creamery, which fronted South Street and Batchen Lane was 79 South Street.

I don't think I heard the actual declaration of war being announced by Neville Chamberlain - but I do remember my mother taking me inside and telling me that war had been declared with Germany. To a 12-year-old boy this must have sounded quite exciting, I suppose.

Life went on as usual, but gradually things began to change. For example the outbreak of war put the kybosh on the age-old tradition of 'eely oilin' at Hallowe'en. I can't remember if all the Elgin schools did this or if it was exclusive to the West End School, which was nearer the shops - but when the bell rang for the dinner break on the day of Hallowe'en the kids flocked en masse through the school gates and ran like the clappers down Mayne Road yelling like banshees 'Eely oil oil gies nuts - Eely oil oil oil

Ian McConachie.

gies nuts'. We rampaged on to South Street - very few cars on the go then - until we reached Batchen Lane where we made a left turn and bolted down the lane, stopping outside Harrison and Reeves Fruit and Vegetable warehouse. Completely blocking the road we repeated the eely oil oil chant over and over again until a man appeared bearing a basket of monkey nuts, hazel nuts, Brazils and walnuts. A great 'Hurray!' went up as he hurled handfuls of goodies into the midst of the cheering children. You can imagine the mad scramble that followed as we made a dive for the nuts scattered all over the ground, gathering up as many as possible with an eagle eye open for a Brazil or a walnut - especially prized items. When no more were seen to be forthcoming we all swarmed back up the lane, through the cross lane, and via Batchen Street to Culbard Street and the loading area of Gordon and McPhail, where more chanting brought yet another distribution of nuts. Having picked up all we could, it was back down Culbard Street, across South Street and down Mutch's Close, where another excellent response was given. Still not satisfied, there was one more stop to make - along South Street to Hall the Fruiterers at the head of Harrow Inn Close where the process was repeated - albeit on a smaller scale. After that, the happy gang of warriors dispersed to enjoy the fruits of their labours. I can't remember that ever happening again: food restrictions, plus other factors due to the war, ended the tradition,

Another change was the darkening of the town. In case of air raids no house, shop or streetlights were to be seen after dark. All houses had to have either heavy shutters closed or tight curtains fitted, and wardens would patrol the town to ensure that all premises were lightproof. No street lights meant that anyone who ventured out during winter nights did so in complete darkness, so a torch was more or less essential - and even this had to have its front glass half covered with black paper or card so only half a beam of light was given; and it had to shine downwards. Headlights on cars had all to be fitted with light shields so that just a small slit of light shone down in front, illuminating only a very short distance ahead.

Identity cards were issued to every citizen, as were gas masks, and both items were meant to be carried at all times in case of attack by the enemy. I remember going to a demonstration by the Army who had placed a canister of tear gas in the Gordon Arms Hotel and invited the public to stroll through the area wearing their gas masks to give them an idea of what a gas attack would be like. And many a one - including myself - came out with eyes streaming due to ill-adjusted gas mask straps.

As prior warning to an air raid a siren was fitted on the roof of the church at the top of Moss Street - later High Spirits pub - and the church itself was turned into a British Restaurant which served excellent 'no frills' meals for workers. It became very popular, with queues forming daily. All signs with the town name on them - be they road signs or shop signs - had to either be removed or painted over to make it difficult for parachutists or other infiltrators to know exactly where they were. The Elgin Laundry at New Elgin Bridge had its name in huge white letters on its roof and those, like many others, had to be obliterated.

In case of invasion, pillboxes began to spring up at strategic areas. These concrete hexagonal constructions were meant to house soldiers, machine guns, and other weapons as part of our defences. Many were extremely well camouflaged - one in particular stood at the roadside at a junction almost opposite the field in which the Eight Acres Hotel now stands. Excellently camouflaged as a cottage, it would have passed very close inspection. There are still one or two of these structures remaining. One was recently removed from Elgin City's ground, and there's another one in Morriston playing field.

To add to the war effort every bit of scrap metal that could be gathered was loaded on to rail trucks and despatched south, where it would be turned into bomb shells and bayonets and other machines of war. A prize target for this was the town's railings. I remember with sadness the removal of our railings at 79, which were plain-hooped affairs, while others in the town were more ornate. There were to be no survivors; they had to go, most of them never to be replaced, their positions still marked on the old dykes with lumps of lead where the railings had been. Everything went, house railings, church railings, along with the WWI tank which had sat in the Cooper Park for years, together with the field guns that stood guard outside the Drill Hall, and the ancient cannon which stood atop Lady Hill. All went to be melted down to aid the war effort. Not only railings, of course, but pots, pans, mangles, motorbikes and anything at all metallic, was rounded up and sent to the melting pot.

All of a sudden the town seemed to be filled with soldiers – Highland Light Infantry, Black Watch, Royal Engineers; all were billeted at Pinefield Camp, schools and other areas. One of the buildings in which soldiers were billeted was the Town Hall in Moray Street and I remember the day that ornate building burnt to the ground in December 1939. We loons watched its demise from the top of North Guildry Street and saw it reduced to a pile of rubble in a few short hours. The army got the blame for the fire but I don't think they ever really discovered the cause.

Not only troops, but also huge army lorries made an appearance on Elgin streets, and caterpillar-tracked Bren gun carriers made a fearful din as they slipped across the town's cobbled streets. I remember one poor lassie who was crushed to death by a carrier that swerved off its intended path.

Aircraft Spotting

A wide variety of aircraft now filled the skies above the town, flying from Lossiemouth and other local airfields. Hurricanes, Spitfires, Tiger Moths and that American Harvard trainer with its ear-shattering, rasping engine noise; Halifax Bombers, Blenheim and Wellington bombers and Avro Ansons and Airspeed Oxfords, distinguishable from each other by their wing tips: one having rounded tips, and the other square. Aircraft spotting now became a great thing with us lads, and one of the boys who lived at the bottom of South Guildry Street formed an aircraft identification group. We all met in an outhouse in his garden and learned the difference between British planes and foreign planes in case we were raided. He devised a sleeve band and a kind of uniform we should wear. I do remember that I was chucked out, either for not obeying the rules or because my family couldn't afford the grey jacket that was part of the uniform.

Waste paper was another valuable commodity for war time salvage with a call going out to collect as much as possible, and we used to go through the town pushing a huge barrow. Benzie and Miller, or Ramsays as it would have been then, allowed us to clear out the old paper from their cavernous vaults in the basement – well, they looked cavernous to us kids. We cleared out piles of paper ... old receipt books and papers from the year dot, and when our cart was full it was pushed down to East End School from where the waste paper would be sent for recycling.

There were many campaigns to raise money for the war effort. Backyard–concerts, dances and other ventures helped to raise cash for the likes of the Spitfire Fund, with a target thermometer in a prominent position in the town centre. At the same time we lads took part in the Government's Dig For Victory campaign and got stuck-in helping to dig up backyards, enabling people to sow and grow their own vegetables.

There seemed to be a great community spirit. A spirit of 'we're all in the same boat so let's get on with it'. Food rationing meant less to eat - at least smaller portions - but the diet was adequate and I can't remember hearing of anyone who'd died of malnutrition due to the rationing process. To us kids the biggest rationing disaster was, of course, the sweetie rationing. When you'd used up all your coupons and it was some time before more were due, you could only gaze into the sweetie shop window and wish. However mums, aunties and uncles were sure to come to the rescue and you'd soon be sucking a gobstopper once again.

My fondest memories of the war years were the many happy trips we made at night when my mother and I used to visit friends' houses. We would set out, often in the darkest of nights, with our torches and make our way to Bishopmill or New Elgin in the pitch dark with only an occasional flash of the torch. We would sing all the popular songs of the moment as we walked along: *The White Cliffs of Dover, Mares Eat Oats (and Does Eat Oats), Run Rabbit, Run, When the Lights go on Again, A Gordon for Me, Pack up your*

Troubles, Goodbyee, and others, until we reached our destination. Singing kept our spirits up in the darkest of nights....and also stopped other people bumping into us.

On reflection very little of the war seemed to affect my life as an Elgin youngster. The only moments of terror were when the air raid siren sounded in the dark of night, heralding an air raid. On those occasions my mother would put out all the lights and we'd sit by the fire in the dark listening for the throbbing noise of German aircraft and feel very real terror when the sound of bombs exploding was heard, even though they were far off. There were few air raids in the area, though some bombs and land mines were dropped at Lossiemouth and in the Elgin area. It was a great relief to hear the 'All Clear' siren.

The only other reminder of the horrors of war was when a relation was killed on active service and when my father, a sergeant in the REME, came home after being evacuated from France at the time of Dunkirk. I will never forget the filthy state he was in and the blank, exhausted expression on his face after all they'd been through to avoid capture by the advancing German army.

I also seem to remember that Elgin had a small prisoner-of-war camp situated on Lossie Green. I can't remember if it contained Polish or Italian prisoners, but each one had a large yellow circle sewn on to the back of his shirt or tunic and I can still, in my mind's eye, see the wonderful mosaic designs they created with painted stones at the entrance to the camp.

At the Playhouse

In 1941, I was 14 and left school to join the staff of the Playhouse cinema where I was employed as a page boy, showing people to their seats, selling ice cream and taking in coats and hats at the cloakroom...all for the princely sum of fifteen shillings per week (75p). Later on I became an apprentice projectionist. In those wartime days, escapism was the thing with Hollywood musicals high on the list of favourite films. One of the first I saw after joining the cinema was '*Down Argentina Way*' with Don Ameche, Betty Grable and Carmen Miranda. You got your money's worth in those days. For a small outlay you could watch a full feature film plus many 'shorts' such as the Three Stooges, Charlie Chase, Andy

Clyde, a Pete Smith Specialty, perhaps a colour cartoon, or one of those wonderful sing-along shorts with the fantastic bouncing ball that kept the tempo. And, of course, the newsreel, which tried to keep up morale by saying how well we were doing when in fact we were in dire straits.

The cinema, of course, had its own blackout problems and large wooden shutters were fixed over the front doors at blackout time. The same applied to the large windows on the emergency stairway, and it was my duty to see that no chink of light shone through.

In the event of the cinema being bombed and incendiary bombs dropped, the building was supplied by the national fire service with buckets and stirrup pumps. The tools for the job also included a special 'bomb grabber', which consisted of a long pole at one end of which was attached a crab-like jaw. The idea was that if you came across an incendiary bomb you would open the jaws of the unit by pulling on the ring, bring the open jaws smartly down on the bomb and snap shut, grabbing the bomb ,which could then be released into a bucket of water or sand. Fortunately no one had ever to try this idea out - not on a live bomb anyway.

Making Omelettes

The cinema boasted a large and very popular cafe and while food was scarce, it still operated. I'm not sure about the general food restrictions, but I do remember that when a further supply of eggs was needed it entailed a journey either to the food office in Moss Street or the egg packing station at the New Elgin bridge. Whichever it was, it involved using the cinema van, complete with a very large galvanised bath in the back. To avoid eggs being stolen and ending up in the black market, they were not allowed to be issued to restaurants in their shells, so the required number of eggs were cracked open and emptied into the galvanised bath which then had to be carefully handled and placed once more in the back of the van. Two of us boys had to sit in the back of the van holding and steadying this massive vibrating omelette as best we could as the van made its way back to the Playhouse. The eggs would be a-sloppin and a-slidin with, I can assure you, a number going over the side.

Another blackout memory concerns the then chief operator of the cinema who cycled to work each day and who was infatuated with a female member of the staff who lived in New Elgin. He decided to walk her home each evening when they were both on duty, and on these occasions I, as one of the apprentice operators, was delegated to walk a discreet distance behind the couple pushing the 'chief's' bike. God only knows why I agreed to this arrangement, but I did, and dutifully pushed the bike along the pavement because, even at the age of 15, I had never owned a bike or mastered the art of riding one - so push it had to be. The pushing ended at the gates where the path leads up to the old cemetery and the pair disappeared up the path after I was told to 'Stay there - I won't be long'. After a few nights, this began to get a bit boring so I took to pushing the bike further up the steep brae, then sitting on the saddle with my feet almost touching the ground and rolling down a short distance. After several such trials, I became more proficient and was soon enjoying my bicycle runs, going for longer trips along the road. On what was to be the final occasion, I was missing when the chief returned from his canoodling session. He had to wait till I returned with his bike and was far from amused. However, I must be one of the few people who learned to go a bike in the blackout.

Patriotism was to the fore in those days and in the cinema there was no mad rush for the exits when the national anthem was played at the end of the evening's performance. Everyone stood stiffly to attention until the anthem finished before making their exit and if, in the course of a film, it was played as part of the plot, the audience would gaze around and, as sure as fate, someone would stand to attention and the rest of the audience would follow suit and sit down again when it ended.

When the Prime Minister Winston Churchill was due to give an important speech to the nation on radio, announcing a victory or yet another impassioned plea for us to tighten our belts, we would couple up an old 'Wireless for the Blind' cat's whisker crystal set to the cinema's sound amplification system and, when the broadcast time arrived, the show would be stopped and the house lights raised. The manager would make an announcement and Churchill's speech was then broadcast over the cinema's sound system. At the end of it there would be a round of applause - the house lights would go down and the show would continue.

VE-Day and VJ-Day saw Elgin joining in the nationwide celebrations with parades, parties and bonfires in many areas of the town, bringing to an end an era which, hopefully, will never be repeated.

From 1945-48, Ian served in the Royal Corps of Signals. Posted to Germany, he saw the destruction retaliatory bombing raids had caused, with whole cities reduced to rubble and homeless children begging in the streets and at the railway stations when troop trains arrived. Later he was posted to Japan and visited Hiroshima, where he saw at first hand the total devastation caused by the dropping of the first atomic bomb only six moths previously.

Crowds turned out to watch Elgin Town Hall
go up in flames in December 1939.
The Northern Scot.

Ronald Shand

SURVIVING ANZIO

The Battle of Anzio began on January 22 1944 with the landing of 110.000 British and American troops in Italy. They took the Germans completely by surprise. However, instead of advancing, the decision was taken to consolidate the beachhead and the delay cost the Allies many casualties. Ronald Shand (b. 1919) is a veteran of both Anzio and Dunkirk. As a young man he was working on a farm near Buckie and joined the TA in 1937. The day after war was declared, he was in the army, and a member of the 6th Btn The Gordon Highlanders. He lives in Buckie.

I WAS SIX weeks training at Keith, then Aldershot and then I was put into the transport section. In January 1940 I was sent to France as part of the 51st Highland Division, and then I was transferred to the 1st British Division. I was stationed on the Belgian frontier and drove the Company Commander. When the Germans invaded Holland and Belgium we moved north of Brussels and took up our first defensive position on the River Dyle; we were there maybe three days – the Germans attacked after two days. Then the withdrawal started. Our vehicles were destroyed and we started walking down the railway line towards Dunkirk.

It was all well organised, but we saw some terrible sights: there were refugees everywhere, people on horses trying to get out, people lying dead in ditches. We took up a defensive position on the outskirts of the village of Bray Dunes. We night-marched along the beaches to East Mole at Dunkirk where we boarded *HMS Harvester*, a destroyer. We were among the last to get off. We got back to Dover and were sent by train to Porthcawl in South Wales where we were given a couple of day's leave, and then I rejoined the battalion in Lincolnshire. We'd lost a lot in France so we had reinforcements and new vehicles. We started training in coastal defence, mostly in East Anglia. We moved to Ayrshire in early 1943 and began training landing off ships; all the vehicles were waterproofed.

I was a Technical Corporal by this time and in March I and two others were sent to North Africa with a load of vehicles and stores – we had to make sure they were stored on board correctly and to do this we were actually signed on as crew. We sailed up the Clyde to form a convoy and set off for Africa – although we didn't know that was where we were going at the time. The ship was torpedoed about 400 miles off Gibraltar and we lost all the

Ronald Shand.

battalion stores and transport. We were lucky the torpedo hit us midships so there was no explosion, but the ship sank.

We managed to get into lifeboats; it was early morning when the ship sank but we were picked up that evening by one of the other ships in the convoy. It had broken down the night before and been left behind – the convoy never stopped to pick up survivors. The ship that rescued us was going to Algiers, but we weren't allowed ashore there until we could be transferred to a troop ship – which was going all the way back to the UK. We landed in Glasgow after being at sea for 14 days in total and were told to report to our Aberdeen HQ for survivors' leave. But when we got there you'd have thought we'd come from the moon. We were interrogated by Intelligence Officers to make sure we really were who we said we were!

I came home on leave, catching the 6pm train from Aberdeen. My brother was home on leave and arranged a car to pick me up at Buckie Station, but I was sound asleep and didn't wake up till the train got to Elgin. I set off to walk to Buckie, but as I got near

Lhanbryde a farmer stopped and gave me a lift. Arriving home, I got something to eat and went to bed, but the next morning people started coming to the door, wanting to know what I was doing home when the rest of the lads weren't.

We were told to report to Infantry Reception Training depot, then put aboard another ship in Liverpool…and off we sailed for Africa again. The 6th Btn was in North Africa, but we weren't allowed to join them. Instead we were put into the 7th Black Watch – it was just one of those things the Army did. After three days I asked for an interview with the CO, and was told there was no chance I could join the 6th Gordons, instead I was put into the 1st Btn in the 51st Highland Division at Sousse. The North African Campaign was just drawing to a close and we were part of the reinforcements. In July 1943 we invaded Sicily – a six week's campaign. About this time Italy capitulated.

Attacked and Driven Back

In October the 51st Highland Division sailed home to prepare for D-Day. My two friends were married and wanted to go home, but I asked to be left behind and join the 6th Btn in Italy, where I was reinstated as a Technical Corporal. In January 1944 we landed on Anzio Beach. There was no resistance when we landed and we went a few miles inland and just sat there…giving the Jerries time to get their forces ready. They attacked us on February 4 with tanks and infantry. The ground wasn't very suitable for tanks: it was a flat area that used to be the Pontine Marshes, but had been drained by Mussolini for fertile farming ground. There were dozens of waddies – dried up water courses - some six foot deep and impossible for tanks to operate. If you dug a trench the water would start coming in.

We were attacked and driven back about ten miles from the sea, and then we managed to hold them. The Germans never got any further. There were some shepherds around but most people had been evacuated. We had very heavy casualties. In our own battalion we lost 70 men and had many more wounded. Three companies were taken prisoner – there was nothing they could do but surrender. We were the only Scottish regiment in the division. The English lost even more men. There were 4,000 troops killed at Anzio, and many Yanks. There are two British Cemeteries at Anzio and an American Cemetery of 57 acres - the Americans buried all their dead in Italy there. I go back often, every two years, with an ex-servicemen's association: I also return to Dunkirk.

Anzio was just rubble when we left it in 1944, it has since been rebuilt, but they still have the narrow little streets. There is a Gordons' memorial, erected where we landed. It was refurbished three years ago and the local shopkeepers are going to look after it: they are grateful to us for what we did. The Germans were responsible for a lot of atrocities in Italy. A party of German soldiers were killed when a dustcart blew up, and their commander retaliated by taking 10 men for every German killed. They took then to the catacombs and machine-gunned 330 of them, then blew up the caves. We passed the spot in convoy and there were wreaths laid out. We stopped; they had just opened up the cave and had a search light, but all we could see was this mass of steaming rags. They took the bodies out and managed to identify all but two of them.

We went through Rome then up through the Florence area and spent the winter in the hills overlooking the Bologna Plains. By this time the war was just coming to an end and our division was pulling back, and we were sent to Palestine. We were three months in the Gaza Strip.

It was April 1945 when I was injured: my Bren gun carrier overturned; I had head injuries, and it took my nose off. I was in hospital in Cairo and they flew out the finest plastic surgeon in the world, a New Zealander called Archibald McIntosh who had worked on badly burned RAF aircrew, to operate on me. He had given a lot of airmen the will to live – he used to take them out to pubs and into civilian company, and make them go out. You always see someone worse than yourself.

I was transferred back to the UK and had various trimming operations in Edinburgh. I was discharged in 1946, got married, and started in the building trade. Then I took an agricultural course and became a farm manager.

My brother Walter, who lives in Fife, was also in the 6th Btn but transferred to Reconnaissance; my brother John was in the Navy and taken prisoner by the Japs. Our brother George was also in the Navy and was on one of the ships taking prisoners off at the end of the war. He asked to see the list and John's name was on it. They are both dead now. My youngest brother, James, was also in the Army and he now lives in Cullen.

William Cordiner

DAD'S ARMY

The television series 'Dad's Army' has made millions laugh, but the antics of the fictional Warmington-on-Sea platoon, under the command of Captain Mainwaring, weren't so very far from the truth, as William Cordiner, Elgin, recalls. A trainee engineer at the time, he has memories of the early days of the Lossiemouth LDV/Home Guard.

LIKE MANY OTHERS, I listened to Anthony Eden's broadcast appeal following the 9pm wireless news on the May 14, 1940, when France was on the verge of collapse. He called for volunteers aged 17 to 65 to form a Local Defence Force, which was of course to be unpaid, but would be given guns and uniforms. The following day on my way home from work, I duly cycled round by the police station, then adjacent to the town hall in Lossiemouth, and handed in my name as a volunteer.

I was directed to report to a retired Army officer, then resident in Prospect Terrace, who had taken on the job of overseeing the formation and training of the local force, and a few evenings later, I found myself, along with some thirty or forty others aged from 16 to 60-plus, doing basic drill in a hall in Clifton Road.

Initially there was absolutely nothing available in the form of equipment or uniforms, and civilian clothing was worn by one and all. At an early stage however, our civilian Identity Cards were rubber stamped with the words 'Local Defence Volunteer' in red, and as numbers grew, we were divided into sections and allocated strategic positions on local roads where we mounted guard during the hours of darkness, stopping and checking all vehicles and pedestrians. By that time we had collected a few air guns, along with one or two shotguns, and had been instructed in how to make 'Molotov Cocktails' (petrol bombs), and also in the 'art of concealment'!

DIY Winter quarters for William Cordiner (right) and his colleagues in the 2nd Tactical Air Force, Holland 1944 - 45.

One fine evening, on exercise a few miles out of town, we were required to conceal ourselves within bomb-throwing distance of the main road in the vicinity of the canal bridge, which wasn't too difficult as there was quite a lot of bracken and whins in the area.

One of the local brass, pretending that his open car was a tank, approached slowly, looking for signs of movement; apparently saw nothing, and was greatly surprised, when, at a given signal, we all stood up – brandishing our make-believe 'Molotov Cocktails'.

He congratulated us on our 'concealment', and told us to line up for a different type of 'cocktail': we were all given two pints of Murray's Edinburgh Ale from the crates in the back of his car. I had not previously rapidly consumed such a large quantity of beer, (he was waiting for the bottles), and so the telephone poles seemed to pass at an accelerated rate as I cycled home that night.

Some weeks later we got our first consignment of real guns – Canadian P.17 calibre .300 rifles – vintage 1914/18 – and before using then for guard duty, we were taken to the Lossiemouth rifle range on the Sunday afternoon and allowed to fire five rounds each. There were five or six targets, about fifty – seventy-five yards distant in concrete butts, and each man was paired-up with a colleague, and took his turn of firing, and marking the targets.

When marking the targets you took up your position in the butt below the target, raised the target on its pulleys, and when your colleague had fired his five rounds, you pointed out the position of each shot on the target with a long marking stick, and then lowered the target, and patched the holes with sticky paper, ready for the next man.

When preparing to fire my first ever rifle shot, the boy next to me, in trying to secure a comfortable position, apparently got some grit or sand up the spout of his rifle barrel, and on pulling the trigger there was an almighty bang, and his rifle virtually disintegrated – the barrel completely splitting apart from back-sight to fore-sight, and the stock shattering, sending pieces of wood flying in various directions. Fortunately, no one was injured.

When marking the target at the butts, after my colleague had fired his five rounds, a wide shot from another rifle sent a bullet through my marking stick, practically tearing it from my grasp, and demonstrating physically the force of a speeding bullet. The marker was in no danger, being below the level of the concrete wall. Unaccustomed to firing rifles, some of us found our ears ringing for about a week afterwards.

A few weeks later the name 'Local Defence Volunteers' was changed, and we were all issued with khaki-coloured arm bands with the new name 'Home Guard' boldly stamped in black letters.

In early October 1940, we were notified that we would be taking part in an Armistice Day Parade the following month, and that a supply of uniforms of various sizes was being delivered in plenty of time. The consignment finally arrived with only a day or two to spare, and we were told at short notice to report to the British Legion Hall that evening to collect our uniforms, consisting of cap, coat, tunic and trousers, puttees, and boots. We got there just as the key-holder arrived, opened the door, and switched on the lights. We all rushed in, and got a momentary glimpse of piles of coats, tunics, trousers etc. laid out on various benches.

At that instant however, the electricity supply failed, and we completed our kitting-out as best as we could in total darkness, being reluctant to lay anything down once acquired in case it disappeared in the darkness.

A Rum Bunch

We all came out with a complete uniform, but looked a pretty rum bunch when we assembled for the Sunday parade in Elgin's High Street, and there was frantic exchanging of coats, tunics etc., immediately prior to the parade. Being tall, my short cavalry type coat was a poor fit, and I was glad to swap it for a long infantry type of coat which was virtually covering the puttees and boots of a short colleague.

And so, into the dark nights and wintry weather of 1940, which became quite severe, with snow and ice and blocked roads. The threat of invasion now seemed less likely, and guard duty and road checks had been discontinued in the early autumn. Winter Home Guard activity became confined to weekly drills and outdoor exercises when the weather was suitable. We had acquired on old water cooled machine gun, as well as a Lewis and a modern Bren, and also a Boyes anti-tank rifle which fired .505 bullets, and these weapons were regularly stripped down and re-assembled.

By the end of the year some of the younger members, including myself, were facing 'call-up', or had decided to volunteer for the regular forces, and so, after seven and a half months in the LDV and Home Guard, I handed in my uniform – only worn for some two months – and moved south to acquire another one.

I joined the RAF and spent two years in Gloucester at station HQ, then in 1943 joined the 2nd Tactical Air Force. We spent 16 months training as a mobile unit, with the task of recovering front line aircraft, in preparation for D-Day, and went in on D10. We were recovering aircraft, which had been shot down, mostly Typhoon fighter-bombers, and were based near St Croix de Grand Tonne, overlooking Bayeau and Caen, which was still held by the Germans at that time.

We were working a 12-hour day, plus overtime, non-stop, and within six weeks had picked up 100 aircraft, repaired them, and put them back in the air. Our CO decided this should be recognised in some way, so he called us all together. He said: "I would like to give you all 14 day's leave; but that is out of the question. I would like to give you a day's leave, but that is also out of the question; but I can give you one extra hour in bed!" We really enjoyed that extra hour.

At the break out from Normandy, we travelled with the British 2nd Army and the Canadian 1st Army into Holland, where we spent the winter. We were still under canvas and asked for winter accommodation. The Germans had blitzed the airfield and as the buildings had been made of wood, there was plenty of wood lying around so we ended up building our own hut.

In 1945 we went on to the Crossing of the Rhine, and after the war ended stayed on for a year as part of the British Army of the Rhine. I was demobbed in May 1946.

George Carr

FROM DUNKIRK TO D-DAY

In 1940, Dunkirk was the defeat and retreat that Britain turned into a victory. 330,000 soldiers were evacuated from the beaches and lived to fight another day, many of them taken off by a fleet of civilian boats. Among them was Seaforth Highlander George Carr (b. 1918) who went on to fight in North Africa, where he was seriously wounded. He recovered in time for the D-Day Landings, but was again wounded. Originally from Newcastle, he lives in Elgin.

I JOINED THE 2nd Battalion The Seaforth Highlanders in 1940 after serving with the King's Own Scottish Borderers, and was sent to France. When we were told to evacuate there was a real panic on, with refugees blocking the roads to the coast; it was a most terrible sight. We were a few days waiting to be taken off, just hiding in the sands – thousands of us – as they could only take us off at night. I was eventually picked up by a minesweeper – I remember the captain telling everyone not to panic; he might have shot us if we had – and was landed at Sheerness. I'm surprised the Germans didn't invade Britain then; they could just have walked in.

In August 1942 the battalion was sent to North Africa; we were on a boat for about nine weeks. We were to take over from some Australians in the trenches. There were Middlesex machine gunners who'd gone off in a lorry and ran into a minefield and were blown up. This was about 200-300 yards from the German line. About 12 of us were sent out on patrol with stretchers to try to get them out – they had pay books and stuff with them that would have alerted the Germans as to who they were. We found them all right: we could smell the gangrene by this time.

We were coming back with the bodies on stretchers when someone must have stepped on an anti-personnel mine and I was badly wounded in the face, leg and stomach – it almost cost me my

George Carr.

sight. My life was saved by a comrade, Kemp from Forres, who carried me through the lines to safety. He was later killed in action. I was semi-conscious, but most of the others in the party were killed. I was flown to Cairo, where I had I don't know how many operations. I was there for about a month to six weeks, but transferred back before the fighting finished.

After rejoining the battalion, we went to Malta to prepare for the invasion of Sicily. It was during the invasion that Jock Mackenzie *(whose story is also recorded here)* and a lot of other comrades were taken prisoner: the Germans set fire to a field and captured them. The rest of us were sent back to Britain in 1943, I got malaria, but recovered, and then we started to prepare for D-Day – we didn't know it by that name then, of course, we just knew it was going to be something big.

I'd been at Dunkirk, but I'd never seen anything like this: the first wave had gone in and cleared the beaches and gave us an easy run, but we were being fired upon. After we landed, we just marched and marched, a good few miles inland. There was a lot of fighting going on ahead of us and the noise was terrific. As we advanced the shells were whizzing over our heads, thousands of them, and the planes were going in to bomb the German trenches. I was scared to death – I was frightened all the time.

We saw German prisoners coming back to be shipped back to Blighty, and there were dead bodies everywhere. I didn't think anything of it; I was used to it by this time. On the fourth night there was an air raid. The 2nd Seaforths were lying in a field not far from Caen; we hadn't had time to dig in when a butterfly bomb – a large bomb filled with smaller bombs – exploded nearby. I was hit by shrapnel – in the same leg I'd wounded in North Africa. I was taken back by ambulance towards the beaches to a field hospital.

The following night, under cover of darkness, I was transferred to an American tanker anchored off shore. I was carried below deck, where I found myself surrounded by wounded Allied servicemen…British, American, Canadian, and French. We sailed at night and landed at Liverpool the next morning. I was one of the first British soldiers wounded in France to be treated in the hospital there. I spent 14 days in hospital, and then went to the Lake District to convalesce.

I was later posted to Pinefield in Elgin, and I met my future wife, Eleanor Cumming from Burghead, at a wartime dance. We were married in 1946.

Rita Marks

NIGHTMARE BOMBING

Moray Tourism Forum chairman Rita Marks has lived in Ballindalloch, where she runs a bed and breakfast business, for the past 14 years. She has Scottish roots, but was born and brought up in Chelmsford, Essex – an area which endured many bombing raids during the war.

WE WERE AN ordinary working class family. I was born in 1939 and my sister in 1945 - my father being incarcerated in the Malta garrison for most of the war. My mother was obviously a 'good girl', not seduced by the glamorous Polish and American pilots stationed nearby. Perhaps the fact that she lived with her in-laws was something to do with it!

I have a vague recollection of my father home on leave at the beginning of the war. I remember him taking me out of my cot and holding me up to see the lights on the Christmas tree. These were real candles in tiny holders and were only ever lit for a few minutes at a time because of the danger of fire.

Because my grandparents were available to look after me my mother had to work during the war. Having been in 'good service' before her marriage she was somewhat intimidated by the raucous factory girls who poured out of their work place twice a day. She went to work in a grocery shop - Luckin Smiths. This was a chain of 'refined' grocers. Years later they were taken over many times and finally disappeared from the scene. All the staff referred to each other as Mr or Mrs or Miss. Customers were Sir or Madam. I loved visiting the shop as there was a network of overhead wires and the sales slip and money from each individual counter would be put in a tube and sent zinging across the shop to the cashier's office.

Our town was the focus of many bombing raids. Hoffmans were ball bearing manufacturers, crucial for armaments, and the other local factory was Marconi's, vital for radio communications and the fledgling radar system. Also, the main railway line to the docks at Harwich passed over a long exposed viaduct. All these were prime targets and the bombs fell night after night. One direct hit on Hoffmans killed the entire night shift of young girls. I don't know if I actually heard them screaming, or if I picked up on adult conversation, or if I just had an over active imagination but I had nightmares for years over this. The girls are all buried in a mass grave in the town cemetery.

Rita Marks in Trafalgar Square.

Our house was in the next street to Hoffmans and suffered bomb damage three times. The first two occasions just resulted in broken windows and an ominous crack in the brickwork. How I envied the neighbour's children who, when the siren went, trekked in an exciting way down their gardens to Anderson shelters with hot water bottles and flasks of coffee and torches. We had a Morrison shelter indoors. This was like a giant iron-framed table that my mother and I slept under in the dining room. My grandparents resolutely refused to leave their beds during air raids. Grandfather had fought in the Boer war and World War I, and Granny had trekked across South Africa in an ox cart, following the drum. No Jerry was going to get them out of bed!

Spoilt Rotten

The third time the house was hit was more serious. The gable end disappeared leaving Granny and Granddad, still snugly in bed, and quite unhurt, staring out at the street in flames. Several neighbours died. The ceiling collapsed on to the Morrison shelter. I don't remember being afraid: I thought it exciting when we were extricated by the fire brigade. I went for the rest of the night to a rest centre manned by the WVS and was spoilt rotten.

While the house was being repaired I was despatched to an aunt in Watford. A week later a bomb destroyed most of the next street. I was moved to the home of another aunt in Alton - and exactly the same thing happened. Whether my numerous relations decided, at this point, that I was a jinx, or whether my mother thought I was just as safe at home I don't know - but home I went.

With rationing food was short, but we fared better than most. Mum would not get involved with the black market but, working in a food shop, she was on the spot when commodities that had been in short supply made a rare appearance. Mum was a keen gardener and 'Dug for Victory' with a will. We also received, once a week, a parcel of fish and eggs from her parents in Lossiemouth. What a tribute to the wartime postal service those parcels were. The boats (all crewed by ancient great-uncles because 'the boys' were all in the Royal or Merchant Navy) would come into harbour at dawn. My granny or one of my aunts would smoke the fish in a little wooden shed in the back garden, parcel it up, take it to the railway station, and it would be delivered next day by the postman. Only once was the delivery delayed and the postman arrived holding a noxious package at arm's length!

I went to school just before I was four. It was a tiny Church School that only took pupils up to the age of seven. The first two classes were at either end of one big room and the bigger children had a separate classroom. Discipline was strict and we had to work quietly - essential with two classes in one room. The lavatories were outside, of course, and were just buckets under scrubbed wooden seats which the caretaker had to empty. We none of us found this strange: we all had outside toilets at home. In our house we had gas lighting downstairs and none at all in the bedrooms. We frequently had to go to the

Rita Marks with her Uncle Paddy' – airman Robert McClean from Northern Ireland, who was stationed at RAF Lossiemouth and married her aunt Elizabeth Main. Paddy lost his life at El Alamein and his son Robert, now living in Canada, was born posthumously.

school shelters when the siren sounded. No creature comforts here though. We were expected to continue with our lessons.

My mother took me to school, on her way to work, on a carrier on the back of her bicycle. We usually met up with another woman with her daughter on the back. I remember them cycling along the road once when a doodlebug came over and the engine cut out. Everyone knew this meant it would shortly come down. Instead of stopping while the doodlebug went on, my mother and her friend pedalled like mad trying to reach the school shelters, with two little girls screaming their heads off at the back. Eventually a lorry pulled alongside and the driver shouted at them 'not to be such daft besoms' and to stay where they were.

Each year on her holiday Mum would take me to visit her family in Lossiemouth. I have an abiding memory of piles of coffins being loaded into the guard's van at King's Cross - the bodies of servicemen being brought home. Passers-by would stop for a moment in respect and men would lift their hats. They all wore hats or caps in those days. We shared a four-berth sleeper, usually with young sailors or soldiers on leave - something that would never have been contemplated before the war.

Eventually peace came. I don't remember much about VJ day but VE day was wonderful. We had a party in the street with trestle tables the length of the road; mountains of food miraculously appeared as everyone sacrificed their rations; the milkman's horse gave rides. There were games for the children and the adults danced to a radio. I won the fancy dress competition as Miss Muffet, probably because of the petrified expression on my face. As a life-long arachnophobia sufferer, I was absolutely terrified of the toy spider dangling from my hat before my very eyes.

Laurie Brander

THE NAVAL PILOT

The Naval Air Branch, later known as the Fleet Air Arm, served in almost every theatre of World War II. It was instrumental in sinking the greatest tonnage of enemy shipping, and was one of the main weapons against the U-Boat. FAA aircrew were also adept at aerial combat, and had many air aces who received numerous honours – including Laurie Brander, Nether Dallachy. His father, the late Dr Thomas Brander, a Lossiemouth GP for 52 years, was one of the two doctors in the town during the war years and was responsible for the First Aid post at the old school at the top of School Brae.

THROUGHOUT THE WAR, night after night, there were Yellow or Red Alerts of air raids and my father had to be at his post waiting for the bombs to fall. When they did, (*the Luftwaffe dropped four high explosive bombs on the town in July 1941*) dead and injured were brought to him from Dunbar Street. They fell just at the back of his house, where he had left my mother in bed, but she was not hurt. We had good, thick bed clothes in those days and she was under them.

One of the bombs fell on Mrs Hay's garage at Redcliff next door: the ceilings came down, the windows blew in, the slates were ripped off - the house was uninhabitable and somewhere else had to be found for the doctor's consulting and treatment room. Arrangements were made to move into an empty house beside St. Gerardine's Kirk and my sister came from the London blitz where she was working for the Royal Free Hospital, then situated in east London, to help them move. Her accommodation was at Wapping, right in the docks area, which took a terrible hammering from bombs. Later she married and moved to a flat at Hampstead where she had her first child. But they had to run from the V1s and V2s to some kindly people in Hemel Hempstead who looked after them till things cooled down a bit.

But I knew nothing of this. I had joined the Royal Naval Volunteer Reserve in 1940 and was directed into pilot training which started at RAF Luton, a muddy field now Luton Airport, flying Miles Magister trainers.

We were accommodated at, but not in, the mansion house, Luton Hoo. Actually our beds were in the attics of the stables where the horses underneath kept us nice and warm and our meals were at the airfield canteen.

Then there was Intermediate Flying Training on Fairey Battle aircraft at RAF Netheravon on Salisbury Plain. I had a powerful dislike for the night flying because there was only one light to be seen, and that was put out when there were enemy aircraft about. We had to saunter around in the blackened sky watching the fuel gauge, hoping the light would come on again before it read nil. Then we had to steer a course from the light to find the very dim glim lamps on the airfield. Radios in those days were entirely useless.

Then it was back to the Navy for Advanced Training at Royal Naval Air Station, Yeovilton, Somerset, on Hawker Hurricane

Laurie Brander.

aircraft, and what a joy they were to fly after the stodgy old Battle. There we were also taught to land on a spot at the right speed in Fairey Fulmars - in preparation for the day when we would have to land on a deck.

Training had taken till the autumn of 1941 when I was ready to join an operational squadron: 888 Squadron of American Grumman Martlets, or Wildcats, as the US Navy called them. But I had never flown one or made a deck landing, so the Squadron Commander was not right pleased to have me joining on the evening before the ship left the Clyde for the Indian Ocean.

An aircraft was put ashore at Cape Town for me to do my first solo on type and again at Trincomalee in eastern Ceylon, or Sri Lanka as it is now. But there was to be no practice flying for me there because a powerful force of enemy aircraft carriers, we heard seven, was sinking merchant ships in the Bay of Bengal and attacks on the island were expected any time.

When they came, all the RAF Hurricane defenders were shot down and the place was devastated. More attacks were expected and I and a few other surviving pilots were ordered to fly Fairey Fulmars which had been hidden in the jungle and were intact. But the Hurricanes had done immense damage to the enemy bombers and their aircraft carriers had to return to the Pacific for replacements where eventually they met their match in the US Navy.

When it became quieter I returned to my ship, *HMS Formidable*, and was allowed to start flying from the deck. We provided air support for the occupation of Madagascar to stop the enemy from operating submarines from there, and there I suffered engine failure and had to ditch my Martlet, luckily being picked up by a British ship. I had a dose of fever and was sent to Colombo hospital to recover.

Meal for the Ants

Passage to Mombasa by merchant ship followed and I joined a group of Navy fliers at an emergency landing strip at Mackinnon Road near Voi in Kenya, left over from the Imperial Airways route from Cairo to the Cape. We slept with a rifle handy in case the bush animals were hungry, but the only damage was from ants – they ate the leather jacket my mother had given me. They left me the buttons.

Then I joined 881 Squadron in *HMS Illustrious* but she was heading for home, where we disembarked to RNAS Hatston in the Orkneys, staying there for most of 1943 but embarking in Carriers as required to supplement their fighter strength when doing North Sea sweeps. They were *HMS Unicorn, Indomitable and Furious*.

This last one had no funnel: gases from the boiler rooms escaped through vents aft on the Flight Deck. Sparks used to fly up from these vents and these could fly up the deck with a following wind. So it was that when I went to man my aeroplane I found it smouldering quietly! The fabric elevator control had caught a spark but it was quickly extinguished by the fire party and repaired by the rigger with a bit of canvas and some paint.

Our relaxation when at Scapa was at the club where we could buy some watery beer. The Orkneys had a glut of eggs and as a change from ship's food we could have our eggs boiled, scrambled, fried or poached. We could even have them hard boiled on the bar instead of crisps. It was from there that I sent an enormous crate of eggs by fishing boat to Lossiemouth for the Church of Scotland Hut where the RAF could get a fry up when needed.

Late in 1943 we embarked in *HMS Pursuer*, a converted merchant ship which never pursued anything – it had a top speed of only 16 knots. Our Wildcats did the pursuing and with some success. Escorting a Gibraltar convoy we were attacked by a force of Heinkel 177 bombers at dusk in the Bay of Biscay. Four of us flew, shooting down two and damaging two others. We had to land in the pitch dark and it was not easy; but we all managed. No ships were damaged.

Then we had a bash at the enemy battleship *Tirpitz* in a Norwegian fjord. We damaged her and she was eventually forced south within RAF range where they sank her with their much bigger bombs. Other attacks on enemy ships in Norwegian waters followed.

At D-Day we were there trying to stop the U-boats from getting into the Channel and I believe we were successful.

Then off to the sunny Mediterranean in August 1944 to attack shore targets before the landings there. My job was to direct the gunfire of British and US battleships against targets ashore. Others in the squadron strafed and bombed. We found the air over Toulon unhealthy from flak, but all went well, and when the army was safely ashore and heading north we went to the Aegean to keep up the pressure and it was there that I was hit in the petrol tank, but well done the Wildcat, it took me back to the ship.

Pursuer took us back to UK to prepare for the Pacific war but I was sent ashore to train pilots for that war.

Lt Brander RN also had a date with the King at Buckingham Palace where he was presented with the DSC in recognition of his success in intercepting the German bombers in the Bay of Biscay.

He later served in Korea as a Squadron Commander and ended his service with the rank of Commander.

Buckingham Palace: Lt Brander RN is pictured with his parents, Dr Thomas Brander and Mrs Brander, after being presented with the DSC.

Laurie Brander

THE BOX

When Elgin Museum was being renovated, the then curator, Susan Bennett, was sorting through oddments in the cellars when she encountered a tattered old cardboard box ripe for recycling. On a closer look she found it had been posted to Levack, 22 Rue Pierre Curie, Paris, by the Red Cross in 1945. She rightly decided the matter warranted further investigation. How did a box addressed to Paris in 1945 finish up in the cellar of Elgin Museum in 2001? The Levacks were relatives of Laurie Brander, and he answers the question with the following story.

THE STORY BEGAN at Rock House, Lossiemouth, the home of Mrs Levack, wife of a sailing ship Captain. She brought Bob into the world who, in due course, became a manager for Cables and Wireless, working in many parts of the world including the Pacific Islands. In the late 1930s he was general manager for the whole of France and living at 22 Rue Pierre Curie, Paris, with his French wife, Therese, and daughter, Minou, their son being at school in Scotland.

They did not run when Paris was occupied in 1940 because, Therese being French, they thought they could be useful to their friends and maybe to the British as well, like 'The Tartan Pimpernel', and Bob thought he might keep his business going, albeit under a different flag. But it was not to be.

Their internment started in the dungeon of Dijon Castle and continued at a pre-fab camp at Vittel in the Vosges Mountains. They could scarcely obtain enough food and warmth to keep body and soul together and their morale sank to the lowest when they received word, and they did receive mail slowly, that their son had been killed while piloting an RAF Catalina over the Bay of Bengal.

The occasional Red Cross food parcel was eagerly awaited and the food was equally weighed out among the prisoners. But these parcels were very slow in transit having to be routed via a neutral country, and the chocolate often crawled out to meet them when they opened the packet. Every piece was carefully allocated to a prisoner.

Rescued in an emaciated state in 1944 by Allied Armies, the Levacks returned to their ruined flat in Paris where Bob set about resurrecting his Cables and Wireless business. Paris was hungry; after four years of occupation food was scarce, so the Red Cross, knowing the situation, sent them another parcel in The Box. But Bob was ill and could not cope, so Cables and Wireless wisely sent a younger, fitter man to rebuild the business and the Levacks set about returning to Lossiemouth. Having no suitcase or kitbag to carry their meagre possessions, what could they use but The Box?

Bob died soon after returning home; Therese lived alone in Lossiemouth for many years, her daughter, Minou, having taken the veil and become a nun in Dumfries. Eventually she could no longer cope and Minou helped her into a home in Aberdeen. They had to empty the house of all the treasures they had collected before the war in their world-wide travels; some articles they wanted to give to the Elgin Museum; but what could they put them in? Of course, The Box.

And that is how a Red Cross parcel box sent to Paris in 1945 came to be in the Museum in Elgin, where it remains among the collection.

Allan Grieve

FIGHTING JAPS IN THE JUNGLE

After the fall of Singapore, the Japanese appeared unstoppable. They took over Burma, leaving the British to withdraw to India – and to plan its recapture. Brought up at Boharm, near Craigellachie, where his family were tenants on the Arndilly Estate, Allan Grieve (b. 1921) was senior fire prevention officer for Grampian before his retirement, and lives in Aberdeen. He is a volunteer at The Gordon Highlander Museum, Aberdeen. Proud wearer of the Burma Star campaign medal, in 2004, he decided to revisit Burma with his wife Isabel, and was taken aback when the young employee at the travel agents' enquired whether Burma was in Spain or Italy. The ignorance of youth inspired him to write his memories of one man's experiences in one of the most difficult arenas of World War II.

ON JUNE 1, 1942, the 9th Battalion The Gordon Highlanders embarked on the troopship Otranto from Shieldhall Docks in Glasgow: our destination unknown.

Ten days at sea, we received a communication to the effect that 'The 9th Battalion Gordon Highlanders had been disbanded and all personnel compulsorily transferred to the Royal Armoured Corps.' We became the 116 Regiment (The Gordon Highlanders) Royal Armoured Corps. We were to proceed to India where the regiment would train in tank warfare for the purpose of re-invading Burma to clear the country of Japanese occupation. This information was classified 'highly secret' and was not disclosed until we reached our first base in Sialkot, in the Punjab – now Pakistan.

Our arrival, after a five-day train journey from Bombay, was somewhat painful. We had been purchasing fruit and other foodstuffs from vendors on the platforms of the stations where the train had stopped. By the time we reached our billets over 50% of the regiment had 'Delhi belly': the local hospital had its busiest time on record.

Our two-month stay in Sialkot was a busy time. I was given responsibility for the exchange of all communications equipment from infantry to armoured warfare requirements. The task involved the carriage of heavy crates on a 500-mile train journey from Sialkot to the Royal Ordinance Depot at Rawalpindi, Northern India, with two transfers at railway junctions en-route.

Allan Grieve (middle row, second right), with local comrades in India in 1943. Pictured (front, left to right) are Lt R. Fraser, Dufftown; Capt. J. McGillivray, Archiestown; Lt A. Gordon, Elgin; and Lt J. Harper, Dufftown. Middle row: Sgt D. Stuart, Craigellachie; Pte F. Fraser, Dufftown; Pte J. Shaw, Tomintoul; Pte A. Keir, Spey Bay; L-Cpl E. McKay, Bishopmill; L-Cpl Grieve; and CSM R. McMann, Dufftown. Back row: Sgt R. Phillips, Dufftown; Cpl A. Gordon, Aberlour; Pte A. Gordon, Dufftown; Pte J. Fraser, Aberlour; and Cpl C. Thomson, Dufftown.

I had no knowledge of the language and little idea of the value of the local currency.

I was given a fistful of rupees with which to pay the local labour force to handle the loading and unloading operations throughout the journey. Having received their pay, the labourers loaded the equipment on to the train at Sialkot and unloaded it at junction No 1, whereupon they informed me that if I wanted the equipment transferred on to the train taking us on the next part of the journey I had better hand over some more rupees: my first experience of blackmail and extortion. Having no option, I got the equipment on board the train only to be confronted with the same demands at Junction No 2. I arrived at Rawalpindi completely broke. I learned a great deal about the Indian on that two-day journey.

From Sialkot the regiment moved south to Hyderabad State and Trimulgary, near Secunderabad. Towards the end of 1943 we took delivery of a fleet of Sherman Tanks – 35-ton weight – and it was with these that we confronted the Japanese forces in Burma.

Each of our tanks had a name painted on the side: 'A' squadron tanks were named after Scottish towns whose name began with A, e.g. Alford, Aberlour, Aviemore;

'B' Squadron chose hills and mountains: Bennachie, Ben Aigen, Ben Lomond; 'C' Squadron was cairns: Cairngorm, Cairn Toul, Cloch na Bein. HQ Squadron chose different names – the CO's tank was Cock 'o the North.

A Rum Hogmanay

Late December '44 we crossed the Burma Border and pushed on into the Kabaw Valley. A detachment of our drivers returned to Calcutta to collect a fleet of new lorries. As it was nearing Hogmanay we gave the drivers money to purchase whatever booze they could find. In addition to a brand new fleet of lorries, the drivers brought back a considerable supply of proof rum. Two days of celebration in a haze of rum vapours left most of us stoned clean out of our mind, with sore heads and stomachs for good value. The remainder of the rum was decanted into the fuel tanks of our jeeps: the vehicles never ran so sweetly.

Now it was time to push farther south through Burma towards Mandalay, Meiktila and Pagan. We had been engaged in skirmishes with the Japs along the way but it was in the Meiktila, Pagan area that our heaviest engagements took place.

The Armoured Brigade, of which we were a part, was constantly moving forward. Our only contact with the outside world was by wireless telegraphy. Our infantry support troops were drawn from the Indian Army, but for most of the time we had the good fortune of having Nepalese Ghurkhas. Without doubt they were most loyal and professional.

The Burmese people had no cause to love the British but they hated the Japanese more. As we passed through their territory, hill tribesmen from different clans would appear out of the jungle, pass on information about Japanese movements, strengths, and location of arms dumps, and then simply melt away back to where they had come from. Their intelligence reports were always accurate.

The Air Ambulance crews flew in, under very difficult conditions, to evacuate the wounded. It was not always possible to get everyone out on the day they were wounded. Dougie Barclay from Lumsden, Aberdeenshire, had both legs shattered when his tank was hit by a Jap 75mm shell at close range. He was taken to a field reception centre to await evacuation. He had no word of complaint; he asked for a glass of water and thanked the medical staff for taking good care of him. The plane scheduled to fly him out was held up due to bad weather. Said Dougie: "I guess they'll get me off tomorrow. I wouldn't like to be an Air Ambulance crewman – too dangerous a job." The next day he died.

At the start of air action one squadron, together with their tank protection infantry, would form the spearhead; the remainder of the regiment would deploy to give covering fire.

At a pre-determined time the forward squadron would disengage from combat and return to the rendezvous point where the regiment was to spend the night. The four squadrons would form a hollow square – a harbour – in which all other vehicles and personnel would shelter. Guards would be posted around the outer perimeter of the harbour to counter any attack by the Japs. In close jungle these attacks occurred frequently.

All vehicles had to be serviced and all cooking undertaken before sunset. No lights were permitted and a total silence had to be maintained during the hours of darkness. In the morning all preparations for the day had to be completed before the harbour broke up. Two trips had to be made beyond the harbour refuge. One was to retrieve the airdrop which would have taken place as near as was practicable. The other trip was to answer the call of nature. Being a mobile force no latrines were dug. Each man would move out, taking his rifle or revolver and his trenching tool. Normally everything was fine except when the Jap Air Force decided to take a look-see; then it was up with rifle and trenching tool in one hand and clutching your trousers in the other you went hell for leather back to the sanctuary of the harbour.

Our emotions were on edge many times, but never more so than when we had to cross the river Irrawaddy. Our 35-ton Sherman tanks were to be floated across on rafts. The river at the point of crossing was almost three-quarters of a mile wide. We crossed at night without the loss of one vehicle. Sadly we lost one officer, Lt J. Lindsay-White, to enemy machine gun fire; another officer, Capt J. Hughes, spent more than an hour in the water, clinging on to a raft before being rescued.

Safely on the eastern bank at breakfast next morning we dropped our guard; possibly the euphoria of still being alive had something to do with it. We were standing out in the open eating breakfast when we became aware of aeroplanes overhead. We paid no attention until one of the lads looked up and commented that there were strange markings on the wings of the planes, something that looked like 'round red discs'! Not a word was uttered but we were under our tanks for protection in double quick time. Old Nip missed a sitting target on that occasion.

The regiment was stationed at Pegu, 90 miles north of Rangoon, when peace was declared. At that time we were intercepting a considerable number of Japanese servicemen and followers wandering desolately back from the Arakan Front, having been deserted by their officers. The soldiers and the followers, some of them girls from the travelling Japanese brothels, were a sorry spectacle.

Although ragged, emaciated and filthy, they were still extremely dangerous. Many had live grenades strapped to their bodies ready to kill British troops if an opportunity arose.

The regiment returned to the UK in November 1945, and was disbanded shortly after. I had to 'soldier on' for a few more months until my demobilisation date in May 1946.

Peter Nicol

THE EVACUEE

Operation Pied Piper, the evacuation of thousands of city children, was the biggest concentrated mass movement of people in British history. Labelled like pieces of luggage, they were transported from the dangers of enemy bombing to the safety of the countryside. Edinburgh was one of the Scottish cities targeted by Hitler's bombers and many families chose to send their children away. Peter Nicol (b.1931), who was commercial manager with The Macallan before retiring, was a war evacuee. He lives in Elgin.

I WAS EIGHT years old in August 1939 when I recall one evening awaking some time after we had been in bed and heard my parents in the downstairs kitchen saying: "We have to get the children away." Not knowing what was going on, I returned to the room where my brothers were sleeping and said to them: "Mum and Dad are going to send us away". My statement caused some panic.

In mid-August Mum, my sister and brothers travelled to Denholm near Hawick and stayed in a farm cottage and then moved into Hawick – my mother and brothers in one house and my sister with an elderly lady nearby. I remember us all sitting around the radio on Sunday, September 3. It was a lovely day and Mr Chamberlain announced that Britain was at war with Germany. Mother, who was sitting at an open window, shouted down to people passing in the street the news we had just heard.

Mother had to return to Edinburgh with my youngest brother Ronald: my brother Derrick and I were boarded with a family in Hawick called Armstrong who had two sons about the same age as ourselves, and we became pupils of Wilton Primary School. We joined the Lifeboys (Junior Section of the Boys Brigade) and were there until late summer 1940. During this time Ronald, who attended the Tynecastle Nursery School in Edinburgh, and all the other nursery children, were moved to a village called Bowling near Galashiels, and my mother and other parents went along to look after them. They lived in the clubhouse of the local bowling club. I recall going up from Hawick by train to see my mother and brother and have recollections of swimming in the nearby river. My sister during this time stayed with relatives in Edinburgh.

One day after school the Armstrong boys, my brother and I were going home. We had to pass a large house with an equally large garden which had several apple trees and a pear tree. We all hopped over the wall and filled our school satchels with a few apples and pears. Unfortunately, when we hopped back over the wall onto the street a school teacher was standing waiting for us. He took it upon himself to take us home and conveyed to Mr Armstrong what we had been up to. The Armstrong boys received a whack, my brother and I, however, escaped with confinement to the house after school for two days, and were banned from attending the next Lifeboy meeting. On reflection, I think a whack would have been better.

Mr Armstrong worked in a woollen and tweed mill that had a shift working system. When he went onto the night shift, which started about 9 o'clock, we walked with him down The Loan and went into a small cottage. In the kitchen an old lady had large pans on the stove and at the open fireside. In the pans there was cooked tripe and for sixpence Mr Armstrong had his small metal container filled with tripe and a couple of boiled potatoes. This was for eating during his break.

Hawick like many small towns at that time had an unofficial greyhound racing track and the dog owners trained their dogs at a round mound called the Moat. They would ask you to hold the dog between your legs, grip the collar tight; they would then disappear round the other side of the Mound and when you heard the whistle you let the dog go. This you were asked to do several times, lasting up to more than an hour. In payment, the owner would give you tuppence to buy a bag of chips.

We returned to Edinburgh late summer 1940 as there did not appear to be any war activities that justified us being away from home. By mid 1941 the bombing of Clydeside and Leith Docks had started and I have vivid memories of going into the communal air-raid shelter with its wooden bunks, where we children were supposed to sleep, and listening to the anti-aircraft guns blazing away. My father, now a special constable, came into the shelter and pointed out a dent in his steel helmet where a piece of shrapnel had struck. Houses in the Leith Docks area had been bombed and a whisky distillery warehouse was also hit. I understand from the stories of older people that as the whisky casks burst with the heat of the fire the spirit was running down the gutters and people were scooping it up in all sorts of containers.

This prompted another evacuation. By this time the Edinburgh Council had built two residential schools south of Edinburgh near the village of West Linton, which consisted of large wooden buildings with classrooms. Each unit accommodated about 16 pupils; every unit had a house-mother and teachers. Mother and father visited at weekends. The school complex was about two miles away from West Linton and we walked to the village to meet the bus from Edinburgh. I recall seeing the bus coming down the road and starting to run as I was excited to see my parents. Rounding the corner of a house where there was no pavement I ran smack into the village policeman who was cycling past on his bike. He hit the ground with me on the top of him, however he was very understanding. A few days after the incident he came up to the school to see if I was all right. My brother Derrick, sister Jane and I were there until mid 1942 and returned once again to Edinburgh.

That was the end of my evacuation years and I was back again at Craiglockhart School, then onto Tynecastle Secondary School. Then the Government announced mid-1944 that it was no longer necessary to blackout windows. I was playing football for the school team and when we came out of the changing room we saw blocks of flats opposite. Instead of blackout windows there were red, blue, green and other colours depending on the colour of the curtains; also the street lights were switched on for the first time since 1940.

In October 1944, 16 pupils from Tynecastle School, along with two teachers, were transported to the Borders. We lived in the local church hall, sleeping on mattresses on the floor and were looked after by three lovely local ladies who reminded us of our grandmother. For three weeks we worked on farms in the vicinity at potato lifting. Working with us on the farms were Land Girls and Italian POWs. The girls shared their sweet ration with us and the Italians shared their lemonade. The farmers paid us a total of £1 2s 6d. It was a wonderful experience.

By VE-Day I was almost 14. The day and evening were spent at the Mound area of Princes Street. It is difficult to put into words the scene – people hugging anyone who passed; dancing to bagpipers; cheering and flag waving: something I will never forget.

On the July 21, 1945 (at the age of 14 years and 10 days) I started my first job as office boy in a travel agency and even then people were making enquiries how they could travel to Holland, Belgium and France to make contact with their old friends.

However restrictions on travel required them to wait a further year.

Eleanor Webster

HARD TIMES

Rationing meant a lean time for most people during the war years… but what if you couldn't afford even the rations? Eleanor Webster (b. 1933), Elgin, had to make do and mend more than most. She was six when her father went away to war, leaving her mother to bring up a young family; but she has many happy memories of those times.

DAD WENT BEFORE the war started because he was in the TA. He went out with the British Expeditionary Force to France on September 1, 1939 – I remember coming home from a walk just days before and Mum crying that Dad was going away. He went into the RASC as a driver. He was missing at Dunkirk for several days. The first we knew he was safe was when the postman, who used to open the window, shouted in 'Dick's OK' – it was a field post card. He came home on leave then went to the Middle East and we didn't see him again for three-and-a-half years. He was in Egypt, Lebanon and Syria, and then he came home on embarkation leave and went off to Normandy and D-Day. In six years we saw him twice.

Mum was left with six children under the age of 12, I was in the middle, to bring up on 37 shillings a week. Over a period of about 10 days her dark hair turned white. Her name was Elsie Donaldson and we lived in Gordon Street, New Elgin. Once Dunkirk was over I never really worried about my father. He was in the Middle East and it was so far away we didn't get news like you do today. My mother had a drawer full of letters from him; they were photographed to make them smaller to send, you didn't get the actual letters, and they were censored. Dad used to draw cartoons for us and we'd sit and read his letters over and over again. We'd never heard of places like Egypt and it was an adventure.

We had a hard time. At times we could barely afford to buy the rations due. My Mother used to sell our clothing coupons. We lived on soups – Mum would get what was called 'a bit to boil', or just bones. She'd buy half a calf's head to make potted meat or brawn, or half a pig's head. We grew our own vegetables: Dad had a great garden already going and we built a greenhouse to grow things. Right from the age of five I'd gone to the tatties with my Mother, but she did all sorts of other work. For a time she worked in the sawmill cutting backs – work which had been done by men before the war.

There were hard times during the war for Eleanor Donaldson (left), now Mrs Webster, with her mother and siblings: brother Bob and sisters Muriel, May, Jean and baby Pat.

Right from the First World War, there had been people singing in the street for pennies. We didn't have pennies, but Mum would take them in and give them soup – you never knew who you would come in and find sitting at the table. 'Forty Pockets' was one of them – called that because he wore so many clothes – and 'Tabby Hector' who collected cigarette ends, another.

The first Italian Prisoners of War worked at the sawmill and Mother brought them home for soup. They used to make rings out of Perspex from the aeroplanes and we all wore them. When Dad heard about the Italians he was annoyed because he didn't think much of them. We also went weeding carrots for Adam of Glassgreen who had German POWs.

Our clothes were bought at jumble sales. The biggest one was Jupp's Sale for Aberlour Orphanage. It was a two-day event. All the toffs donated clothes and we'd go up with a pillow case. Mum used to make things from old clothes – she made a skirt from an old coat. There was also the Shilling-a-Week Mannie who came from Inverness with a suitcase full of clothes. The only time we had new clothes was for Sunday best. We were poor but always clean and tidy. On a Sunday we'd get our hair washed in the big sink and put in rags to make ringlets.

Stewed Tea and Gulls' Eggs

People went to the gasworks to buy cinders; they'd take an old pram or wheel barrow, or just a sack across the bar of a bike. Mum would go to the woods where they'd cut down trees and cut the roots which were full of resin. We burned anything we could get. Tea was always in short supply so we'd make several brews from the same leaves. Till the end of his days my Dad always liked his tea stewed.

Sweets were rationed and on a Sunday at the beginning of the month there would be a queue at McKenzie's shop at the foot of School Brae. We sometimes joined them to buy Highland Toffee, Jersey Cream – a sort of tablet – macaroon bars and sherbet dips. Our ration books were spread around several shops so you'd get what was going. We never had a joint of meat, but our meals were supplemented by a lot of rabbits – my brother went out with ferrets - and gull's eggs, and there was fishing for trout in the Black Burn.

There was no such thing as Christmas dinner, but there was a dairy in Gordon Street and Mum used to help pluck the chickens and in return would get an old boiler which she'd use to make soup, then roast. I don't remember getting toys, but I was desperate for a doll. Mum used to bring sticks home and we'd make dolls from them while my brother would whittle aeroplanes.

I remember several plane crashes, at least three, and my brother and sisters were quite blood-thirsty about them. We'd hear them coming over and realise there

James 'Dickie' Donaldson.

was something wrong. My brother Bob would dash off on Dad's bike and was sometimes there before the crash. There was one went down on the golf course and you can still see the dent. My brother and his friends got there and found burned trees and bits of bodies all over the place. For ages after children went around with empty matchboxes with a hole in the bottom to push a finger through, telling everyone they'd picked up a bit of a body. Bob once came back with a pile of pennies welded together, the heat had been so intense. We were always coming back with bits of plane. You could have made a whole aeroplane out of the bits in our shed.

We used to walk to Lossiemouth in the summer; all the other kids went with us, and we'd have pieces with jam, if we had any, and carry milk in a lemonade bottle. I remember once an airman stopped, he had a little Austin car. He said he'd give Mother a lift, and the baby, but before he could stop us we all piled in – about ten of us.

In about 1940 or 41 they started school dinners. Gracie McDonald was one of the cooks at New Elgin, cooking in premises that I think are now the library. Meals cost 1s 10d a week, but after the first two children in the family, the rest got it free, although even that was a struggle for Mum to pay. We had two courses, either soup or pudding and a main course, and we had to eat everything. I've always hated carrots, but I had to eat them. We had 'frogs' eggs' – sago pudding – and semolina with a spoonful of jam in the middle, and sponge pudding with 'jam sauce', which was just watered down jam. The main course would be mince – we had a lot of mince – or fish pie. They were ingenious what they did with what they had. We were always hungry: we'd pinch swedes from Bilbohall Farm, take the tops off and eat them – we plundered a lot. I was a coward and usually kept watch while the others went after apples and such.

Albert Slorach was the headmaster, coming straight from university when the headmaster Mr Jamieson was called up. He was so dark and wore a pin stripe suit, we were sure he was a German spy!

In 1944, it was the 100th anniversary of the Co-operative movement – the co-op was in South Street where Munros' is now. They formed a choir for the celebration and it was so successful we gave concerts for the Welcome Home Fund; it was called the Co-opy Choir by everyone. I did my first solo in Fogwatt Hall and there was a piece in *The Northern Scot* which Mum sent to dad in Egypt. He wrote back that it was 'a hell of a long step from Fogwatt to Holywood!'

On August 6, my 12th birthday, I was at the Academy. They dropped the Bomb on Hiroshima, and that was the end of the war.

It took a bit of getting used to when Dad came home. We'd watch him shaving, fascinated, but we didn't like him sleeping with our mother.

Ian Webster

REMEMBERING THE FIRE

Ian Webster (b 1930, a former policeman, had a relatively privileged childhood growing up in Elgin, but one incident from the war years is clearly remembered.

MY FATHER HAD a tailor's shop, Websters, at 32 South Street, Elgin, and we were quite well off during the war. Dad tailored uniforms for officers and did alterations for the Army and the RAF. He was also an agent for Elgin Laundry and the forces sent stuff there. If anything went missing I was sent to the laundry (in New Elgin) to find it.

Bogs o' Main was a satellite airfield and there were several crash landings. We'd get on our bikes if we knew an aircraft was in trouble and race out there.

When the town hall in Elgin went on fire we got quite close. Just a week or so before my Mother had taken me to see the Pirates of Penzance in the town hall. My father was in the Auxiliary Fire Service, I don't remember him being at the town hall, but he was there when Gordonstoun went on fire. The fire station was on Old Mills Brae and as far as I can recall they didn't have a fire engine as such, but a tender pulled by a great Rolls Royce car.

A spectacular picture of Elgin Town Hall at the height of the blaze.
The Northern Scot.

Sandy Turner

THE AGGRESSIVE SPIRIT

Born at Auchnarrow Farm, Knockandhu, Glenlivet, in 1915, Alexander (Sandy) Turner served with the 6th Battalion TA The Gordon Highlanders before joining the regular army a couple of years before the war started. Of the 10 years he served in the Scots Guards, four of them were spent in North Africa, where he was awarded the Military Medal for bravery. He now lives in Tomintoul.

I WAS IN Egypt, in the desert at the beginning of the war. What I remember most is the sun and the heat...and the comradeship: in a battalion we were all friends; we looked after each other; our lives depended on each other.

We were bombed and shelled for weeks on end. We never got hit by our own side, but there was a saying: 'When the British planes come over, the Germans take cover; when the American planes come over, everyone takes cover.'

The food was just enough to exist on, but one day the platoon commander told me, as the sergeant, to take a section to a certain map reference to see if any Germans were on patrol. He added that we should also look out for anything that would give them a change of menu in the officers' mess.

When we arrived, two gazelles rose up: I fired a burst from a Bren gun and knocked the legs from one of them. Having been on a farm, it was nothing to me to kill an animal, and we hung it up on the back of the truck and bled and skinned it. A couple of the guardsmen said it was cruel and they wouldn't eat it, but they changed their minds later when they could smell it cooking. We ate it. It was lovely...and we forgot all about the officers' mess.

During leave, I went to Cairo and saw the sights. The barracks in Cairo were alongside the Nile and it was easy to reach the pyramids. It was possible to go right inside and see where the tomb was – the sarcophagus was empty and looked like a horse's trough.

When we were in Italy, a house had been taken over as an observation post and was being heavily shelled. We were dug in nearby and our officer said he was going up to see what was happening. The house took a direct hit. After things quietened down a bit I went up to the house. The door had been blown out and I looked inside: everyone was dead, lying there covered in dust. I went back out and was standing on the door – it felt a bit wobbly, and when I lifted it up there was the officer's head underneath.

Sandy Turner at Buckingham Palace after being awarded the Military Medal by the King. He is accompanied by his wife Margaret and brother Donald.

Sandy was in Damascus when he heard he had been awarded the Military Medal for 'complete fearlessness, great initiative and a really aggressive spirit' when leading a platoon in an attack on an enemy position at Taquo Plateau, Western Desert.

The citation continued: 'While going ahead of his forward section with another sergeant and one guardsman, Sgt Turner captured in succession two Germans and two lorries with anti tank guns and their complete crews. Though our own shells were falling close, he continued to advance and was engaging the enemy who were retreating when their main position, some 400 yards in his rear, was captured by his company. His bold advance was instrumental in the capture of the company's objective.'

My parents, William and Jane, were among many families in Moray who took in evacuees.

My mother and father took in a family of four boys from Musselburgh – the youngest not even at school. They were treated as part of the family and ate their meals with everyone else, but there were some evacuees who were badly used.

There was one family at Tomintoul took in two boys who were so unhappy they ran away – they walked 14 miles to Grantown before they were found. It was their job to empty the pot with scraps for the hens, and they would eat the food in it. There were others who enjoyed their time here so much that they came back to visit, and there is now a Braes reunion for those boarded out in the Braes of Glenlivet area.

Towards the end of the war my parents moved to Rhynie. Coming home on leave I stepped off the train and saw a girl leading a cow – she said she was in the Land Army, which I knew nothing about, and she was taking the cow up to be serviced, something she did every year. I said couldn't one of the men do it, to which she replied: "No, it's got to be the bull."

Betty Turner

THE SEASICK WREN

Betty Turner (b.1921) joined the Wrens in 1941, but never really found her sea legs, although she has happy memories of her war years. She now lives in Tomintoul.

I WAS WORKING in an office in Edinburgh when the war started. I felt I should do something, and I'd always had a notion to join the Wrens – I don't know why because I get sick just looking in the washing machine.

Because I'd worked on a GPO switchboard I was sent into the Signals and went to Evanton in Ross-shire, where there was a Royal Navy base and an RAF base for training air gunners. However, my fiancé was in the south of England so I put in for a transfer to try to be nearer to him – and got posted to Orkney.

I started to make my way to Kirkwall, but only got as far as Thurso. There was an oversight: my paybook did not have my photograph in it, and the north of Scotland was a very restricted area. I stayed in Thurso overnight so that they could arrange for someone to meet me at the other side, and the next day I went down to the ferry. It was my intention to write some letters during the crossing, but I'd never been to sea before and no sooner had we left the harbour than I began to feel violently ill.

I managed to get down below to a toilet, where I was sick, sick, sick. Eventually a sailor came and knocked on the door to see if I was all right. He said I had to unlock the door…what a sight I must have been! But he was very kind: there were no berths on the ferry, but he put me to lie down on his bed and brought me a cup of tea in a great big cup, it was like a bowl. I drank it and said it was like nectar. He said it should be – it had half his rum ration in it. So not only was I sleeping in a sailor's bed…but I was under the influence of alcohol as well!

When we got to Scrabster he had trouble waking me, but the

Wren officer was waiting for me at the top of the gangplank…what a beautiful sight she was; she was immaculate, and I was a mess. She was very kind, and got me into the car; whereupon I immediately felt I wanted to be sick again. The next I remember, I was in this big dormitory, aware of all these Wrens looking down at me; I must have looked dreadful.

I was two years on Orkney. We had really good Naval quarters, always lots of hot water and lovely food; and the people were wonderful. Then I got married and lived in Edinburgh.

I have very happy memories of Orkney and would like to go back, but I just don't think I could face the crossing again.

Nan Mavor

A FORRES TRAGEDY

On the afternoon of November 7, 1940, tragedy struck when an aircraft crashed into a Forres garden, killing all seven members of crew. Nan Mavor, now in Elgin, was working for her father, Adam Milne, in his shop in Tolbooth Street.

I DIDN'T HEAR the plane coming, just this great 'woomph' as it came down. I ran out and saw boiling black clouds with rosy red centres over the shop. I thought it was a house on fire at first, and then the bullets from the plane started exploding and zipping back and forth, just like bees. It was lucky no one was hit. The fire brigade arrived within minutes and quickly got the poor lads out, but there was nothing that could be done for them.

The plane, a twin-engined Whitley bomber, is believed to have taken off from the long defunct RAF Forres airfield – a training station for bomber crew at Pilmuir. It was said to have been trying to avoid the town and make for Roysvale Park when it came down in the gardens of Fern Villa, a block of houses. The backs of two of the houses were severely damaged, but no one on the ground was killed – and that was nothing short of a miracle.

There were normally children playing in the gardens – George and Caroline Nicol, Alan and Elizabeth Ross, and Jim Leiper – but that afternoon two of their mothers had taken them to Elgin, I think to see a Disney film, which was a very lucky escape. The plane must have nose dived into the garden at the last minute, it took up such little space, and it hit the ground with such force that I believe one of the engines is still down there, buried in the ground.

During the early days of the war I was considered by my father to be too young to go out with boys, but my friend, Amy Fraser, and I worked at the Townswomen's Guild canteen twice a week, washing dishes and clearing tables – doing anything. Miss Murray and Mrs Angus were in charge of the canteen, and we were always willing to stand in if anyone wanted a night off.

There were dances held somewhere or other most nights of the week: in the Town Hall, Drill Hall, Masonic Hall and People's Hall, but Amy and I were 17 before we were allowed to attend...and then just once a week – although we would often slip in for half-an-hour on our way home from the canteen. Charlie Campbell and his band were favourites – Charlie was a local hairdresser. The dances were always packed, with no room to dance, just to circle the floor. That was all right until some Canadian airmen came in with the jive – that cleared the floor and caused rows, and we thought there would be fights. The MC, Mr Stephen, called a halt one night, and the band and he went away and had a discussion. They decided they would give the jivers every fourth or fifth dance – he said these would be for the 'jitter-buggers only'. That caused a laugh because there was no swearing then.

The ruined buildings at Tolbooth Street, Forres, following the
Whitley bomber crash in 1940.
Courtesy of Arthur Grant

Once when someone was getting married, all the groom's pals were sent off on some scheme and couldn't attend. People had handed food in for the wedding, and no one wanted it to be wasted, so we were sent out with an open invitation to any troops we happened to see to come. On another occasion, the Townswomen's Guild gave a party in the Castlehill Hall, but again the troops were sent on a scheme and we were dispatched to see who we could bring in. I met this really nice New Zealander who came to be one of the family. Mother always invited everyone home – she did for them what she hoped someone would do for her own sons, and everyone I had a date with had to come home. If any soldiers were passing our front door, Mother would fill her big brown enamel kettle with tea and put cups in a basket and go out and give them a drink. Then the next lorry would come along and the kettle would be used again – same cups, no one minded.

Head of the ARP in Forres was G. R. Mackenzie. He was so top-notch in the ARP that when the war ended people were disappointed he never had a chance to put his training into practice.

There were huts for aircrew at Anderson Crescent and Macdonald Drive, and they used the small metal bridge at the ford by my home to go over, so we usually had lots of company home from the canteen – I persuaded my Dad there was no need to be waiting for me. One of the soldiers was from Aberdeen; he was in the Royal Artillery and was called Eddie. He came back a few years later after he'd been wounded to stay at Sanquhar House, which was a convalescent home. He went back to war, but was killed at Wadi Akarit – I saw his death notice in the paper. It was such a shame.

Everyone dreaded receiving a telegram during the war years. My father was also a postman, and when a dreaded telegram came telling of a serviceman or woman killed in action, the postmaster, Mr McMurray, would ask him to drive him to the address so that he could deliver the news personally. On the way, Dad would give him some family background, so that he knew the circumstances of the bereaved before he arrived.

This consideration was repeated in other towns: in Burghead, for example, postmaster Duncan MacKenzie always notified the minister of whatever church the family belonged to, and the pair would deliver the telegram together. Mrs Mavor's husband, Bill, who comes from Burghead, said everyone always knew when they saw the postmaster and a minister walking along together that they had a terrible duty to perform, and some heartbreaking news.

I was a member of the Girl's Training Corp during the war – I had hoped that this would eventually lead to joining the Wrens, but that was not to be. I was chosen by the Corps to represent Moray and Nairn at a big gathering in Gloucestershire. It was quite an adventure – we stayed overnight in Aberdeen, then travelled down by train. It was packed with troops. When we arrived we were put up in a village hall: we did tests and helped at a nursery school, and we challenged a local boys' school to a cricket match.

Late in the war, Amy and I cycled over to attend a fete at Altyre House, which had also been taken over by the army. There was a fortune teller – Jean the Batchie, who was well known for her psychic powers. She told me some remarkable things. I was already going out with Bill by this time and he had sent me a letter saying he would be home in the May of the following year, but the fortune teller told me I'd have a

Nan Milne, now Mrs Mavor, proudly wears her Girls Training Corps uniform; her brother Harry was in the ATC.

ring on my finger by September. She was right – they dropped the Bomb, Bill was home early, and we got engaged that September.

When the war was over, I remember the Sutherland boy, whose family lived over the shop, coming home. He had been a Japanese POW. They sent a taxi to bring him home from the station, and all the men from the shops carried him upstairs. So many people came to hand in things for him.

My own memories of the war are very happy ones, on the whole, and I feel guilty about that in a way, when so many suffered.

Norman Black

BUILDING BRIDGES

Norman Black (b. 1921) took part in 'Operation Neptune', code name for the navy's activities on D-Day. Some 4,100 Allied craft of all kinds were given the task of transporting the ground forces across the Channel, getting them ashore, ensuring the flow of supplies and communications, and taking off the wounded. Norman, who lives in New Elgin, sailed with 702 LCP(L) Flotilla from their shore base HMS Tormentor near Southampton on June 5, 1944.

I JOINED THE Navy the previous year; I'd been in a reserved occupation working for Elgin Central Engineers but, because everyone was in uniform, I persuaded my employers to let me go. I wanted to join the RAF, but the army and the air force had taken all the motor mechanics in the country and I had skills the navy were desperate for.

The LCP (L) (Landing Craft, Personnel, Large) was one of the smallest sea-going vessels in the Royal Navy during the war, and on this occasion we'd been given the task of providing smoke cover for the Allied Landings. There were 12-15 boats in the flotilla; we were ready to go the day before, and just sat in these small craft. It was a very rough journey and I was glad to see the French coast, I was so seasick.

I have a log of the whole operation, kept by a colleague, which records that we sighted the Normandy coastline at 5.40am on June 6, although we had seen the flashes of bombs and guns throughout the night. At 9.30am we heard over the radio that the invasion had started.

The flotilla was supposed to provide smoke cover for amphibious tanks, but in the event the tanks were never launched because the weather was too bad. We spent that first day and night laying smokescreens of chlorosulphonic acid as Allied cruisers bombarded the German positions and wave after wave of troops went ashore…all the time we were under attack. This went on day after day, with little respite, although on Sunday, June 11, the log happily records: 'wind south-west force 2. Sea Calm'. It wasn't to last: on June 18 we again had to endure gale force winds overnight and were unable to take on a fresh crew when dawn broke.

(As history now records, two artificial harbours, with the code name Mulberry, were constructed to facilitate landings on the Normandy beaches. Less well known are 'gooseberries' referred to in Norman's log. These were the Mulberry breakwaters constructed from 70 obsolete merchant vessels, previous amassed at Oban, sailed under their own steam to Normandy, and sunk in shallow water.)

Helping to keep the army on the move, Naval landing craft built bridges across major rivers as the Allies advanced through Europe.

The log also records a Liberty ship being hit by a mine; 'on fire aft; 200 missing'…that LSTs (*tank landing ships*), beached to unload cargo, were sitting ducks for shell fire until they were refloated with the next tide. Twelve were killed…that a barrage, started ashore at Caen, gave the smoke boats 'a warm time'…and that human torpedoes were spotted; two probably sunk. On Sunday, July 9, more than a month after setting sail for Normandy, we returned to the UK for a complete refit and some leave before resuming our duties.

In February 1945, 702 was about to be disbanded when it was

suddenly revived, became 821 LCVP Flotilla, and dispatched to North-west Europe for the final stage of the war and the Crossing of the Rhine. We were sent to Antwerp in *HMS Northway*, a Landing Ship Dock; we were shelled on the way. When we arrived at Antwerp we were welcomed by a buzz bomb and a rocket, close enough to be unhealthy. We spent three weeks there under V1 and V2 bombardment – one day they were coming over in streams and I thought the Rhine couldn't be worse than this. After launching trials we joined up with the army for the Crossing of the Rhine where, among other tasks, we combined with the Royal Engineers to construct a Bailey Bridge. The boats were taken in army tank transporters, so we had no accommodation and just had to get what we could, sometimes staying in farmhouses. We stayed in a Dutch home one night and heard that two Jerry spies had been caught wearing British uniforms...but it turned out the 'spies' were RAF officers.

US Rations

After Holland we moved on to the Elbe and joined up with the US 9th Army. There were about four or five of us and we went up to their depot for rations – they gave us enough for about 200 people, even chewing tobacco. We lived quite well; we were out in the countryside and one night had turkey and potatoes, peas, pears, jelly and tea for supper. There were also live pigs: we picked one up and sat it between us in the back of the car. It wasn't alive for long.

The US Army offered to commandeer a large house for flotilla accommodation, but when Lieutenant Stephens, our CO, realised that a German family would be turfed out as a consequence he refused to accept the accommodation. He was a New Zealander and a very nice guy.

We got a bridge across the Elbe but we weren't allowed to use it. The war in Europe had ended and the other side was now Russian territory. There were a lot of refugees trying to get across from the Russian side, but all we could see were these thousands and thousands of Russian troops and their horses – it must have been a cavalry regiment.

On May 23, 1945, we arrived at Ostend, and three days later boarded *HMS Oceanway* at 6am. We dropped anchor in the Solent at 6pm.

Men of the Navy's landing craft flotilla queue up for rations.

Among Mr Black's wartime souvenirs is a book published in 1944 advising service personnel – now almost assured of victory – on how to behave on German soil, particularly when in contact with civilians. Here are a few extracts:

The book warns against responding to hard luck stories: 'Some of them may be true, but most will be hypocritical attempts to win sympathy. For, taken as a whole, the German is brutal when he is winning, and is sorry for himself and whines for sympathy when he is beaten.'

Of Hitler's success in gaining power: 'It seems strange that such wild ideas could impose on a European nation in the 20th century, but woven into Hitler's doctrine are many deep-seated "complexes", such as hatred of the Jews, a desire to domineer over others and a readiness to believe that they themselves are being persecuted.'

The nature of the Germans: 'When you meet the Germans you will probably think they are very much like us. They look like us, except that there are fewer of the wiry type and more big, fleshy, fair-haired men and women, especially in the north. But they are not really so much like us as they look.'

What the Germans think of us: 'The British do not work so hard as the Germans or take their work so seriously...But on the whole the Germans admire the British.'

About sport: 'The Germans have only taken to sport during the last 30 years, but they are keen and capable performers. They learnt most of their sport from the British. Soccer is the most popular game, but it is played less vigorously than in Britain...'

And a warning about the women soldiers might meet: 'Numbers of German women will be willing, if they get the chance, to make themselves cheap for what they can get out of you...Most of them will be infected.'

Norman Black (right) with members of crew as their landing craft is loaded up ready for land transportation.

Roderick McIntosh

THE GUNNER

Roderick McIntosh (B.1918), Elgin, is a Normandy veteran. He worked in the timber trade before the war and had married his wife Nancy in 1939. He was working at RAF Kinloss putting up hangars when the war started.

I WAS CALLED up in 1940 to 136XZ Battery - rocket guns – and after being in Orkney for a time went to Clydebank. It was bad there. There was a big shake up, and awful bombing.

I volunteered to be a ship's gunner in the Maritime Regiment, probably because my brother Angus was already in it, although I aye fancied a ship.

My first posting was on the Stranraer to Larne ferry, transporting American troops. They were a good crowd and I remember they came off the boat singing 'A hunting we will go'. My next posting was to the *Empire Rider*, a merchant ship going all round Britain with cargo. I remember later being told by a Burghead fisherman that the boat had been captured from the Germans, but I don't know if that was true. Then I was posted to the Liberty ship *Saminver*.

Liberty ships were designed for 'Emergency' construction by the United States Maritime Commission and were named after prominent Americans. The Saminver was on loan to UK - one of many.

So far, my war had been uneventful, but that was to change. We went into Normandy four hours after the first landings on D-Day, taking troops, supplies, tanks - everything. We saw a bit of action then. We knew it was the invasion. Planes were going over dropping silver strips to mix up the radar, and you couldn't see the sea for ships. Back and fore for weeks we went, and not much sleep. One night, coming back from France, we lost seven ships in a convoy of 15. Flares went up and we were easy targets for the U-boats. We speeded up - we were supposed to stop for the pilot to come on board when we reached the docks, but we just went right on in.

When we were loading up we'd hear the fly bombs coming over. One fellow said: "If that engine stops then it's going to hit us". The engine stopped and I thought that was it, but it went into the water.

When the V-bombs were hitting London, I was in barracks, housed in Nissen huts at East Ham. We were in bed, covered by our great coats because it was so cold, when a V-bomb just missed us, but it blew both ends of the Nissen hut out - the blast just went straight through.

The biggest surprise of the war happened one day when I was looking out of the barracks window and saw my brother - we ended up gunners on the same ship. The saddest was getting a telegram to say my brother Joe, in the Black Watch, had been killed in Crete.

Roderick McIntosh, his wife Nancy,
and their son Roddy.

BACK YARD CONCERTS

Children were expected to do their bit for the war effort: Chrissie Stewart, now Mrs Mitchell, Garmouth, held back yard concerts in the garden of her grandmother, Mrs Elizabeth Milne, High Street, Lossiemouth.

I'M SURE WE weren't the only children to do concerts, but I remember in 1941, when I was 13, raising £8 5s for the Minesweepers – we probably chose them because most of the local fishermen went into the Navy, and the fathers of a couple of the girls and my uncle were in the Minesweepers.

War time back yard concert players: (back row, left to right) Chrissie Stewart (now Mrs Mitchell), Etta Stewart, Mary Taylor, Jean Stephen, Elma Smith and Mildred McKenzie; (second row) ? Stewart, Jean Laing, Betty Stewart, Helena Grant, Muriel Foules, Isobel Cairns, and the boys Peter Stewart (Chrissie's brother) and Jim Ainsworth.

We had a silver collection – which meant the least anyone could give was a silver 3d – and crowds would turn out. Granny would supply some chairs; there was a garden seat, and a wall to sit on. Granny had an old stone wash house, where we would practise, and we'd hang a pair of red curtains on the washing line.

I'd organise friends – some of us were in the same class – and their brothers and sisters. We'd sing songs, recitations, my sister Betty would play the cello and I'd give a violin solo. Some of those involved were my brother Peter, Etta Stewart, Mary Taylor, Jean Stephen, Elma Smith, Mildred McKenzie, Jean Laing, Betty Stewart, Helena Grant, Muriel and David Fowles, Isobel and John Cairn who came from Glasgow and were billeted up here, Pat Stewart, Irene Gilbert, Isobel Finlayson, Marjorie Allan, Marjorie Taylor, Jim Ainsworth, and the Cameron brothers from Elgin.

I also played with Kim Murray's Strathspey and Reel Players: we made recordings for the radio six times, performing in a hall in Lossie Wynd in Elgin…each time the composition of the players changing as more and more young men were called up.

All in their Sunday best: some of the children who
performed in backyard concerts.

William Sim

THE ROAD TO ROME

William Sim (b. 1919, d. 2004) wrote an account of his wartime experiences not long before his death, and his daughter, Mrs Irene Black, Elgin, has kindly allowed me to use extracts. They show that, even in the midst of a World War, and thousands of miles from home, it is possible to see a well kent face.

IT WAS A Friday, September 1, 1939. I was cutting corn with the horse and binder on my father's croft and when my mother came down with my afternoon tea she said: "I'm afraid you will soon be away, there is talk on the radio of declaring war." Being a member of the Terriers (Scottish Horse) we would be liable for early call up, but little did I think I would be away that evening. We had to report to the Drill Hall at 6pm, I can't remember if we stayed there that night or not, but I know we entrained for Dunkeld on Saturday morning at 10am with lots of weeping wives, mothers, sweethearts and such like seeing their loved ones off; yours truly had no one, and I thought this the end.

When we arrived in Dunkeld we were billeted in the Institution. We had lots of fun for a start as some of the horses had never been ridden and some of the soldiers had never been on horseback. This is where the farm lads had the only advantage over the 'Townies'.

Training consisted of being up as soon as reveille sounded. You then proceeded to feed the horses, and then you groomed them. It was then time for our breakfast. We had to parade with all our equipment, that being our helmet, gasmask, rifle and sword, we also had to have our horse saddled and be on the parade ground ready for inspection by 9am and Lord help you if anything didn't pass the inspection! We then mounted and moved off in formation to the imaginary field of battle, which to us was great fun but in reality would be a real disaster.

Just before Christmas we moved down to the Midlands of

William Sim.

England to a place called Welbeck Abbey. The reason we had moved was because we were to disband the horses and form an artillery regiment. We still trained with the horses but they were going away in small lots everyday until, I think, the month of March saw the last of them. By this time the regiment was divided into two. The first half, which consisted of the Elgin and Perthshire lads, formed the 80 Scottish Horse RA. The Aberdeen and Dundee lads formed the 79 Scottish Horse RA. We were then made up to strength with an intake of English conscripts.

Late 1941 we moved to Norwich, then in February 1942 we entrained at Norwich: we did not have a clue as to where we were going. All kinds of rumours were flying around. Most of us had one wish - not to be sent to the Far East! I should add that before we set off for the train we had been equipped with a tropical kit that contained shorts, light shirts, long socks and a pith helmet.

When the train came to Peterborough we went in the direction of Scotland. There were a lot of cheery chaps, especially the Scots, thinking that they might be able to visit their relatives. That was wishful thinking! The Glasgow lads had already guessed that we were bound for Gourock, the place for ships. Our ship, the *Strathaird*, was one of many waiting for us. There were five large troop-carrying ships, two battle ships plus two cruisers, six corvettes and a few other odds and ends.

We disembarked at Aden and marched to the railway station, and then we were on our way to Egypt. We arrived at our destination and were billeted near the pyramids in large tents, eight of us to a tent.

The tents were in rows out in the desert on the sand, it was lovely on your bare feet as the sand was hot with the strong sun. There were rows of tables with forms to sit on out in the open air for us to have our meals. When we had our meals there were containers with loads of small eggs (we would call them pullet's eggs I guess). To avoid getting diarrhoea you had to eat as many hardboiled eggs as you could - I ate so many I had to go and make a nest!

Fur Coats and Dresses

Eventually, our equipment arrived safely and we started to do manoeuvres in the desert. After a short time some of the drivers, me included, were sent to Alexandra to learn how to seal up our engines so as they could travel in water, not deep water, maybe a couple of feet. We knew there was something afoot. A week later we set off for Tripoli where we were to embark for the invasion of Sicily. We packed into a few troop carrier ships and set off for our first real action. We landed safely at the port of Syracuse without any incident. We then spread out on the land and took up our firing positions. We had eight guns in our Battery with a hundred pound shell that was very effective. My job was to drive a signal truck accompanied with a sergeant and five signallers. We laid a telephone line from the command post where the guns were, to the observation post up among the infantry. Once the line was laid we usually stayed about half way between the two points so that if the line went dead on either side of us it was easier to reach.

Sicily was captured in a relatively short time. Messina was the last big town before we crossed over to Italy. The majority of the civilians had hastily vanished by the time the British advanced, leaving their shops, etc. unlocked and unattended. One shop in particular, selling ladies' fashions, became too much of a temptation for some of the lads and they helped themselves to fur coats, dresses and other such items to take home to their loved ones. With me being in charge of the truck, I told them there was no room for any extras on board but I relented when they said they would just take one item each. I did not take anything because I did not think my mother would be pleased. The goods were stored in the truck until we had landed in Italy.

The piece of water between Sicily and Italy is not very wide but there were ships waiting to transfer us across. One of the sailors in our boat was a Birnie loon, Bob Thomson, and we were able to have a good blether. We attended the school together, and later he became manager of Brackla Distillery near Nairn. His father was horseman at Glenlossie. There were a lot of troops landing at different spots along the Italian coast. We moved on as the Jerries and Italian soldiers were moving back rapidly to try and form a defensive line. So it went on like this for quite a spell, advancing every day until we finally caught up with them, then the battle started all over again.

We arrived at a marshy place after we had been in Italy for two weeks. Our truck had laid a line from the guns to the observation post; they were maybe about 4,000 to 6,000 yards apart. Our halfway shelter was in a big quarry where we brewed our tea and cooked our meals. We had been in this position for two weeks when I had to exchange trucks. The marshy position was full of mosquitoes and a lot of the drivers contacted malaria and had to go to hospital. The trucks pulling the guns had to have two drivers each and because they were short of heavy drivers the captain took me off my one and put me on to one pulling the guns, this was because I had been trained to drive the large ones too. A young fellow just out from England took over my truck. I had only been off my signal truck for four days when my ex-companions drove into the quarry for their lunch and a German shell landed right on top of them and killed the lot. Poor fellows, they were never to get home with the fur coats and other things they had stowed in the truck, it all went up in smoke. The malaria did not last long, a few days in hospital and the men were back on duty again. A new signal truck arrived and I was back to driving it again with a completely new crew.

A Lucky Chap

The night before we withdrew from the front line our signal truck was up beside the infantry (Green Howards) an English Regiment, and we were being shelled something terrible but, luckily, the only damage was a piece of shrapnel which pierced one of my petrol tanks and I lost about six gallons of fuel. The hole in the tank was about two inches; dear knows why the truck did not go on fire. When I went back to HQ to get it welded again the mechanic thought I was a very lucky chap!

When we withdrew from the front we knew there was something up because they were dividing up the troops. After a few days, only the troops that were really essential, such as the gunners and drivers with their trucks set off to a port on the east. A few hours at sea then, in the early hours of daylight, the vessels dropped a ramp and you drove into the water and kept your motor going, if you stalled you were stuck there! After landing we were told 'you have invaded Anzio'.

There were three main roads leading to Rome and we occupied the middle road. Alex, my brother, and his regiment occupied the lower road nearer the coast. We had very little resistance and managed to deploy ourselves in the positions allowed us. All the roads led to Rome and our purpose was to advance and cut off the supply of material and such like on the road to Cassino and allow the British to advance. But the Germans fell to our plans and instead of having 6,000 Germans against us we had 60,000, so we had some battle for three months.

After three months in Anzio we started to break out: morning after morning, eight hundred guns on our side opened up on the Germans for two hours, heavy, light and everything that had shells! That was only our section. I don't know how many guns the Americans were firing. It was a long three months tied to the same spot. We had a few killed and some taken prisoner but, when we did advance, the scene was terrible: the number of Germans lying dead or wounded together with the dead horses was a gruesome sight. Because the Germans were running short of petrol, they used to take the horses from the Italian farms to transport their food and other goods. We were just glad we didn't have to stop, as the stench was terrible!

My brother, Alex, came to see me in Anzio; I was unaware that he was not far from us so it was a pleasant surprise to see him again. Then, a few weeks later, I got a lift on the back of a motorbike and went to see him, thinking this would be the last time I would see him in Italy, but no, on the way to Rome we passed them as they were waiting at the side of the road. I think that was their last action in Italy as they were going back to England to prepare for the invasion of France.

The Germans had fled by now and left a clear field for a while. We came to a place outside Rome and were told we were staying there for a three-week break. We had time to rest and recharge our batteries. We were only a few miles from Rome and we were allowed out to visit every day.

Back in action again, we were well inland, near Pisa. Having previously seen the Sphinx, Colosseum and the Vatican it was an added bonus to see the Leaning Tower of Pisa. Pescara is a large port on the coast. We passed through it but never stopped. It was here that George Marshall was killed. He was a school friend of mine, one of two brothers. George had been on duty all night and had entered his tent to have some sleep; he had not long laid down when a German shell exploded a short distance from his tent and a bit of shrapnel hit him on the head and killed him outright. George was a sergeant and he had just got married before he left Britain. He was one of the nicest men you could ever meet. We often had a 'news' together; George's father and mother were great friends of my parents It was very sad. Many years later Hamish Proctor (*an Elgin councillor for some years*) visited his grave, which according to Hamish, was very well looked after. He was most surprised at the number of Scottish graves that there were in Italy.

A small place called Perigola was a nice stop for us; the people seemed more friendly than usual. Of course, after Mussolini was killed in Milan the people seemed to relax towards us.

We kept going up north and the Germans were withdrawing very fast at times, then they would have a stand again but not for long, our superiority was beginning to show. By the end of April the war was over. After three months we moved down to Rimini. We had little to do there apart from guarding a few prisoners of war (Germans). One afternoon one of the clerks asked me if I would like to go on holiday to a place just outside Venice. I asked him to put Henry and my name down on his list. There were only two going from our battery, but he was a good friend of ours so this helped our case. The island was called Lido de Jesolo. One evening we were being entertained to a pipe band, I said to Henry that I thought I knew one of the pipers and he suggested that we speak to the chap after he finished playing. Right enough, when we approached him and I asked him if he was Bill (Willie) Finlayson, he said yes. During my last while at school this chap worked for A. Legge at Wardend Farm just up the road from our croft. He was one of twin boys; they came from Lossiemouth and had worked on different farms before they both joined the Seaforth Highlanders before the war. His brother Alex, who was also a piper, was on the island too, so we went about as a foursome, much more fun than just the two of us. Alas, the ten days went by too fast and we had to go back and join the regiment again at Rimini. (*The memories of another Finlayson brother appear elsewhere in this book.*)

My father and mother had four sons in the war all in different regiments and we all came back. John (Jack) the eldest, was in the Royal Signals and spent most of the time in England; Alex was next, he was in the 6th Seaforths, but I have mentioned him before; I come next but you know all about me! Last of all was Jimmy; he was only 14 when the war started and when he did eventually join up I can't remember which regiment he was with.

Sometimes, when I think back to the narrow escapes I had, I just think how fortunate I was.

Donald Allan

D-DAY WITH THE ARGYLLS

Among Donald Allan's World War II souvenirs is the jagged piece of metal that almost cost him his life. The former Argyll and Sutherland Highlander was 'somewhere in Normandy' when a shell went off close to his lorry and a chunk of shrapnel went through the windscreen.

I WAS CALLED up in February 1942 at the age of 18 and became in the Argylls what I'd been in Civvies Street – a lorry driver. I served as a mechanic and got sixpence extra a day for that, driving a lorry and looking after other machinery. Before D-Day I was at Tilbury Docks. The V2 rockets were coming over, though we didn't know what they were at the time. We took shelter under the lorry…it was only later that we discovered there were proper shelters.

We went off on a big boat on the first day of the invasion: the airborne lot had gone in first. The weather was rough and we lay off the coast for a couple of days before being put ashore on landing craft. The Jerries were shelling us and some got knocked out. Our first objective was supposed to be Caen, but we never got there. We were surrounded by German SS troops in the woods for three days. (*Fierce fighting ensued, and regimental records show that the Argylls were eventually extricated from their tight spot by the tanks of the Scots Guards, commanded by William Whitelaw, later Viscount Whitelaw, Leader of the House of Lords and former Tory Home Secretary*). We were told to get out as best we could. I was preparing to take a wounded lad out in my lorry, but I was told by the sergeant that it wasn't an ambulance. Anyway, I just carried on and the lad was later transferred to a real ambulance and then to a field hospital.

Getting out wasn't easy: there were deserted and damaged vehicles all over the place and we had to keep stopping to clear the way. It was during one of these halts that I had my close shave with the piece of shrapnel. I'd left the driving seat and was standing at the side of the lorry when a shell went off. I was thrown several yards by the blast, but the man next to me was killed and 19 others were injured. If I hadn't got out of the lorry, I'd have been killed – the piece of shrapnel just went straight through the windscreen. I picked it up and kept it to remind me of my lucky escape.

Donald Allan.

It was my job to take rations up to the front at night. I had to find my way there without lights, so it was OK if there was moonlight, but not if it was really dark. I was taking rations up to a mortar platoon one night. They sent someone down to show me the way. We found what we thought was the road, but then saw something white ahead...we were driving into a minefield.

We got back on track and made it to the platoon, but after I'd delivered the rations I had to make my way back by myself. Suddenly I spotted eight Germans, but when they saw the lorry they ducked down behind bushes. They didn't know it was just me in the lorry, but they weren't taking any chances, thank goodness.

I remember the discomfort of life on the battlefield: never being able to take your clothes off; shaving in cold water; trying to sleep through the noise of the shelling, either by digging in or getting under the lorry. But I'm grateful that, unlike many others, I came back unharmed. It was just a bit of luck I got off...all I ever had was a poisoned finger.

Grace MacBeath

BOMBS AND BROWNIES

Grace MacBeath, Elgin, was a small girl in London in 1939, and remembers her usual holiday with relatives in Scotland being cancelled as the war clouds gathered.

MY FATHER HAD been transferred from the B.T.H. in Glasgow to London, so I was born in London and in 1939 instead of our usual holidays with grandparents in Glasgow and Bathgate we stayed in London and visited various museums, the zoo, and a trip down the Thames etc. and on occasions I heard this strange wailing noise. On enquiring what it was, my mother said that they were just practising and it would be a warning to go to the shelters, which were being built on the streets round about.

I remember that on Sunday, September 3, my father was painting the outside of the house and at 11am he came in and turned on the wireless and we heard Chamberlain say that we were now at war. In due course an Anderson shelter was delivered in sections to our door and Dad dug up the flower bed in the back garden and made a deep hole to half bury the shelter; it was then covered up with the soil dug from the hole. (We had had the choice of shelters and my friend along the road had a Morrison shelter which was like a large metal table with wire mesh round the sides, leaving room to climb in and where they had all their bedding.) Later my brothers and I were playing 'Doctors and Nurses' in the kitchen - my younger brother being the patient and lying on the table-topped mangle with the old curtains hung over the pulley above him, as a hospital bed. Mother came through and took down the curtains and said she had to put them up with the other ones to keep the light from showing outside. We did not have 'blackout' curtains upstairs so we got ready for bed downstairs and folded our clothes neatly and put them on a chair in the bedroom so that if the sirens went at night we could grab our clothes. Only when we were all on the landing with bedroom doors shut, would the light go on.

Grace MacBeath with her mother and brothers
during that last summer of peace.

After a year or two, Dad moved the dining room table etc. into the 'parlour', usually used on high days and holidays, and one double and a three-quarter bed were brought down from the bedrooms. One night my brothers and I were sitting on the double bed knitting squares for blankets when we heard the drone of a German plane. Within seconds we heard this loud whistling noise and we dived under the bed and there was a terrific thump. Next day we learned that the houses on one side of a street in Hendon, just across the other side of the park from us - there was an aerodrome there, now a museum - had been flattened. Those that saw this particular episode said it was just like an express train coming down. I wonder now whether it could have been some kind of rocket.

Luckily we only had one window blown out before we moved from London. This particular night we were not in the shelter, it being not long after tea time, and we were sitting round the fire. When we heard the loud thump, the water in the goldfish bowl on the piano slopped from side to side and nearly came over the top - we were fish sitting for our friends who had been staying with their granny for a month or two - and next day at school some boys had pieces of parachute from the landmine which had come down some three streets away. Of course, we all had to go round next day to see the crater.

My Dad took on another allotment - we now had three - and he planted six apple trees at the back of the garden. It was decided to keep hens - my grandparents had a farm and Dad knew all about hens - and as we were a family of five we could have five hens. The hen house was duly built and we went to buy the hens, which we called Ann, Betty, Cynthia, Daisy and Edith. A little while later we increased the number to seven when two war workers were billeted on us, so Fay and Gertie joined the other hens. The billeting officer said that with three bedrooms we could squeeze up and take two war workers, and we had them until we left London in 1943. I think they must have gone into the shelter built out on the road as there was not room for them in the Anderson shelter.

Sleeping in the Shelter

With three allotments, fruit trees in the garden and hens, we never went hungry, although we often went to school rather tired in the morning if we had been kept awake most of the night with the bombing. One girl in our class turned up even although the back of her house had been blown out when a bomb fell in the garden. If all was quiet at night, we stayed in the house, otherwise bombing went on for two or three weeks and we would sleep in the shelter. Sometimes we heard shrapnel falling and we used to look for it in the morning and take any trophies to school. Each morning we would count the number of RAF planes as they flew over in 'V' formation on their way home from bombing raids to see if they were all there. We children could tell the difference in engine sound from the German bombers and the British planes. Even yet, after sixty years, I still get a funny feeling inside if I hear an unusual engine sound, especially through the night.

In the early months of the war a lot of the teachers were called up or volunteered for the services so sometimes we went to school in the morning and others went in the afternoon. I even remember a teacher coming to the house and the boys next door and our friends round the corner would sit round our dining table and do sums and writing. When things got more organised we went to school as normal, carrying our gas masks, which we had to keep with us at all times. I remember that there was a shortage of paper and we resorted to slates and slate pencils for a while. If the siren went we trooped into the shelters - long and narrow with benches down each side. During the commencement of what turned out to be the Battle of Britain we went to the school shelters. Various mothers came and collected the children as the 'all clear' had not gone, but my mother and our neighbour's mother did not arrive - my younger brother was at home and couldn't be left. At 4pm the teachers told us to run all the way home, which we did, and found our mothers on the door step almost in tears wondering what to do about us. We looked up and saw the fighter planes chasing the others across the sky.

I was a Brownie when the war started and although we kept going through the war, sometimes there were very few of us. I and another girl were working for our 'Golden Hand', which was the First Class, and if you got this you could 'fly' up to Guides. Quite often there were just the two of us and we used to meet Brown Owl in one of the shelters built on a street corner. We eventually flew up to Guides, and although we had a few cook-outs, camping was suspended during the war.

As my father, then in his forties, was in a reserved job, he was not called up but was out several nights a week on fire watch. My mother had to attend first aid classes so that she could help out if there were any casualties nearby. The playing field along the road had been taken over and made into an army camp and one night a lorry full of ammunition had been hit by a bomb and the driver was carried along the street on a stretcher, but was taken in by the lady two doors along, otherwise it would have been our house.

When we were in the shelter during night raids, we could hear the countdown for the anti-aircraft guns in the camp - 5. 4. 3. 2. 1 FIRE! We children used to talk to the ATS girls on duty at the camp gate, especially the Scottish ones, and we were asked if they could come to our house for a bath as they only had showers on the camp. Thereafter we had two that came each Sunday afternoon for a bath, and to wash their hair, and then they stayed for tea.

One of the men that Dad had worked with in Glasgow had set up his own Electrical Engineering firm in Morecambe and he had managed to trace Dad to London and offered him a job in

Morecambe. I remember that my parents spent many nights in 1943 drafting out a letter to Ernest Bevin, Minister for Labour in the coalition parliament, in order that Dad could be released from his job and take up the one offered to him. After a few weeks of watching for the post, permission was granted and we moved to Morecambe in May 1943. There were very few raids in Morecambe and I could not understand why people did not go home one day when the siren went when we were on the beach.

On our way home from school one day in June 1944 I noticed buses lined up outside the station and word soon got around that they were for the evacuees. As soon as I got home I asked Mum if we could please have one - London by this time was being bombarded by the V l rockets and had we still been there we would have been evacuated (my grandmother and aunts in Bathgate had already offered to have us but mother preferred us all to stay together and she did not want to leave Dad on his own). We duly went down to the Institute in Heysham where there were still a few children left with labels tied to their coats, and we came home with Carol aged nine. She slept in my bed with me, I had always wanted a sister, and she stayed until the war ended in May 1945.

That was a great time of celebration and all the children round about enjoyed a Victory Party in one neighbour's garden. It was lovely to see the tables full of meat paste and fish paste sandwiches, jammy buns and even jelly and ice cream! We managed to get up to the farm at Bathgate again for our summer holidays and we were there in August when the war with Japan ended. Two kittens born at the farm that week were named Monty (for General Montgomery) and Vicky (for victory). It was still some time before rationing ended and it was well on into the 1950s before houses were being built to buy and furniture that was not 'utility' was available - just in time for us to get married and set up home.

Robert McLean

THE DESERT RAT

At the outbreak of war, maintenance and repair of Army equipment was mainly in the hands of individual regiments. In 1942, REME (Royal Electrical and Mechanical Engineers) was formed, and many men with existing skills were transferred to its ranks. Among them was Robert McLean (b. 1919), Lossiemouth. He was born and brought up in Forres, where his father owned a motorcycle shop, and trained as a mechanic. After being called up in August 1940 to the Royal Army Service Corp, he transferred to REME when it was set up. He was to spend four years in the desert, where REME was to face its first test: restoring vehicles and equipment to battle readiness to break the Afrika Korps and the Italian Army.

WHEN I WAS given my medical I was told my eyesight was Grade 3 and someone said they wouldn't take me in the services, but they did. My pay was 7 shillings going up to 14 shillings, but we only ever saw 10s of it – we had something taken off for 'barrack damages'. I never did any damage, but they took it off anyway.

I was sent to Post Said where we did a lot of square bashing, then to Alexandria with the 30th MT Co. Then I was sent to Mersa Matruth.

We were moving in convoy, with someone on the roof of the truck all the time to watch out for aircraft. We were machine gunned by Messerschmitts and dive bombed by Stukas. If we saw planes coming we got out of the truck and dispersed as quickly as possible – the Germans were mainly after the trucks. Rommel chased us up and down the dessert a few times. We had very little in the way of transport to start with, then Montgomery came out and he had everything.

My job was working in the base workshops synchronising aircraft engines to fit into small tanks: they were death traps. If they were hit by armour-piercing bullets they just went up in flames because of the high octane fuel; men had no chance of getting out.

We were mainly recovering damaged vehicles and re-conditioning them. One day we were progressing through the dessert when we met trucks coming towards us at full tilt. I said to the sergeant we must me going the wrong way, but he said: 'No, Jock, we're going this way.' They were throwing gear off the trucks and one stopped and the lad said the Germans were at their backs, but the sergeant would not be shifted and we kept going. It

Robert McLean.

later transpired that the fifth column (*subversive agents*) had been at work, getting troops into a panic, and they only stopped when someone fired a salvo…so the sergeant was right and we were going the right way after all.

Getting water was a job. We had water bottles which were supposed to do us about two weeks. Monty had all the comforts in the desert: a caravan; lots of water for a bath. We kept ourselves as best we could. The first thing you did when you stopped was to dig slit trenches, then get the tin dixies out and brew up for tea in a sand box. Tea was always full of sand, the sand got everywhere. Some of the water tins had once contained petrol, so the water didn't taste too good either.

If you were in a place for any length of time the officers said you had to use a 'thunder box', but if a thunder box wasn't available, you just used a shovel. Dysentery was commonplace and we all got diarrhoea. They gave us tablets to fend off malaria, but some wouldn't take them because they turned the skin a bit yellow – but I took all I could get.

A reconnaissance plane came over every night taking photographs, but it was too high up for the fighters to reach it. The

RAF stripped a Spitfire down to the bare essentials to try to get it up high enough, and it did. The Junker came down not far from us and we went over to get souvenirs.

A group of Desert Rats take it easy.

After El Alamein there were a lot of casualties, but Montgomery had things well in hand. We were in Tripoli and were told General Lyon was coming so we all mustered…and Churchill and Montgomery turned up. It was a real morale booster after living so long in the heat – our eyebrows shot up.

We had to adapt tanks and trucks for the invasion of Sicily, and it was quite a job waterproofing them. We were in Salerno for a while and visited the Vatican where we were invited for an audience with the Pope, Pius XII in St Peter's. He spoke to us in various languages, to all denominations. We were in action most of the time, but that was a break in the conflict. In barracks we'd catch chameleons – you could just pick them off the branches of trees – and keep them to catch flies. They were very amusing. I was in Germany for several weeks – I saw Dresden flattened – working at an ILOB factory at Schleswig-Holstein. Some German tradesmen volunteered to work with us. They were quite willing because they knew the end of the war was coming and they were keen to co-operate.

From Germany I had 'agricultural leave'; my brother had a farm and I was able to come home to help him with the harvest.

When I had my discharge medical, my eyesight had miraculously improved to Grade 1!

After the war I got a job at RNAS Lossiemouth and later at Invergordon, but I'm still on the Army Reserve list…so I could be called up any time!

Robert McLean in Egypt.

Marie McLean

THE BANK TELLER

Like so many people, war brought about a change of occupation for Marie McLean nee Anderson (b. 1922). In 1946 she married Robert McLean, a young soldier she'd met in the church choir, and the couple now live in Lossiemouth.

I WAS WORKING in J. R. Geddes Drapers in Forres at the beginning of the war – my wages were 8 shillings a week. We sold everything: millinery, coats, dresses, materials, wools, and haberdashery. It was very formal. We had to wear a hat to work and when we left...although we usually ripped it off once we were away, and we had to have a buttonhole. If a customer came in, the manager would say, "One forward, please!" for us to serve.

When war was declared, I didn't want to go into the services. I'd heard you had to strip naked to be examined by a doctor, and that put me off, so in 1940 I got a job in the Bank of Scotland, replacing a man who'd been called up. There was great camaraderie, not like in the banks today, although the hours were long and we didn't get home till the books balanced, even if that meant staying till midnight. Our bank paid the wages for the servicemen at RAF Kinloss, all except for the officers who had accounts. Once a fortnight a girl had to go round all the banks in Forres – there were five: ours, the Royal Bank, the National Bank of Scotland, the British Linen Bank, the North of Scotland Bank, and the Bank of Scotland, and collect all the English notes. Usually just one girl went, carrying a leather bag for the money. We'd walk back through the streets carrying £2000-£3000, a lot of money then, but never thought anything of it. But a vehicle with an armed guard would collect the money to take it to RAF Kinloss.

George McKenzie was in charge of ARP and was very strict. My father, Adam Anderson was a lieutenant in the Home Guard – he'd been wounded in World War I. I remember him saying how

George would be disappointed if Forres didn't get at least one bomb...I think the only bombs that fell were up the Findhorn somewhere. George held a practice one day and let off a gas cylinder outside the bank: we all carried gas masks with us and had to go outside wearing them. After the test was over one of the bank staff brought a bit of the gas canister back inside for curiosity. In a wee while all our eyes were streaming and we had to go home...but not until after we'd balanced up.

Marie McLean.

One night an ARP warden, he was a postman, came round and whispered something to my father at the door, and my father went off with his gun, very mysteriously. I think there was rumour of an invasion, but he never said anything. We locked the door. There was a shotgun in the house and I decided if anyone came I'd use it...but I didn't know how to fire it.

My father was strict so I wasn't allowed to go to any of the RAF dances, only the church dances. I was in St Lawrence Church Choir. One Sunday, starting at 9am, it was full of troops and an Irish chaplain preached and they had communion. I think it must have been prior to D-Day. We knew there was something big going on.

William Grant

BOATING, SHOWS AND FOOTBALL

War was quite an exciting experience for many young boys. William Grant (b. 1931) and living in Elgin, remembers the good times.

I WAS NINE when the war started. We lived in South Guildry Street and I remember being told there was an important announcement being made - we didn't have a wireless so I went down to my Aunty Jessie's to listen to it. It didn't mean a great deal to me at that age.

William Grant.

My father was called up. He did guard duty with the RAF, but didn't find that very exciting so eventually became a mid-upper gunner in Halifaxes – not dropping bombs, but metallic strips to disrupt enemy radar. He'd been an insurance agent and my mother did his work while he was away to keep his books going.

The day Elgin Town Hall went on fire in December 1939 I remember there being a lot of smoke. I ran down to my granny's at 51 High Street, went upstairs and watched the fire from there – I saw the town hall tower collapsing, it was quite exciting. There were discussions about how the fire started – the Seaforths were billeted there – and it was said later it might have been an electrical failure, but no one really knows.

Boating on Cooper Park pond: William Grant, his mother and brother early in the war. Later he worked as a boat attendant.

I was employed at the boating pond in Cooper Park: my job was time-keeper – I think people got 20 minutes for sixpence – and we were always busy, even during the war. We had double summer time, so the boats kept going until later at night, there was no stopping at teatime and going home in those days. There were lots of troops wandering about; they always asked me if I had a sister! One day I remember a company of them came running across the park with their rifles and ran straight across the pond, they were on some sort of exercise. After we'd finished with the boats we'd got to the shows, which were held in a corner of the park. There were the usual things, including a boxing booth.

We also went to the cinema. I remember being at the Playhouse one night with my Granny. They were showing *'The Light that Failed'* with Ida Lupino, which was pretty tense. The tension built up so much that I fainted and had to be carried out to the foyer where I was laid out on a couch. I didn't know until much later that I had a heart deficiency.

I went to the football - there was a game every week in those days because the 30th Training Battalion had a team and they played when Elgin City was away. There were no holidays as such, but my aunt had a property at Blackhills where we went in the summer. Everything was very basic, no toilet and you had to go up the road to fetch water. I really didn't want to go. I was at Springfield School, which was paid for, so schooling wasn't disrupted during the war. I'd just jump over the wall to get to school.

My grandfather, George D. Grant had a grocer's shop at Braco's Banking House in the High Street – now a cycle shop. Everything had to be weighed out, nothing came pre-packed, and so he would cut butter from a huge slab, and weigh out a pound of sugar. My granny used to boil a big ham to sell in the shop – ham today doesn't taste anything like my granny's ham. I did help in the shop for a while, but didn't like it. I did the message side and had a proper message bike. My great-uncle Alex retired from the railway and he became the message boy. He must have been the oldest message boy in Elgin, but he was very fit.

I don't remember being worried about my father when he was away to the war, although my mother did tell my brother and me that if anything happened to him one of us would get his watch and the other his bike.

When the war was over I was told my mother and father were going away on a second honeymoon and we would stay with my granny until they got back.

James Coutts

THE RABBIT CATCHER

*Reserved occupations were not uncommon during the war –
someone had to stay behind and run essential services, but Hetty
Milne's father, James Coutts, had an exceptional occupation. Mrs
Milne, who lives in Elgin, recounts his story.*

LONDON AND MANCHESTER, Birmingham and Liverpool –
I knew nothing of these cities except as destinations for the many
crates which lined the stations throughout the north of Scotland.
The wooden crates were packed full of freshly caught and cleaned
rabbits destined for the butcher's shops in those beleaguered cities.

My father, James Coutts, was a professional rabbit trapper and,
as such, he was in a reserved occupation during the war years. As
a young man he had left home and travelled the countryside as an
itinerant worker. While working in the Glenlivet area he met
Chrissie MacKenzie and they were married at Achbreck Church on
Christmas Eve 1931. They set up home in Burghead and had four
of a family. During the war years, Dad didn't get home very often.
There was no petrol to spare for home visits but when he did
arrive, our living room became a sort of mini factory. All the traps
and snares he needed for his work had to be repaired to make sure
that there would be no undue stress on the animals if they were
caught on a snare which did not do the work properly. Mam would
lay out the material required for the snares and dad would prepare
the sticks and brown binder twine needed for the pegs.

This was a time of wartime restrictions and early blackouts so
by the light of a single paraffin lamp they would carry on
working, Dad whittling and shaping the wood to make the new
pegs to support the snares and Mam winding the shiny copper
wire at an even pace to keep them taut. As we got older, we girls
learned how to put in the brass eyelets which ensured that the
snares ran smoothly.

When he was away from home, dad worked in places as far apart as Invermorriston in Inverness-shire and Strathdon in Aberdeenshire. With regular stops he worked on the farms and estates of Moray, Banff and Strathbogie, in a rota system and each time he had to negotiate a price with the farmers. While in the Inverness area he had regular 'digs' at Assich Croft in Croy, known locally as 'Bumbers'. The traps and snares were set up last thing at night and the trapper was always careful not to leave his scent on the trail. When Mr Rabbit came out for an

Rabbit catcher James Coutts helped to feed Britain during the war.

early breakfast, he'd go lolloping along the track and was caught in mid-jump, quick, easy and painless. By the time the trapper did his rounds at first light, the animal was dead. Each carcase was then gutted clean and paired off and, by the time the Inverness train arrived at Cawdor station, they were crated and ready for transportation to the towns and cities of England.

Housewives, desperate for something to feed their families, queued for hours daily, waiting for the butchers' shops to open. Very little meat was available and a consignment of fresh rabbits meant that the shop could open for a couple of hours. Gangs of city boys would sometimes raid the countryside but their methods of poaching were frowned upon. Carcases were riddled with shot and no busy housewife could face the challenge of cleaning up the meat before cooking. Where these men got their ammunition from was a mystery, black market I suppose. To the professional it was a matter of pride that all his products were cleanly caught and he had to make sure he got them to the markets as early as possible. No matter where he was working, there were always a couple of crates with his labels still on them, returned to the station, from those city butchers who were hard pushed to keep the housewives supplied with meat of any kind.

Of course, my father was not the only one supplying rabbits to the markets. Young farm lads were always eager to help the trapper and, when he had moved on, they would set up a few snares and any rabbits not required at home were transported to the nearest game dealer over the handlebars of their bikes. When my uncles came home on leave from the army they were always glad of an excuse to get out of the house. They would borrow a few snares and head for the fields; it helped them to recuperate before being sent back to the trenches.

Many of the railway stations my father used were closed down in 1963 but a few are still in use as tourist attractions. The train has returned to Dufftown and Keith. The old granary at Ballindalloch Station on the Speyside Way is going under extensive repairs at present. Happily, Nairn and Huntly are still part of the railway network which once transported the many crates of fresh rabbit to the households in England.

Hetty Milne

THE RABBIT CATCHER'S DAUGHTER

Hetty Milne (b.1932), an author in her own right, has also contributed her own memories of growing up in Burghead during the war.

I REMEMBER THE BBC relay station at Burghead on the south shore of the Moray Firth almost disappeared under a sea of green and brown paint. The five bright lights on the 500 ft. steel mast which pierced the northern sky were dimmed for the duration of World War II. The miles of sandy playground from Burghead to Findhorn became a desert as a double row of huge concrete blocks marched along the shoreline, connected by great fat rolls of barbed wire. Observation posts and concrete shelters with their gun-slit eyes appeared overnight all along the bay and on the back shoreline. The slappy and the sinkies, both favoured spots for swimming, also had their share of concrete while the harbour area was out of bounds to the Broch bairns. Iron railings disappeared from the walls around gardens and the school playground, while the iron barred gate in the high wall around the so called Roman Well was replaced by a strong wooden door.

The annual burning of the Clavie ceremony, held each January, was barred until further notice, and the black tarred cairn on top of Doorie Hill was now imagined to be the bridge of a ship out on the Atlantic Ocean. Children from the age of 12 began working in the 'tattie fields'; back yards, which had never seen a spade before, became fertile gardens while vegetable plots down by the railway lines were well sought after. Fewer single women caught the bus into Elgin for work as they left their native town for a job with the Land Army or Timber Control; some went on to the railways and others served with NAAFI at home and abroad. I remember the ration books and clothing coupons, I also recall the sounds of the dredger as it worked to deepen the harbour entrance and the drone of aircraft as they left Kinloss for their early checks over the Moray Firth. It was 1943 before I was old enough to get exemption from the school to go tattie lifting. Before that, I made my own contribution to the War Effort. From the age of nine I was able to help my father in his work as a professional rabbit trapper. During the school summer holidays our family always headed for Glenlivet where our Granny Mackenzie lived. Petrol was rationed so we had to travel by bus to Elgin, train to Dufftown and by bus again to Tomnavoulin. While living at Granny's house we children had to take home the peats from the moss to keep the fires burning. All water had to be carried from a well down by the burn some distance away. Granny, mother and aunties all knitted for the army comforts. Nothing was wasted: jumpers and cardigans were drawn back and re-knitted as socks, gloves and balaclavas. We fast growing children had to be content with hand-me-downs.

Father's day started at daybreak. As soon as the first streak of light pierced the sky, he was out checking his snares which had been set up last thing at night. An experienced man knew exactly where to set his snares to get the best results. By the time he came back with his game bag bulging I would be up and ready to get started. Each animal was held firmly by the back of the neck and the belly fur smoothed down before my father slit the carcass with the sharp tip of his knife. Next he put his hand inside and pulled out the gory contents and threw them into a bucket by his side. The heart and liver were kept as a tasty bite for the ferrets he sometimes used in his work. A quick slit in the hind legs enabled me to join two rabbits together and hang them inside the wooden crates, ready for transportation to Manchester or Birmingham.

My mother was very ill during the summer of 1942 so we stayed on the croft for longer than usual. We were back home when our brother was born in November. I remember one day my grandmother, against her better judgment, allowed us to take the old wind-up gramophone out into the sunshine. There was an assortment of records but the one I remember clearly was *Over My Shoulder Goes One Care'* sung by Jessie Mathews, who later became Mrs Dale of the long running radio programme, *Mrs Dale's Diary*. Back home at Burghead, we had missed all the excitement as a plane had come down just outside the harbour wall. The army began to move into Burghead. My uncle Rob Mackenzie and his pal Allan Grant from Tomnavoulin arrived unexpectedly at our house. They had been billeted at Gordonstoun and this was their first chance to visit. A dance was arranged for the soldiers. My mother thought I was too young to go to the dance but when one of the lady volunteers asked if I might come and help in the kitchen, that was a different matter. I washed dishes all evening in the cramped kitchen in the Drill Hall, there wasn't much chance of getting down to the dancing until the last half hour.

Hetty Milne (centre) and her sisters
Kate and Betty.

I remember the smell of disinfectant that came from the rough khaki uniform of the soldier who eventually asked me up to dance. Some of the bigger girls in our street were there and I remember how they used to come to our house and my mother would help them draw the line on the back of their legs to mark the seam on their liquid stockings. They had a great time raiding each other's wardrobes for the best blouses and skirts and summer frocks for the dancing.

Keeping Ferrets

Auntie Jean came to stay for a few days. We three girls enjoyed having her teach us the words of the latest songs. *'You Are My Sunshine'* was one. I asked Jean if she knew *'Bonnie Charlie's Noo Awa'*, which we'd been learning at school. Her eyes filled with tears and our singing was over for the time being. I didn't know that Uncle Charlie, who was a piper in the army, was in Libya in North Africa at the time. When my father came home there was always a rush to get the wet and dry batteries charged up for the wireless. While he was twiddling with the knobs he always passed the things I liked, *'Big Bill Anderson and His Rocky Mountain Boys'*, and *ITMA* with Tommy Handley. He preferred to go through the squeals of the high frequency stations with the skirling operatic singers until he could find Lord Haw Haw, who sent propaganda messages to the nation.

In Burghead, while most back yards were turned into productive gardens, our yard was a bit different. During his travels around the countryside, my father put in an order for a load of backs to be delivered to our yard. I would gather some bigger girls around me and, under the pretext of building houses, we leant the longest and heaviest backs against the wall which surrounded the yard. If set out properly we could have a nice space between the dyke and the planks. We made tables and stools by just using suitable pieces of wood. When we were sitting down and pretending to play house, Mam would bring out some scones or pancakes, still warm from the girdle.

When our pals set off for home again it was time for me to get to work. I would set up the saw-horse and while Mam held one end of the cross-cut saw, I held the other and we set to sawing the long pieces of wood into short lengths to fit inside the grate where Mam did all her cooking. There was a big hack block where we could split the logs into manageable sizes and two axes, the smaller one for splitting kindlers which were dried inside the box in the old fashioned fire grate.

Also in our yard there was a hutch where Dad sometimes kept the ferrets he used in his work. I remember one night going out to the hill below York Tower at Newton near Elgin. Our purpose this time was to work with the ferrets. You can always tell when there are rabbits in the warren by the amount of fresh sand at the entrance to the burrows. The tackle this time was a bundle of nets and a .22 rifle. The nets were set out to cover the rabbit holes leaving only one or two clear. Everything is done in silence, the ferret is placed inside the free hole and the rabbiter sits back with his gun ready. My father had a keen sense of hearing and could hear the movement of the ferret at work. He knew when the quarry had been disturbed and was ready to shoot as soon as the rabbit appeared at the uncovered hole. One clean shot in the head made sure of a meal for one of those families down south. Each bullet had to be accounted for when applying for more ammunition. Before going out to work, the ferret was fed just enough to take the edge off his appetite so that he would chase the rabbit without resorting to feeding while still underground. Does this all sound a bit gruesome? Don't forget those hungry children in the cities.

The country housewife had her own scarcities; not much sugar for jam making, flour and eggs in very short supply and no corner shop to run to for a tin of Spam. Rations for one week for each person: 4oz tea; 8oz sugar; 2oz butter; 4oz margarine; 2oz lard or fat; 4oz bacon; about half pound of steak and three pints of milk. Children got extra milk at school and, wait for it, one egg per fortnight. Ration books with 20 points per month were also part of the allowances but there wasn't much you could get for that. Sweets were rationed and shopkeepers tried to save them for their regular customers. Tinned food was very scarce. Coupons were also required for buying clothes and women had to make do with what they had, adding a touch of colour or a piece of lace to give their old clothes a bit of glamour. Rabbit was a great stand-by for any household. It could be used in different ways, just like chicken today, stewed, pot-roasted or boiled. My granny had a mincing machine which she clamped to the side of the kitchen table and, when she had made some pastry - using the grey flour that was available eked out with some oatmeal - her pies were the best in our world. We enjoyed vegetable soup made with boiled rabbit.

My sister Kathleen, two years younger than me, has reminded me of the view from the skylight in our bedroom. When she was about five years old she was standing on tiptoe on top of the chest and pulling herself to her full height and peering through the narrow slit left open for fresh air. She remembers clearly the sight of sleek, grey battleships out on the Moray Firth as they headed for the deep haven at Invergordon. It was never completely dark in our tiny bedroom. When we lay in bed and watched the stars, we could sometimes see the searchlights sweep across the northern sky.

Chrissie lived at the bottom end of the town and we lived at the top end. She would sometimes come and join us as we played our street games with skipping rope or an old tennis ball. As darkness came down we would eventually move inside to the light of one single paraffin lamp. When it was time for Chrissie to go home, we would step out into the dark where there wasn't even a chink of light showing from any windows. I'd go down the street with her most of the way home then we would part, each going our separate ways but both running in the middle of the road. Of course, there were no cars at that time but there was always the fear that someone, or something, would jump out to frighten us as we passed dark doorways or garden gates.

Bigger boys and girls played different games from us and we would sometimes hear their voices shouting eerily in the mist as they played Smoogle or Hide-and-Seek. I never understood the rules of Smoogle but I can still imagine the spooky sound of their voices in the blackout as they roamed the outskirts of town. Wintertime slides on 'Torchies Brae' were great fun for us wee ones until the bigger teenagers arrived to spoil our play.

We young people were very sheltered from the tragic circumstances of war. There was no television in our homes bringing the awful pictures of what was going on in Europe and Africa, but I recall the one time my father took us to the pictures in Elgin. The Gaumont British news was showing the fires burning in London after the Blitz, and we three girls set up a terrible noise as we ran from our seats and had to be restrained by staff until our Mam could get out of her seat. Dad hurried out to bring the car round from where he had parked. There were no pictures in Burghead and, I can tell you, it was a long time before we were taken back to the Elgin Playhouse.

Doug Smillie

OUR DAILY BREAD

Rationing during the war didn't just affect the public – bakers had to be enterprising if they wanted to continue to give their customers good service. Doug Smillie's father, Robert, started his bakery in Elgin's High Street in 1927. When war broke out, his eldest son Len was exempt from military service to help run the business; two sons went away to the army, and the youngest, Douglas, was still at school. Still living in Elgin, where he continued to run the business until his retirement, these are his memories.

I MUST HAVE been about 11 or 12 when Len said he had been to Austins the Bakers to see a demonstration on how to make a 'utility' loaf. All the other bakers were there, and in the event of an invasion they were told they had to go to Austins and produce these loaves 24-hours a day. The bread was brown and didn't rise much.

I remembered an old retired baker came back to work for us, and a baker from Aberdeen came to us as a result of redirected labour. He had worked with the Co-op in Aberdeen and his job had been to put the puff pastry on steak pies, that was all he did. He made lovely puff pastry, but how many steak pies did we have during the war? He found it hard at first, but given time, learned a few things, and my father and he ended up appreciating each other.

I left school in 1943 and considered working in a surveyor's office, but my father pointed out that once the war had ended, men would be coming home to these jobs and I could end up out of work. And so I became an apprentice baker.

We used to do things to eke out the rations: we had lumps of prepared sugar beet – it looked like lumps of brown coal – which we boiled down to make sugar. We used soya flour and almond essence to make marzipan, and we also extended fats by creaming them with soya flour. One of my jobs was to 'cure' eggs in waterglass when there was a glut of them, and that would help to see us through the winter. We also had wonderful stuff called sprayed dried eggs from America which made beautiful jobs of sponges and Swiss rolls.

There were lots of wartime weddings. If someone was getting married then the customer would save up some of the ingredients and bring them in for us to use to make a wedding cake. If they brought icing sugar, we'd decorate the top with a little icing.

Smillie's bakery van was a commandeered vehicle – it could be used for deliveries during the day, but at the weekend it was commandeered by the Home Guard for active service.

It was wrecked one weekend and, as it was impossible to get a replacement, the bakery resurrected two trike vans, and I used them to make deliveries.

Queuing became a way of life – if you saw a queue you joined it...and found out later what people were queuing for. War was a great leveller.

We had a little tea-room upstairs, which was very popular with the soldiers because it was so cheap – my father used to say he hoped someone was looking after his boys the same. At weekends the boys from the camp would be queuing up the stairs and one or two farmers with them on a Friday, for bacon, eggs and sausages. My sister Muriel did the cooking and my aunts helped.

At times we felt that the war was very far away. It was only when someone had a tragedy that it struck home.

The arrival of evacuees was an exciting event for Moray schoolchildren. His wife Catherine, neé Mackay, remembers at the age of 12 rushing down to Elgin Railway Station to see them arrive.

We'd been told they were coming, and they arrived carrying their cases and their gas masks. I think they came from Edinburgh.

I remember one family taking in six evacuees: they didn't all stay throughout the war; some went home after a while. Some evacuees were adopted by their host families; others kept in touch, even after leaving Moray.

Charles Finlayson

BOSOM PALS

The five Finlayson brothers were well known in Lossiemouth – all played the pipes as their father, grandfather, and great-grandfather before them had done. And all five proudly served their country in World War II. Donald, the eldest, became a Flying Officer in the RAF and baled out over the English Channel during the Battle of Britain. He won the DFC and Bar. John was a CSM in the 2nd and 7th Seaforth Highlanders: he was badly wounded at Arnhem. Both Donald and John have since died.

William and Alec, the twins, both served in the 1st Battalion The Scots Guards: William was blown up at Salerno, but survived and now lives in Blythe, Northumberland; Alex lost an eye in North Africa; his home is now in Aberdeen. Charles, the youngest, was a sergeant in the 6th and 7th Seaforths. He was wounded twice, in both France and Holland. He now lives in Banff and these are his memories of the happy times.

I COULD WRITE numerous stories about the various things that my brothers and I went through during the war, being in the infantry – that's where it all happened – but it's too sentimental. It always ends up talking about our pals that didn't make it, and we eventually start to cry. I like to tell the stories about the things we did for a laugh and the funny side of the army. This is an example of what we used to get up to for a laugh.

When the 6th Seaforths were mobilised in September 1939 they were billeted in the Drill Hall at the Cooper Park (now part of Elgin Library). We were all lined up for church parade on the Sunday morning. The RSM was waiting patiently for the CO to arrive for inspection of the boys, when he noticed that the flag was flying at half mast on the flag pole....then what the hell is that flying at the top of the pole? Oh no, it can't be – but it is! A pair of lady's bloomers.

The boys started laughing but the old RSM was spitting fire and vengeance on the perpetrators of such a deed before the CO's inspection. He tried long and hard to find the culprits but that was a well kept secret...and the bonnie lassie that walked home to Bishopmill minus her bloomers (no bikinis in them days) kept her secret too.

I had three bosom pals. We marched together, the four of us. We all smoked Woodbines in packets of five. Our pay was 2 shillings a day with the stoppages off that. When we moved to Forres we landed on our feet – the officers' mess and billets were in the Carlton Hotel; we were in the Drill Hall and eventually up in the Hydro. The officers' mess sergeant approached our pal John, whose father was a gamekeeper, and asked if he could supply anything to supplement the menu in the officers' mess –pheasants, rabbits, hares etc.

The Finlayson brothers: Donald (centre) served with the RAF and won the DFC and Bar; John (top left) and Charles (top right) were in the Seaforths; and the twins Alec (left) and William were in the Scots Guards.

We landed on a really good thing. John didn't mention it to his father, no, the four of us went out twice a week poaching on the Cawdor Estate. Our pal John was a good teacher at the poaching and our pal Eric the butcher was a crack hand at plucking the pheasants, ducks, partridges, pigeons, hens, hares and rabbits. Eric was a real professional at the presentation and getting them ready for the cooking pot – he used to buy the white mealy puddings for the stuffing. My job was to bury all the feathers, hare and rabbit skins, leaving no evidence.

The officers' mess were being fed like royalty; I can still remember the price-list: pheasants, hens and ducks 1s each (5p in today's money!), partridges, pigeons, woodcocks, 9d each, large hares 1s, rabbits 6d pair, 15 to 20lb salmon 3 shillings.

One day we were at Findhorn putting up miles of barbed wire and filling sandbags for gun pits. We stopped for midday break – two slices of bread and cheese and water out of the water bottle we carried. There were many seagulls around and one of them made the fatal mistake of splattering John across the shoulders. A crack shot, he duly picked up his rifle and had it down in a minute. We were going to bury the carcass but Eric stopped us and suggested John take down another one and make a brace. So he did, and Eric dressed them as ducks and handed them in to the officers' mess. It later on materialised that during the meal in the mess the CO commented that the ducks tasted a bit strong, but the mess caterer replied that that's what happened when ducks had access to salt water.

Those seagulls were some ducks!

I am the only one of the four that survived the war and can only speak of the good times and the laughs we had together.

Bill Lindsay

THE OPTIMIST

The fall of Singapore to the Japanese Army on February 15, 1942
was probably Britain's worst defeat of World War II. It was an
indication of the speed and savagery with which Japan was to
conduct a war that only ended with the use of the atomic bomb in
August 1945. The surrender of Singapore also ushered in three
years of appalling treatment for the Commonwealth POWs who
were caught in the island military base. Director of Education for
Moray and Nairn prior to the re-organisation of local government,
Bill Lindsay was commissioned in 1939 and joined the 73rd Heavy
Anti-aircraft Regiment guarding Rosyth Naval dockyard, but life
was not very exciting and so in the Autumn of 1940 he volunteered
for service in Malta – where all the action was, he thought. He
never did discover exactly how Malta turned into Malaya, but on
March 11, 1941 he arrived in Singapore and was posted to a
regular Ack-Ack Unit – the 3rd Anti-aircraft Regiment.

THE FIRST WARNING I had that something was about to happen
was when on one of my rare visits to the cinema in Singapore a
notice flashed on the screen instructing all troops to return at once
to barracks. The next day we had instructions to cut down some
rubber trees which might impede our view, which certainly showed
that things were being taken seriously, and that evening we were
even allowed to lay out some live shells round the gun pits!

The night the causeway connecting Singapore with the
mainland was blown, we were told that we must move our gun site
and be all set at Teloh Ayer Harbour. Things were now looking
very black. On the Monday the last of the Hurricanes had fought
magnificently against heavy odds; on the Tuesday they had flown
off to Sumatra. On the Wednesday morning just before first light
we were awakened by a smash and grab bombing raid on a nearby
oil tank. We stood to in case there should be a repeat. Soon we

heard the low droning of a heavy plane coming in from the south. We then saw it was flying navigation lights and probably flashing what was the recognition signal of the day if there had been one. It was coming straight towards us and was a sitting target, but my spotter suddenly said, "It's a Catalina". I had to do a quick piece of thinking. We had been instructed to treat all planes as hostile and this Catalina could well be flown by Japanese who had captured one or two of our planes. I had no time to seek guidance so I made the big decision – I decided the

Bill Lindsay.

plane was friendly, passed on the news to the next gun site and in a few moments saw the plane land safely. I learned later that the plane carried General Wavell (*Supreme British Commander of the South-West Pacific Region*) who had arrived to give a 'backs to the wall' talk to the troops. If I hadn't disobeyed the Army command and had brought down his plane I'd have regretted it all my life.

On the evening of the 15th, Singapore capitulated. The following day we marched to Changi.

Towards the end of June, hearing that a party was going to Thailand, I volunteered to go on it. I thought there might be some chance of food working there rather than doing nothing on a starvation diet in Changi. We travelled, packed literally like herring in a barrel, in steel coaches on a three-day nightmare journey to Banpong, to the west of Bangkok. We took it in turns to sit at the openings in the heat of the day. Our job was to be unloading railway supplies at a marshalling yard which was to be the start of the railway to Rangoon. We lived in long, low bamboo huts thatched with attap. Our beds consisted of bamboo slats a foot or so off the ground. Life was tolerable for a while, but with the monsoon trouble arrived. The huts were up against the railway embankment and there was no drainage so that the site became first a quagmire, then a pond, then a lake.

The water was soon lapping our beds. It was a long miserable walk to the latrines at night and one can imagine what happened. The place, too, became a gathering ground for frogs, and one could see floating past one's bed all sorts of nauseating things and imagine more. Yet I distinctly remember one night looking out and seeing the reflection of the moon in the water so that it really looked beautiful and I recalled lines I had learned at school – 'Two men looked out through prison bars – One saw mud and the other saw stars', and I determined as far as possible that I would see stars. And being an optimist, I usually did. Fortunately, we were not to settle long in this camp, and my last recollection is of a doctor in gumboots, with the water lapping round him, performing an operation on a makeshift table of slats.

The Friendly Thais

The Thais were very friendly to us. Often when we were out on working parties they would come over surreptitiously and slip a packet of cigarettes or some fruit into our hand. In fact the Thais were so friendly that the Japs shot two or three 'pour encourager les autres'. I remember one occasion when after pushing heavily laden lorries through the streets in the heat of the afternoon, a Thai woman came out to my group at the end of the column with a bowl of iced coffee and straws. It was nectar indeed! The day before I was to go up country to the jungle I slipped off round the corner when the guard in charge of the working party was not looking to see if I could find something to spend my fortune of 50 cents on. In a store I saw a cake of Lifebuoy soap. I went in and asked the little girl in charge what it cost. She told me one dollar. I showed her that all I had was 50 cents. She then went and consulted someone at the back of the shop and coming forward with a smile handed it to me saying: "I give you".

For the next few months I was in the base camp at Kanburi, a small town on the River Kwai. The work was still hard: mainly collecting stones from the river bed to act as ballast for the railway, but the meals were more regular. The highlight came when it was heard that there was to be a distribution of mail. I was sent to Nong

Pladuk to collect it. First I had to sort it out and it will not be difficult to understand that the first letter of the alphabet I started with was the initial letter of my own name but I seemed to be the only officer for whom there was no mail.

PARTICULARS OF HOLDER.

NAME (in full) WILLIAM FRASER LINDSAY

Rank or Appointment. Lt. R.A.

Issuing Officer

Signature of Holder.

Date of Issue 28 JUN 1941

Little more than six months after this pass
was issued giving Bill Lindsay authority to
be anywhere in Malaya, he was a prisoner
of the Japanese.

Hygiene was a constant problem. No words could possibly portray the utter filth of the latrines. Our closest friends were lice: we could not get rid of them. Finally it was decided that every person in the camp should have everything he possessed put into a steam oven. This was done and we were cleared. Unfortunately, the person who put my knapsack into the oven did not notice that my only pair of boots was there. When I returned they were ruined! Next to lice came bed bugs. We soon found a way, however, of getting rid of them. From time to time we took out the bamboo slats, which formed our beds, ran them through a flame and we were free for a while.

Flies were a constant menace, and it became a rule that every sick man in hospital should have a fly swat to help to keep the flies down. The Japs even saw the sense of this because it affected them and they offered rewards for every quinine bottle full of flies that they were given. It takes a long time to fill a quinine bottle, but quite a lot of useful dollars accrued to the sick because of this. One day, however, a curious Jap thought he would look inside one of the bottles and saw that those flies were very dead indeed – too dead! Instead of being disposed of they had been saved to add to the next day's store!

It was now the late autumn of 1944 and the railway was almost completed. Soon the men from the south – the Thailand party - would meet the men from the north, the Burma party, in the region of the Three Pagodas Pass and the line would be joined. At this time we were working 27 hour shifts. We would get up in the morning at first light and after breakfast of rice porridge and tea would make our way to the trucks, fit men and sick men alike, and then we would trundle down the line as far as it could go. Sometimes the sick would be sent back at this stage. We would work till about mid-day when we would have a break for 'lunch', consisting of a rice and vegetable rissole and hot water. We would then work all afternoon in the blazing sun until about dusk when we would have the evening meal – the one thing we lived for. This consisted usually of rice and vegetable stew with a little meat in it. Then by the light of flares we would start again and go on working all night until the next shift arrived the following morning after nine.

A Letter From Home

I got my first letters from home in January 1944 – the last time I had received letters was in early December 1941. The main information I got was that my people at home had received one of the two postcards which I had so far sent them. This was a great relief.

One day I was the officer in charge of a working party and went down to collect the spades. To my amazement I saw a number of Japanese soldiers sweeping the path of leaves. I could not understand why they were doing the job instead of us and I thought it best to turn my head aside and appear not to see their humiliation. Unfortunately I failed to notice the new Jap

Commandant who had arrived through the night. He gave a great shout and motioned me to come towards him. He was very thickset, almost as broad as he was long. He motioned to me to come right up to him and the next thing I knew was that I was lying on my back about six yards away. I got up, and he motioned me towards him again, and like a fool I went. He repeated the same performance. My bones were aching, but this time I had the sense to shout out that I was the officer in charge of the working party and I was left to carry on.

At night we could hear allied planes on their way to military targets in the vicinity of Bangkok. Our camp was situated next the marshalling yard of Nong Pladuk, where we had started two years before. One night I listened to the planes coming over and it seemed that instead of going on to Bangkok they were circling the camp and I knew that what we had always feared was about to take place – the marshalling yard was to be bombed. Our side of the camp escaped, but a stick of bombs hit the huts on the other side killing over 100 POWs. No other incident in the whole of the three and a half year's captivity did more to lower morale than this raid.

However, there was one consolation. The following day I was in charge of a small party that was sent to assist in the other camp. Before I went the CO told me there was a rumour that a plane had dropped a pamphlet. He told me to try and see it with my own eyes, memorise it, and report back to him personally. I saw the pamphlet which had been dropped outside the camp and been brought in by a Thai. On the top it bore the inscription 'Cheer up, boys! It's in the bag!' On one side was a map of Europe giving the allied positions and on the other a map of the Pacific with the same information. It was the first real news we'd had had for over two years and renewed our hopes.

In January, 1945, we moved back to Kanburi which became an officer's only camp for the first time, apart from a few Jap-employed men. One of the POWs I met was Bill Barr Cochrane, who made me some trousers out of a kit bag, but I didn't know him then.

Life became increasingly more difficult. The Japs were losing the war and knew it, and knew that we knew it. Every plane that passed over was an allied one. When they passed low we used to cheer until the Japs issued an instruction forbidding us to laugh or cheer when allied planes came. The Japs did everything to break our spirit. Once we were confined to our huts for a week. The tension mounted. Many were sure that one day the Japs would turn their machine guns on us and liquidate us.

Home for Christmas

In July we made our last move. First we went by train to Bangkok. When in Bangkok station that night a Japanese troop train with wounded and sick stopped opposite our truck and a Japanese shouted to us in English: "You'll be home for Christmas!" We hoped he was right – and he was.

First, however, we were to have a forced march which I shall never forget. For a day and a night we marched to a new camp to the north-east of Bangkok. We were very weak and carried all our possessions on our back, few as they were. We helped to carry each other's loads, but the march was too much for some. I remember that at the entrance to the camp one man just could not get up. In fury the Jap guard urinated on his face, but even that could not produce the necessary last effort.

At the mid-day break one day we noticed that our guards were very excited and were talking and gesticulating. One was drunk and was putting his arms round some of the POWs and saying: "All soldiers friends", etc. When we went back to the camp in the afternoon one of our number who had stayed at the bamboo pile during the 'lunch' break, said to us in subdued excitement: "What do you think of this?" A Thai came over to me and said "Tokyo finisho" and wrote on the ground 14.8.45. He also muttered something about a great bomb.

During the night a Dutch party arrived and a doctor said that in Bangkok station someone had whispered to him that the Japs had capitulated. The next morning the senior British officer approached the Japanese and asked if the war was over. At first he talked about a truce, but eventually conceded that the Japanese had capitulated, so the officer said: "I take over from now," and he did.

Later that day a smartly dressed British officer appeared from nowhere and was closeted with the senior British and Dutch officers. Suddenly word came round that this officer would be going back immediately to Bangkok and would be pleased to take any letters we had. This caused a laugh, because the Japs had taken all our pens and pencils recently and we had no notepaper. By a stroke of luck, however, I had picked up a pencil the day before which a Jap must have dropped. I took a letter which I had received from home and wrote a brief message to my parents between the lines. I then folded it into an envelope, gummed it shut with rice, tied it up with pieces of thread from my knap-sack and addressed it home via Army Post Office Air Mail. Within ten days it was delivered to my home in Scotland and I still have it!

The next day we saw planes dropping food parcels to another rank's camp nearby and we were told that in a few days we would be taken to Bangkok.

Thousands of troops had their home leave delayed so that we POWs could be shipped back at the earliest possible date. I travelled on the *City of Worcester* calling at Colombo, Suez and Gibraltar, eventually arriving at Liverpool. The next day I was proceeding north in the train and that evening in my home town. The whole crescent was lit up in welcome. After nearly five years I was home.

I don't bear the Japs or the Korean guards any ill will. The worst in men as well as the best comes out in wartime and life in the jungle wasn't funny for the Japs either.

It all happened a long time ago and when I think of it now I remember those who never made it home or whom I shall never see again, and all the friends I had who would willingly share their last dollar with me and did so.

Rita Ross

KNITTING SLIPPERS, MAKING KNICKERS

Three days after war broke out Margaret Watson's father went away to sea. Now Mrs Rita Ross, New Elgin, she remembers those days clearly, although she was only six at the time.

MY FATHER, ALEXANDER, was a Lossiemouth fisherman, but he was in the Naval Reserves, so he was one of the first to go. After he left we went to stay with my grandmother in Bishopmill. Being just six it didn't really register with me where he was going, but I remember going to the station to say farewell. He was at Dunkirk, in the Mediterranean, Egypt and Tobruk.

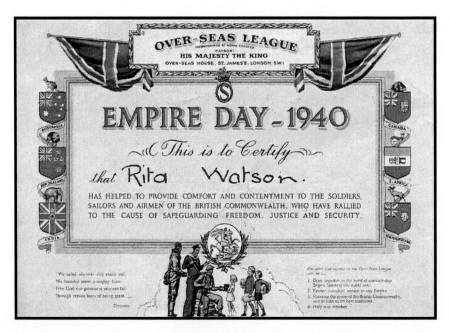

A colourful card was sent to children who'd done their bit for the war effort.

I don't remember having a hard time of it. I do remember the blackouts, so in winter we could only get out to play when the moon was shining. At school we were told we had to practise for air-raids. When the bell sounded we were to run as fast as our little legs would carry us and go home. We were to ask our mothers what the time was. I never did find out why, but I suppose it was so that the school would know how long it took us to reach home, and whether we'd have time to get home if there was a real air raid. We lived quite near the school, so it was easy for me.

A Lossiemouth fisherman, but now in the
Navy, Alexander Watson would have treasured
this picture with his daughter Rita.

Because we'd moved in with Gran and Granddad and two aunts and an uncle, we had plenty of rations. When dad came home he always brought lots of chocolate, and I also got fruit – bananas, grapes, peaches, things others didn't get at school; they would run round and ask for a bit.

As far as I was concerned, war was an adventure. We stayed near the woods and collected cones and bits of trees for firewood, and we went to the gas works with an old pram to get cinders – it was a long walk, but distance was no object. We also walked to Sunday school at St Columba's and to the Gospel Hall in Murdoch's Wynd for a lantern slide show in the afternoon.

When I was seven we knitted squares for blankets for Empire Day at school. We also collected silver paper, and empty metal toothpaste tubes. Nothing was wasted. I even knitted slippers, and I sewed a pair of knickers in green check.

I liked going to the pictures every Saturday morning. It cost thruppence. We'd see *Flash Gordon*, but have to go back the next week to see the next episode, but it was mostly cowboys and Indians. I remember seeing *Pinocchio* at the Playhouse – it was always a treat when the film was in colour. We'd be standing in the queue waiting to go in and someone would shout: 'Halls have got crisps!' and we'd all dash along to Halls the greengrocers.

We had an accumulator battery for the wireless, but Granddad ruled the roost and we were only allowed to listen to the news. The library was still on the go and I had my *Beano* and *Dandy* to read. All the teachers at Bishopmill School were women, except one, Mr Paul. At playtime we'd get Horlicks to drink in winter – it made me sick – and I was given Virole to keep me healthy, and wore an iodine locket and a liberty bodice to keep warm. It was something you never questioned – and I never got ill so they must have worked.

James Chisholm

STANDING ROOM ONLY

Working as a fireman on the railways still involved doing one's bit for the war effort, as James Chisholm (b.1924), Elgin, can confirm.

THERE WERE AROUND 100 employed at the railway shed in Elgin with the old LNER (*London and North Eastern Railways*). It was a reserved occupation; a few men tried to volunteer for the services but were turned down.

Fireman James Chisholm onboard his LNER steam engine.

You never knew where we'd be going. We might be taking troops, tanks stores, or ordinary passengers. It was always something different. One particular time, we went to Aberdeen to pick up mules for the Indian Army training in the Cairngorms. We were told to go to Broomhill beside Boat of Garten where a squad of Indian troops started unloading the mules. They tied them heads to tails, and one white man on a great brown horse led the whole string of mules away.

I lived in digs at 237 High Street, where there were 10 lodgers. My room had four beds in it. With being on shifts someone would get out of bed to let someone in for a sleep - accommodation was short and we didn't think anything of it in those days. It would be frowned on today.

The landlady was good, but sugar was short so she said we could either get sugar in our tea, or a pudding. Most of us went for a pudding - I've not had tea with sugar in since. It cost 30 shillings a week, but I think my wages were just 45 shillings so there wasn't much left.

Train crews received special rations because we had to take a 'piece' with us. This meant extra cheese which was pooled on a Monday so that the landlady could share it out through the week.

I remember that the trains were always full, standing room only - there was no other way to travel. At Aberdeen the guards would be pushing people in, the carriages were jam-packed. There were trains stopping at all the places right along the coast, and going up to Mulben and Dufftown.

LNER railwaymen at Elgin during the war years.

Nan Rennie

THE LAND GIRL

The Women's Land Army played a crucial role in Britain during the war by helping to provide Britain with food at a time when U-boats were destroying many merchant ships bringing supplies to Britain from America. Now living in Inverness, Nan Rennie's home was in Elgin for many years although she was born near Ebbw Vale in South Wales in 1921. She worked for a firm of Jewish tailors in London before the war, and it was in the city there that she first encountered British members of the Nazi movement.

THE PEOPLE I worked for were very good employers and never mentioned the problems in Germany to me. One day I'd been out for a walk with my older sister, Kathleen, who was also working in London when, by mischance, we encountered a rally of Blackshirts led by Mosley. We had to pass through them, and it was a frightening experience, especially as I worked for Jews. My mother came up from Wales when war was declared and insisted my sister and I return home. I wanted to join one of the armed services, but my father said no, so my sister and I went into the Land Army. I did eight weeks training at Carmarthen Agricultural College. We were supposed to train in various sections: dairy one week, poultry the next, and so on, but I went into cows and stayed there. I liked it, although before the war I didn't know one end of a cow from another. It was hard work, and we used muscles we'd never used before.

Land girls are always shown wearing corduroy jodhpurs, bottle green pullovers and cream shirts with a tie, but that was our dress uniform: we were more often in dungarees. After college I was posted to a farm at Cwmbran. There was another Land Army girl, the farmer, his wife, and two children. The wife had no idea about farm life and the food was dreadful. She couldn't even boil potatoes, and knew nothing about seasoning. I think her husband felt sorry for us because he used to buy us buns when we were on the milk run. We'd get up at 6am, eat porridge full of lumps, and then go straight out to the cowshed. We had to milk the cows by hand, and deliver the milk round the town, ladling it into jugs - no bottled milk in those days. We also worked in the fields and we had two big shire horses to look after. One day I was sent out to a field with the horses harnessed to a big roller with me sitting on top. There was a steep slope, which we went up OK, but coming down the horses started galloping, anxious to get home. I tried criss-crossing to and fro to slow them down, but they wanted to go straight down. Luckily a young man was passing, saw I was in trouble, and took over.

Eventually Gwen, the other girl, complained about the food so much that we were moved. I went first to a farm near Newport, and then very soon to a big house at Chepstow. I'm not quite sure how they justified having a Land Army girl, they were very well off and had a personal maid, cook, kitchen maid, chauffeur, gardener and gardener's boy - this was when there was a war on, mind! I had to look after two cows, milk them and make butter. I also looked after chickens, and the family's four dogs - two fox hounds, a spaniel and a terrier - and when the son of the house came home from the army on leave I was expected to look after his hunter, all 17-hands (I was five-foot-two!). I said I had no intentions of doing the latter, so his batman had to do it. When I'd finished my chores with the animals I was supposed to help in the garden. None of the lawns were turned over to vegetables, as ordinary people were expected to do. Sometimes troops marched across the grounds on exercise.

Serve Yourself!

The family didn't seem to go without anything, and still held dinner parties. One night the maid was off and the cook asked if I'd serve at dinner. I said it wasn't my job, but she had a struggle walking so I agreed to help... but I just put the food on the table, they had to serve themselves: there was a war on, after all! When the air raid warning went we'd go up onto the balcony to watch the German planes going over. There were never any bombs dropped near us.

Nan Rennie.

There were dances, and we'd go to the pictures often. Once the air raid siren went while we were in the cinema; a lot of people got up and left, but we stayed to watch the end of the film, although we were a bit apprehensive. In October 1940 the Land Girls were invited to a dance at the army barracks in Chepstow. I was already going out with an army dentist at the time, but this Scot was sitting at the next table and he arranged to take me home. We got engaged at Christmas. He was due leave and wanted to take me up to Scotland to meet his parents, but my father wouldn't let me go on holiday with him without getting married first! So we were married on January 12, the day before my 20th birthday. We had a church wedding by special licence. I wore a new powder blue dress with a darker coat and hat. My younger sister Doris and cousin Miriam Williams were bridesmaids, they wore what they had. You couldn't get sugar for icing, but my mother made a sponge cake and covered it with chocolate, and that was my wedding cake. The wedding car was loaned to us.

We rented rooms in Chepstow after we married, but they didn't have any cooking facilities and I was only allowed a scuttle of coal a day for heating - and it was winter. When my husband was posted I went home to live with my parents, and our daughter was born there in October 1941. When my husband was posted to the Isle of Wight I took rooms in a big house near Southampton. The owner, Mrs Obie, had a large garden - the tennis courts had been dug over and planted with potatoes - and I helped in the garden when I could. The first time I went to stay, it was quite a built up area, but I later went back and you could see across the town to the docks - it had been so badly bombed.

Most of the war I spent either in South Wales, or in Aberdeenshire with my husband's family. I travelled up by train with the baby. The trains were always crowded, even travelling first class. There were people standing in the corridors or sitting on their suitcases, and always lots of servicemen and women. The train would stop at almost every station and there would be trolleys serving tea, but everyone took sandwiches with them. In rural Aberdeenshire there always seemed to be plenty of food and rationing didn't seem to be the problem it was in the south where if you saw a queue, you joined it – and discovered later what you were queuing for! I usually took butter and eggs back to Wales with me after a visit north. My father-in-law would shoot a brace of hares and I'd tie them together, put a label on them, and post them south. Whisky was scarce, but I always managed to get some for my father, who was an invalid, and I'd post that - it was so much easier to post things in those days, and everything arrived the next day, despite the war.

When the war ended I was in Aberdeenshire. We were expecting it, but it was a big relief. I went back to Wales and there were street parties – everyone gave whatever they had from their rations, and we pooled the lot. There was a strong camaraderie then that has sadly disappeared.

Ken Gill

BOMBED BUT BUOYANT

Plymouth suffered tremendous damage in World War II: it was described as the worst bombed city in the country. Air raid control centres were organised underneath the guildhall and Devonport market, and in early summer 1940 the blitz began. Ken Gill (b. 1926) formerly of Hopeman, now Rothes, lived through it.

I REMEMBER THE day war was declared. We'd been looking through the gates of what should have been our next school – I was going up to secondary school that year and should have started the next day – but we never got to go there because it was taken over as a hospital, which is what it had been in the Great War, too.

I joined the Civil Defence in Plymouth a year before war started when I was 12, we knew war was coming and they would take you at any age. I was a messenger boy at a Report Centre and when war broke out it was my job to open up the market gates when the sirens went so that people had access to the shelter under the market. Sometimes people would get there before me and were wondering why it wasn't opened, but there was another gate just round the corner they could use. Another job I had was to keep the escape hatches from the shelter topped up with water – the lids had a sort of lip round the edge. This was to stop gas leaking through. There was a bicycle to generate electricity in case the power went. I tried it a few times, but even for a young blood like me it was hard going. I couldn't keep it going long.

I used to go out on my bike to the wardens' posts with messages. One night I was riding along – no lights, of course, because of the blackout when all of a sudden I found myself flat on my back, stunned, and a policeman peering down at me. "What are you doing down there, boy?" he said. I was in a bomb crater.

Plymouth was the heaviest bombed city in the country, and that's not just me saying that. One day a friend and I went up to the park shelter to have a smoke when the Germans started dropping incendiary bombs on the park. The ground was soft and many of them failed to explode, so we started collecting them. My friend had an arm full and ran home with them to his mother. He couldn't even open the door his arms were so full, so he kicked it open and ran in to show his mother what he'd got...and all she said was: "You've been smoking again, haven't you?" Sometimes the incendiaries would come in through the roof and my father would throw them out of the window quickly.

Ken Gill (left), with a fellow Civil
Defence messenger, endured the
bombing in Plymouth.

A lorry would come and take a load of us children up to Lee Moor to cut bracken. This was put under netting to disguise the chalk ground as they thought the Germans were using it as guidelines.

Imagine what it was like, going into the shelter one night and coming up the next to find everything gone, cinemas, houses, everything. It was like looking at a different land – there was nothing there but rubble. It took me 20 minutes to go home usually, but one morning it took an hour, I had to take so many detours. The night before my mother said she'd got an egg for my breakfast – you couldn't get eggs – and I was looking forward to it, but when I turned the corner, the house was completely gone. I always think of my mother when I see an egg.

The family were all in the Anderson shelter. I found the cat and put it in my jacket, where it was clawing me, it was so frightened. My father was a warden on a firing range and he had a hut. We slept there on the floor until another warden took us to his cottage at Crafthole. There was my sister and her four children, my mother, father, myself and my brother who was home from the Navy after being operated on, all sleeping in a two-bedroom cottage. I don't know where the owners slept. It was seven miles to Plymouth, but my father said I still had to go to school, so I walked it – only to find the school had been evacuated, and I'd no idea where they'd gone. I had to walk all the way back. I was 14 by this time and waiting to hear the results of my exams to get into the dockyard, but Dad said I couldn't be idle so he got me a job at Tregantle Fort as a batman to officers training in gas warfare. There were a lot of civilian batmen, but I was the youngest – the others were mostly old soldiers. One day we were told a plane was in trouble, it was flying up and down the beach, unable to get sufficient lift to get up over the cliffs. It crashed into the sea and a warden swam out to help. After that we used to swim out regularly to get souvenirs from the sunken plane.

A Family Flee

One morning I went to the fort and saw a passenger plane sitting on the slope above the cliff. A policeman was guarding it and he said a French test pilot had managed to save up the fuel to fly his family out and bring them to England. I often wonder what happened to that family. It was very brave of him. I imagine he didn't dare to fly further inland in case he was shot down.

After a few months we were told that ATS girls would be doing the job from then on, but Dad said I still couldn't stay at home doing nothing. The owner of the cottage was called up and I got his job as warden on the range, with my own hut. My father had been in the Great War. One day we heard an explosion and he said it had been a mine on the beach. It was roped off but exploded and four sergeants were missing. All we found were their buttons, with pinholes in them, and a pair of boots with the feet still inside. We took the boots. Mum asked where we'd got them from, and we told her from someone who didn't need them. We wasted nothing; everything was so hard to come by.

There were a lot of Polish fighter pilots about. They were fantastic; you could see them up there fighting. At the cinema, they were always allowed to go to the head of the queue. Everyone thought they were marvellous.

I heard I'd passed for the dockyard and became a shipwright apprentice in November 1941. There was a raid one night, and we were all sitting in a massive building where they did the moulding for the ships - it was like a hangar only 10 times bigger. We had candles. Suddenly we heard this big crash and someone said that a bomb had hit us, but there was no blast. We crept down to the other end of the building and suddenly came in contact with metal. A voice called out: "Where the hell are we?" It was an American landing craft, which had crashed right into the building - they must have been confused in the raid.

A friend of my mother's was evacuated to Torquay with her child to escape the bombs. One day a policeman came to the door with a letter for my mother: the friend had been machine-gunned by a plane as she was walking along the street and had been found dead with the letter in her hand – she'd been on her way to post it. Rather than send the letter to us, the authorities delivered it with the explanation.

An RAF friend of my brothers was killed when his plane crashed: I was a bearer at his funeral. I was a bearer at a lot of funerals.

I had a girlfriend called Hettie Bunny, and going to work one morning she showed me a nose cap of a shell. She'd been in bed the night before when a raid started. People used to hang on to see if it was going to be a big one; if so, they'd get up and go to the shelter. Eventually she thought she'd better get up and was just out of bed when the shell came through the roof and hit the bed, straight through it. She probably saved my life by stopping to show me the shell... we heard a crash as we were talking and the building I would have been walking past if I hadn't stopped collapsed.

One night I was taking her home when we saw this chain of lights coming along the road towards us. I pulled her into a doorway just in time...they were incendiary bombs; we'd never even heard the plane.

I joined a new Report Centre in 1942 and instead of a cycle I was taught to ride a motorcycle. We were all madcaps, and would race to get the best bike. One day we had to learn a route to escort the fire brigade. All the best bikes had been taken and I ended up with the one we called The Crab because it went funny round corners. I was lagging behind everyone else because of this. A water tank had been damaged and the water spilled over the road had frozen. They all hit the ice and came off their bikes, but I saw it in time so I had the last laugh.

I was due to go into the Navy, but it was D-Day and they cancelled it. After the war I was a carpenter on troop ships, and then passenger ships.

Mona Clayton

NAZIS OVER LOSSIEMOUTH

Mona Clayton, nee Colvin, (b. 1922), now living in Canada, worked in Lossiemouth Post Office during the war. She met her husband Herbie, who was with the Canadian Air Force based at Lossiemouth, and after the war went with him when he returned to Canada. Her brother, William Colvin, was at Arnhem, and she recalls being worried about him. His story is also told in this book.

MY DAD DIED just before the war started, and the Colvins were all very upset but we all just carried on helping each other cope. My job was said to be necessary so I stayed and helped Mum as much as I could. We had many service men at Seaview including one Black Argyll and Sutherland soldier from Sierra Leone.

When we thought the Germans would be invading, we all listened to Winston Churchill on the wireless: he gave us hope

My most vivid recollection is of the Nazi plane I saw coming up from the East Beach and round the harbour. I was fixing the blackout on my bedroom window and nearly fell off the chair when I saw the Nazi sign on the plane. It bombed the aerodrome but was shot down and the crew are buried in Lossiemouth Cemetery. I remember the Polish Army billeted in the Baptist Church and their voices singing in the evening – the Polish Army built the concrete blocks at the West Beach.

I remember spreading pig manure with Mother when an air raid siren went off. We kept on mixing it in as Mum said she could never come back to it (It was awful stuff!).

I was away in Aberdeen when the houses in Dunbar St were bombed in 1941, they missed the Coastguard Station.

I was very lucky to have an American boyfriend in the RAF who could get chocolates and I sure enjoyed them during the picture shows. Local dances during the war were always so crowded. Ian Tocher's band played.

Jimmy (my father's older brother) was at the 13th General Hospital in Cairo for years. He was with the BEF in France and got out of France at St Malo a few days after Dunkirk. He was in the RAMC.

I was kept very busy at the Post Office as we had all the Air Force mail to look after.

I was on duty at the Post Office on the morning in 1945 when the plane crashed and killed so many members of the Flood family. It was quite an explosion.

Rene MacDonald

ON THE GEORGE CROSS ISLAND

Maltese by birth, but now a 'full-blooded Scot' – she has lived in Moray since the end of the war – Rene Robinson was one of four sisters, and was still at school when war broke out. In recognition of the islanders' suffering and endurance, Malta was later awarded the George Cross. Rene met her husband, retired Elgin GP Dr John MacDonald, when he was stationed on the island during the war. They married when she was just 19.

WHEN THE ITALIANS started dropping bombs on Malta in June of 1940 I was nearly 15 years old. Although the war had begun the year before, we had nothing to fear then from the Germans. My dad worked as an electrician in the engineering department of the Royal Navy's Malta Dockyard. The engineering department was deep inside the steep, densely populated hills and cliffs which surrounded Grand Harbour, between moorings at Bighi, Dockyard Creek and French Creek.

I was a pupil at the Royal Naval Dockyard School, at Verdalla, a palace of The Knights of Malta, but it was quickly closed when it was revealed that directly underneath, filling the dungeon, was a large Naval explosives store.

The first bombs dropped by the Italian Air Force did little damage. At the beginning there were no fighter aircraft on the Island, but Gladiator biplanes of the Fleet Air Arm crated up for transport to Egypt were unpacked and assembled - the famous trio Faith, Hope, and Charity. Their pilots gave those Italians a bit of a fright, which persuaded them that they could not just 'take over' the Island of Malta. Its defences were reinforced and the Navy returned. But my school days were over.

By this time the Germans had arrived in Sicily, just 60 miles away, and the real bombing of Malta began. Bombers took just 20 minutes to fly to the island: 10 in a Messerschmit.

I couldn't wait to join the RAF as a civilian assistant and on my sixteenth birthday I was accepted and trained. In the War Rooms, deep inside the rock beneath Valletta, I worked on the 'plot', a very large table on which were pin-pointed the size, altitude, direction of approach – the bearings – of all the enemy bomber and fighter formations as they flew towards the island. It was exciting work and I was so proud to be called a 'plotter'. We never knew how long the raids would last and the rule was that we stayed on duty until there was a lull in the bombing.

Getting to and from work was often in the middle of an air raid. I was trapped once when a bomb almost hit us and we were rescued from the rubble by some Navy lads who had been boozing in a nearby pub. But my most horrific moment came when our friend 'Big Bill' Piercy, a Merchant Navy Officer, and I accompanied my sister Joyce, who was a year my senior, through Valletta to Grand Harbour where she used to catch a ferry across to Bighi, where she was a lady cipher assistant – a 'cipherine' – in Naval HQ. We had just reached Customhouse Steps when a German raid started. We took shelter in a warehouse. Big Bill held us in his enormous arms and said: "Girls, start praying, because we need God's help to stay alive!"

My oldest sister Betty was a nurse in King George Fifth Hospital in Floriana. She was the first of us girls to be married. Her husband was in an RAF Bomb Disposal Team. He started to sleep walk, and Betty found herself one night being ever so gently lifted from their bed – she knew that she should not waken him – and laid very carefully inside a chest of drawers.

Joyce and I joined a concert party billed as 'The Raffians' and we toured the RAF messes and performed at the historic Manuel Theatre in Valletta to a wider audience. We made our costumes from enemy parachute silk and mosquito netting and very fetching they were.

When I was seventeen and a half I joined Joyce as a 'cipherine' in Naval HQ which had by then moved to War HQ inside Lascaris Bastion. Girls in the Woman's Royal Naval Service (The Wrens) were not drafted to Malta until much later and local British girls manned the cipher machines. Entry to HQ was by pass only; it was guarded night and day against possible saboteurs.

To go to work we ran from our flat in Vincenti Buildings at the posh end of 'The Gut' to the top of Strada Reale (now Constitution Street) then down a poorly lit stairway carved inside the rock which led to the War Rooms. We felt safe there while the bombs fell on Malta, but always worried about Dad in Dockyard and Mum with our youngest sister Sheila at home. Ted Robinson, my Dad, had been in the team which was reconditioning the Floating Dock and was the last man to leave it when the Luftwaffe sank it. He was a fine man. He earned the respect of his workmen who called him 'Sant a tuila' - the tall saint.

Food and Boyfriends

It was not all blood and bombs. We were young. 'Captain Caruana's' was the place to be with our pals, for the two important things in our lives were food and boyfriends. One was severely rationed. The other was not.

Luxuries such as eggs were bought from Gozo women who sold at the doors. Mother was always pleased to let us bargain in Maltese with them when at other times she forbade it. 'It will ruin your English,' she said. Eggs were kept for a hurried departure into the shelter. Mum would say: "Quick! Fry an egg on bread and bring it with you." In the communal rock shelter deep under the British Institute at the end of the street we had our own family cabin where we would live and sleep until the all clear. Dad paid workmen forty pounds to cut it from the rock. We had bunks, magazines, a primus stove and electric light. My best friend 'Pat' Cameron was killed by bomb blast. She was found dead sheltering behind a wall, covering her face with one arm, without a mark on her! She was a pharmacist's assistant with Collins the Chemist in Strada Reale.

There were thousands of Navy lads and Submariners; Army and Air Force men on the island and boyfriends were two a penny. Three of the lads I liked best were killed and I remember them well. Mike Janvlin was a Submariner whose boat was reported missing; Ronald was an Army captain killed by 'friendly fire' on the beach-head in Sicily; Mike Malone's plane crashed into the sea when, it was thought, he became oxygen-starved.

Did I weep for them? Of course I did, bitterly. But life could be very short in those days. And we were all so young! Derek was in the Fleet Air Arm. He appeared at the flat one evening with his face and hands painted in red ink, a silly grin. He said he had been painting the town red! Later he confided that he had just been awarded the Distinguished Service Cross. He was about 22 and we were great buddies. I wonder where he is now.

All my boyfriends were well behaved, except one. He was an officer called Peter in the Royal West Kents and should have known better. I was born in Malta but my parents were Kentish folk. He had asked my father's permission to book me into a hotel for the night as we were going to a dance beyond the creeks and the ferries stopped at sunset. He promised to take care of me. I was in my nightie when I heard him knocking. I must have had suspicions about him for I had made the door fast with a securing chain. He asked to come in and took his pistol from its holster. I told him where he could put his pistol and locked the door. There was a telephone in my room - a winding-up, old-fashioned thing, but it worked. I rang Philip, a Naval doctor friend, told him what was happening and he roared round the creek on his motorbike, rescued me and drove me home. I couldn't explain to my mum, and as we girls had all been forbidden to ride motorbikes, I got a right good telling off!

My parents were bricks. We were not allowed to go out with any boyfriend unless they met him, and despite rationing, mum and dad gave super parties Whatever their rank, all were welcomed at the top flat No. 27 Vincenti Buildings, although Pete, Joyce's fiancé, wrote on their visitor's book: 'This is a strictly Naval establishment but Pongos and the RAF will be tolerated. The drop from the window into Bakery Street could be unpleasant.'

Vincenti Buildings had a charmed life. It was hit, but the bomb did not explode. Joyce persuaded her Peter to make use of his rank and rescue some of her clothes from the flat. His Radio Officer's stripe was the same colour as the Bomb Disposal badge. He appeared at the top window and Joyce's blouses, cami-knickers and other important feminine requirements came floating down to the street – and mine too. The wicked man.

I met John after my mum and dad had given him the once over at his housewarming party when he took possession of a roof flat near his 'Dressing Station' in Malta Dockyard, where he was one of the doctors. He had been in and out of Malta in his destroyer during 'Operation Husky' - our invasion of Sicily - and said he had admired Joyce and me from afar. He was a conceited chap and paid dearly for it.

He had the nerve to arrive at our flat one evening in his 'number ones' and asked me to tie his bow tie for him. He was taking a Naval nursing sister to a dance and I would have quite liked to have been asked to go to it. They had hardly arrived at the Marsa Club when a phone call stopped him in his tracks. "Surgeon Lieutenant MacDonald, you are required to attend an Able Seaman R for Robert, S-O-U-L, at his home. He is bleeding badly from a haemorrhoid." John had to leave his nursing partner and spent a couple of hours at the other end of Malta fruitlessly searching for an address which did not exist. Then the penny dropped. That name! And who could have sent him on this wild goose chase? Who indeed!

Next week he took me swimming in The Blue Grotto, challenged me to a race up a cliff, which I won, and then proposed marriage. Ten days later we were married in St John's Episcopal Cathedral in Valetta, and a fortnight after that he was off to the Far East. Japan surrendered when his warship was revitalling in the Seychelles, and back he came to me – with a ginger beard that I did not like.

"But I must have my captain's permission to shave it off," he argued.

"I am your captain now!"

That was 60 years ago; five children, thirteen grandchildren and one great-grandson later…and I still love him to bits.

A guard of honour for Surgeon Lieutenant John MacDonald
and his bride Rene following their wedding in Malta.

John MacDonald

U-BOATS AND ROMANCE

Retired Elgin GP Dr John MacDonald – better known in literary circles as Charles Mackie, author of novels with the Wolf of Badenoch as a central character – served in the Royal Navy during the war. However, his major victory in 1945 was to win the hand of a girl he'd met on Malta.

'The marriage of Miss Irene Robinson, 27 Vincenti Buildings, Valletta, Malta, and Surgeon Lieutenant John MacDonald, RNVR, Northview, North Street, Elgin, Scotland, took place in St John's Episcopal Cathedral, Malta, on June 27, 1945.'

THIS WAS THE peak of my Naval career!

From shore base HMS Drake in Devonport I became the doctor to some 200 men in the Destroyer *HMS Witherington* and after working-up from Londonderry. We performed anti-submarine patrols in the NW Approaches and then became part of the Gibraltar Anti-Submarine Force. Two very dramatic events occurred during my career as a Naval Doctor, and both involved *HMS Witherington*.

We teamed up with *HMS Wishart*, a sister ship and engaged and sunk a U-Boat in the Straits of Gibraltar, taking all of her surviving crew aboard as captives. This is what happened: suddenly, the ringing note of the anti-submarine detection apparatus changed to the double-echoing, ping ping.

"Asdec reporting contact," came the calm voice of the leading hand at the controls. From the Bridge, "Action Stations" followed by the scream of the Klaxon.

When I first joined ship I chose my station in action forward of the after depth charge party in the shelter of the bridge structure – halfway along the ship and near the engine-room companionway. The method of attack later changed from full speed ahead to a creep approach. We had by that time seen what a homing torpedo from a pursued U-boat, tuned in to the high frequency sound of the attacking ship's propellers, could to us when we found *HMS Chanticleer* with her stem blown off lying in the anchorage at Pico in the Azores, and it was a sobering sight.

Wishart beat us to it. The black flag sprung from her masthead.

"*Wishart* attacking sir".

Almost immediately came the huge white eruption of the sea behind her and the dull thump of her exploding depth charges. The attack continued after nightfall. Then, at last, "Submarine surfacing".

"A Gun, fire star shell!"

"Sub showing the white flag."

"Cease fire".

In the blackness of the night the tiny lifebelt lights of the German crew flickered like fireflies and the calls "Camarad!" drifted thinly from the heaving sea. The sub had gone to its watery grave.

I visited the survivors, huddled on the steel floor in the tiller flat. We were searching for a second sub and the erratic motion of the ship matched the varying roar of her propellers in that cramped space. A Naval seaman stood guard with fixed bayonet. I recognised him, Hussey Yeo, a Devon man extraordinary whom punishment seldom allowed ashore. The smell of Naval duty-free tobacco hit me when I stepped inside.

"Able Seaman Yeo, where did these men get their cigarettes?"

"I gave them, surr."

"Against regulations to frat with the enemy."

"Aye, aye sir – but the poor buggers needed a smoke."

I had no German. I pointed to my red stripes – "Doctor. OK?"

Smiles creased the enemy faces – "Ja, Ja. OK, OK!"

On September 8, 1943, Italy surrendered. The submarine war in the Mediterranean was not over. German U-Boats still tried to force an entrance at the Straits of Gibraltar.

We were operating from Malta; then came a dramatic signal: "*HMS Witherington* will take the surrender of the eastern flotillas of the Italian undersea fleet on September 10, at 1300 hours. Rendezvous such and such a destination."

It was a scorcher of a day. At noon we sat motionless at the rendezvous. Grey-blue sea stretched in all directions to the horizon. The ship was at action stations, guns manned, depth charges primed.

My action station, changed since we encountered *Chanticleer*, was forward, below the bridge at the door of the Asdec cabin. There I could hear everything - and the ship's doctor would not necessarily be blown to smithereens at the first counter-attack!

I could hear the Asdec operator in his cramped sweaty quarters relaying to the bridge a string of underwater bearings. There were 10 submarines and they surrounded us in a wide arc, but there was nothing to be seen.

"This is weird!" remarked the First Lieutenant. "We have fought this enemy for three years."

"Stand by Action Stations!" said the Captain quietly into the ship's communication system. " 'A' gun, swing 180 degrees, slowly." And to his First Lieutenant, his Number One: "Just to make sure they know we mean it!"

The Captain had his chronometer in his hand. Punctually, at 1300, 10 black, sinister shapes broke the surface, neatly spaced in a perfect circle, with us in the centre.

A Leading Seaman called the bearings.

"Trust the Ities to put on Grand Opera for us!" said Number One.

A conning tower hatch broke open and a white flag was raised to its small mast.

"Standby *Witherington* to receive surrender," said the Captain, his voice a shade louder than usual.

"Signalman. Make to that boat," – the aldis lamp began to chatter – "Follow me in line ahead."

And to Grand Harbour in shattered but unbeaten Malta, we led them.

The rest of my dogwatch in the Navy was uneventful – very occasionally there were times to be afraid; and fun, yes, especially when courting!

To quote Ronald Regan: "A man's gotta do what a man's gotta do". But when I met Rene I quickly learned that this had not been just a man's war.

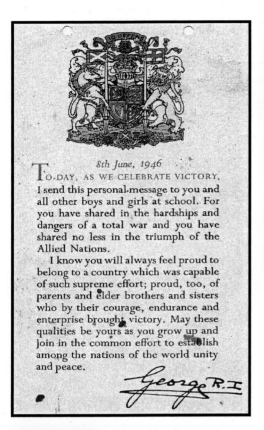

8th June, 1946

To-day, as we celebrate victory, I send this personal message to you and all other boys and girls at school. For you have shared in the hardships and dangers of a total war and you have shared no less in the triumph of the Allied Nations.

I know you will always feel proud to belong to a country which was capable of such supreme effort; proud, too, of parents and elder brothers and sisters who by their courage, endurance and enterprise brought victory. May these qualities be yours as you grow up and join in the common effort to establish among the nations of the world unity and peace.

George R.I

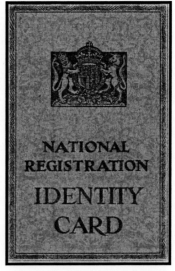

NATIONAL REGISTRATION
IDENTITY
CARD

Above: Everyone was issued with an identity card during the war. Even children were provided with their own cards.

Left: A message from the King was sent to every child in Britain for Victory Day.

Somewhere in Normandy: a soldier of the 2nd Btn The Gordon Highlanders.

21 ARMY GROUP

PERSONAL MESSAGE
FROM THE C-in-C

To be read out to all Troops

1. The time has come to deal the enemy a terrific blow in Western Europe.

The blow will be struck by the combined sea, land, and air forces of the Allies—together constituting one great Allied team, under the supreme command of General Eisenhower.

2. On the eve of this great adventure I send my best wishes to every soldier in the Allied team.

To us is given the honour of striking a blow for freedom which will live in history; and in the better days that lie ahead men will speak with pride of our doings. We have a great and a righteous cause.

Let us pray that " The Lord Mighty in Battle " will go forth with our armies, and that His special providence will aid us in the struggle.

3. I want every soldier to know that I have complete confidence in the successful outcome of the operations that we are now about to begin.

With stout hearts, and with enthusiasm for the contest, let us go forward to victory.

4. And, as we enter the battle, let us recall the words of a famous soldier spoken many years ago :—

> " *He either fears his fate too much,*
> *Or his deserts are small,*
> *Who dare not put it to the touch,*
> *To win or lose it all.*"

5. Good luck to each one of you. And good hunting on the mainland of Europe.

B. L. Montgomery
General
C.-in-C 21 Army Group.

1944.

'Good hunting!' A D-Day message to the Armed Forces from General Montgomery...

SUPREME HEADQUARTERS
ALLIED EXPEDITIONARY FORCE

Links: De Glorieuze Kruistocht. Het inspirerende vlugschrift van generaal Eisenhower op de vooravond van de invasie in die.

Rechts: Deze persoonlijke mededeling van generaal Montgomery, bevelhebber van de Geallieerde grondtroepen, straalt optimisme en vertrouwen uit.

Soldiers, Sailors and Airmen of the Allied Expeditionary Force!

You are about to embark upon the Great Crusade, toward which we have striven these many months. The eyes of the world are upon you. The hopes and prayers of liberty-loving people everywhere march with you. In company with our brave Allies and brothers-in-arms on other Fronts, you will bring about the destruction of the German war machine, the elimination of Nazi tyranny over the oppressed peoples of Europe, and security for ourselves in a free world.

Your task will not be an easy one. Your enemy is well trained, well equipped and battle-hardened. He will fight savagely.

But this is the year 1944 ! Much has happened since the Nazi triumphs of 1940-41. The United Nations have inflicted upon the Germans great defeats, in open battle, man-to-man. Our air offensive has seriously reduced their strength in the air and their capacity to wage war on the ground. Our Home Fronts have given us an overwhelming superiority in weapons and munitions of war, and placed at our disposal great reserves of trained fighting men. The tide has turned ! The free men of the world are marching together to Victory !

I have full confidence in your courage, devotion to duty and skill in battle. We will accept nothing less than full Victory !

Good Luck ! And let us all beseech the blessing of Almighty God upon this great and noble undertaking.

Dwight D. Eisenhower

…And a similar message, although phrased rather differently, from the Supreme Commander of the troops invading France, Dwight D. Eisenhower.

A fellow pilot puts the finishing touch to 'Fifi' as Eric Phelp
admires his work from the wing of the plane. Fifi was later
shot down, her pilot bailed out and was taken prisoner.

NOTICE.

1. When you join your Unit you should take with
   you:— YOUR RAZOR

   Your Gas Mask.
   Your National Registration Identity Card.
   Your Ration Book.
   The enclosed envelope N.S. 124 completed in
   accordance with the directions at the top.

2. Before you leave to join your Unit you should
   take or send (or ask your employer to send)
   your Unemployment Book (including Exempt
   Persons Book) to the nearest Local Office of the
   Ministry of Labour and National Service. The
   Local Office should be informed why the book is
   being surrendered. You should keep a note of
   the number on the book.

N.S. 34.   (5574) Wt. 9001—4008 500,000 4/40 T.S. 677

A conscript was warned to take his gas mask and ration book
with him when called up… oh, and not to forget his razor!

Betty Brander

ON THE HOME FRONT

Life on the Home Front was hard, particularly for women left to bring up families on their own. Betty Brander (b. 1915) lived in King Street, Elgin for 55 years, including the war years.

I WAS PEELING potatoes at about 11am on the Sunday and I heard the church bells ringing for church when Chamberlain declared that we were at war. Six weeks later, my husband John, who worked at the Cathedral as a mason, was called up to the Royal Engineers, Bomb Disposal. We had one child, Muriel, and I was left to bring her up on £1 0s 48d – less than £1.50p in today's money – but everyone was in the same boat and you didn't think anything of it. There was no keeping up with the Joneses in those days. You helped one another and everyone was very kind – if a neighbour was short they'd come and borrow a bit of food.

When rationing started you got 4oz bacon or ham, 8oz sugar, 2oz tea, 8oz meat, 2oz cheese, 2oz butter and 4oz margarine, 2oz cooking fat a week; one shell egg every two weeks and a packet of dried eggs every four weeks. When you went to the shop you had to wait while they weighed everything out for you. Corned beef cost 2d for half-a-pound. You could buy under the counter if your face fitted. If you could get a knuckle bone then you'd boil it up and make broth. We didn't have fridges in those days. I had a wooden safe which was kept in a cool corner, but there was never anything left over. A boat load of bananas came into town one Saturday: the children were excited, but when they got them they didn't know what to do with them – they'd never had bananas before.

Everything had a utility mark, bedding, everything. I remember buying a pair of sandals for Muriel at Greenlees shoe shop, they cost 1s 11d. I never stopped knitting, scarves, balaclavas, and little finger-less mitts. I knitted for everyone. I was very good at darning socks; I won a prize for my darning. You never threw anything away.

Our only heating was a coal fire, and coal was short. I'd take an old pram about once a week and go to the gasometer at the east end of Elgin to buy a bag of coke for 9d. I had a gas cooker, and gas lamps, no electricity; there was a penny meter. All the washing was done by hand in the tub, using a scrubbing-board and a bar of soap – you just got so much. Muriel came home from school one day and said the teacher had remarked on her dress and how nicely starched it was and asked what her mother used. I said: "You know what I use, Muriel? I use the water from boiling the rice." You saved up all your laddered stockings and boiled them up so they all came out the same colour, that way you could wear them.

Housework was hard work, the grate had to be cleaned with black lead; the fender polished. I remember all the toffs in the big houses at Borough Briggs used to have their carpets hung out in the spring and they'd get someone from Andersons and England to come along and beat them.

I don't remember listening to the wireless much, except hearing Lord Haw Haw. Oh, the things he said, you knew it was all lies. I worked at Bilbohall Hospital in the kitchens and stayed there for almost 50 years. During the war I worked from 6am to 6pm; Muriel stayed with her Gran or my sister-in-law. You walked everywhere. I walked to work each day, and with the blackout that meant having to grope your way – you couldn't have a torch. I remember they had double summer time so that there were longer daylight hours to work. I used to pick up the rolls early in the morning from Morrice the Bakers.

There were troops at Pinefield and one day Muriel was going to school and saw a soldier. She said "I think that's my Dad," and it was – he was home on leave. He was mostly in London, but also in Germany and the Hook of Holland. When he was in London we'd go down to see him. We left here at ten-to-two in the afternoon and got into King's Cross the next morning at 8am, when Dad would be waiting for us. The fare cost £8. 0s. 6d for the two of us, but the army paid. The train was always full of troops and stopped at every station. I blessed the Salvation Army; they were at every stop with trolleys and cups of tea.

I remember running from the doodle-bugs in London, and seeing some dreadful sights – Ormond Street Hospital was bombed and you could see the beds hanging out of the windows.

I used to post *The Northern Scot* to my husband. I had a special way of folding it up and tying it with string. When my husband came home at last he had £68 gratuity, a suit, shoes and a trilby hat.

Betty Brander, her husband John (who was in Bomb Disposal, Royal Engineers), and their daughter Muriel.

John Rennie

THE LUCKY GORDON

John Rennie (b.1913), who lived and worked in Elgin for many years and is now retired and living in Inverness, was a Sergeant with the 2nd Battalion The Gordon Highlanders serving in Singapore when war was declared. As a seasoned regular, he was sent home to train others, and so missed the fate of so many of his comrades.

WHEN THE WAR in Europe broke out in 1939 we were given jungle training, then I and one other Gordon were sent home on HMS Cairo as instructors. We arrived at Plymouth and I reported to a Railway Transport Officer. I was supposed to be joining the London Scottish, but he said if I was a Gordon then I must report to the Gordons, and gave me a warrant to travel to Keith where I reported to the CO of the 6th Gordons, a TA Btn. I was put up in the Seafield Hotel in Keith – I think it cost 16s a week. I spent two weeks with the 6th Gordons, instructing them on how to use a Bren gun – they'd never seen one before. I'd had one visit home in eight years and my family was just a few miles away near Peterhead, but I wasn't allowed to go over to see them. Then the London Scottish, 2nd Btn, started asking what had happened to me and I was sent to London, Buckingham Gate. We messed at Wellington Barracks. I spent three years with them, in and around London, and they were a fine bunch of men. I hoped we'd go into action together, but it was not to be.

In 1944 I rejoined the 2nd Btn The Gordon Highlanders, which had been reconstituted with the 4th Btn in Orkney after being scuttled at Singapore. They had suffered heavy casualties after the Normandy Landings, and were now at Estry near Falaise where I was to join them with my friend Captain Donald Spence – I'd been commissioned by this time and promoted to Captain. We disembarked at Mulberry on August 12 and were picked up by trucks and driven 100 miles. We saw the results of the fighting so far: Bayeux had been declared an open town and was undamaged, but Villais Bocharge was devastated. I joined A Company as second in command to Major Duke, B Company, 2nd Gordons, 227 Brigade, as part of the 15th Scottish Division. The battalion at this time was commanded by Roddy Sinclair, Earl of Caithness.

We pulled back to Maltot to prepare for the crossing of the Seine. There had been a massacre of Canadian POWs at Maltot and the Canadians had retaliated – there were many dead Germans lying unburied.

On August 24 the

John Rennie.

Division started to move forward towards the Seine, but the roads were crowded with upturned German tanks, TCVs and burnt-out three-ton trucks. The Germans had used a lot of horses for transport, and for miles the ditches were piled high with dead horses. You could hardly take a step without stepping on a dead German. The stench was horrible.

Around about this time, we had a parade: Montgomery presented my close friend Angus McPhail with the MC and told us "Nothing on Earth can stop the war being over before Christmas." How wrong can you be?

It was thought there would be no opposition at the Seine, and on August 27 the crossing began. We only had enough boats for one company to cross at a time. D Company, of which Donald Spence was 2nd in command to Major Max Tindal, was ahead of us and started across while we lay in a ravine waiting. When they were more than half-way across, the Germans opened up on the five boats, each contained 12-15 men, pouring machine gun bullets into them. It was a most horrible sight: we could see the boats being machine-gunned and there was little we could do about it.

Some of the lads were diving into the water to try to escape; some reached the bank and were taken prisoner. Donald Spence was shot dead – he never left the shore: as 2nd in command of D Company his job was to see the boats loaded. He took a bullet straight through the forehead; I think perhaps it was a stray bullet. We had known each other all through our service. He is buried at Bayeux and many years later I visited his grave. In total at the Seine two of our officers were killed, five other ranks, 45 wounded and 30 missing.

We fired HE and smoke shells from six-pounder guns into the far bank, then withdrew to another crossing, formed up at Muids, then headed for Le Thuit. A Company was having it fairly easy and I was sent over to Frettville to see what was happening. While I was away our HQ was mortared, killing one of our stretcher bearers and wounding several others. The Germans were pulling back all the time.

We went through Belgium like a dose of salt and into Holland. At this time Montgomery's fiasco at Arnhem had taken place and we were involved in the 'sideshow' at Gheel where we lost one officer and had 49 wounded. We had some trouble at a place called Best, where we suffered 26 killed – I was still 2nd in command of A Company at this time. A and D companies led the attack and we suffered heavy casualties on the open heath; we reached the railway embankment, but could make no further progress. The Germans had dug in with machine guns and mortar under railway carriages and we had difficulty locating them. We were ordered to pull back; I grabbed a 2" mortar and fired smoke bombs at the German positions so that we could get away. We lost two officers, 25 other ranks were killed, a total of 54 wounded and 63 missing. Quite a number of men were captured but relieved the following day. There is a memorial to the Division at Best.

At Tilburg I was given 48 hours leave and went back to Brussels with my friend John Thomson and a Canloan officer (*a soldier 'on loan' from Canada*) from The Royal Scots called Jake. There was a club for officers of the Rear Army HQ in Brussels, and as you went in there was a chandelier someone had made out of parts of a Nazi aircraft. You could still see the Swastika. Jake looked up, pulled out his revolver and emptied it into the chandelier – officers were diving for cover under the tables. We got him out of there fast.

Shelled by Our Own Guns

We took Tilburg easily, but Meijal, which followed, was shocking. There was a Division of Americans on our flank and the Germans practically over-ran them. We came across an abandoned American 'half-track' and inside was a pair of galoshes – the Americans were issued with galoshes. Unfortunately, they were both for the left foot, but I still wore them for a long time after. We wasted nothing. We were heavily shelled by our own guns at this time and took shelter in the semi-basement of a farmhouse. Our CO ran back to Battalion HQ to tell them we were being shelled by our own guns. My batman, a little Yorkshire man called Richardson, and I captured a German who was just about to fire a Panzer Faust into the farmhouse. He turned out to be a Pole and was only too pleased to surrender. He kept saying we were his Allies, but he was wearing a German uniform.

About this time a Battle Training School was set up at Genval near Brussels for training junior NCOs, and Major Douglas Duff and I were sent there as instructors – there were a lot of reinforcements coming in who had no experience of fighting. What they didn't realize is that in battle nothing goes according to plan, and you have to be able to make immediate adjustments. We started a scheme called 'Snap Orders'.

It was a nice change for us, and I was lucky I missed some of the worst fighting of the war clearing up the Rhine banks. But Battle School didn't last very long for me. I spent Christmas 1944 there, but on February 22 Major T. Gloster, Commander of C Company was killed and I was recalled, promoted to major, and given command of C Company. I was very proud to join C Company, where I had spent all my early service in the Gordons. My first battle in command was to be the crossing of the Rhine.

The night before we made the crossing I shared a billet with another CO, Kilpatrick, in a mining village. We told the old lady in the house that we would be sleeping with our clothes and boots on, so not to put sheets on the bed. What we didn't know was that in Flemish 'sheet' means 'shit' – no wonder she had a peculiar look on her face. She was very welcoming – all the Dutch were – and we shared our food with her…they had so little, and were in a hell of a state, both in Holland and Belgium. Kilpatrick was killed the following morning.

The Rhine was bordered on both sides by flood banks. We crossed in Crocodiles (*amphibious armed personnel carriers*) or storm boats – I was in a storm-boat – and lay up on the river side of the opposite bank. My job was to take Haffen – the Seaforths had already tried and failed. There was open field between us and Haffen and the Battalion Commander had said that B and C Companies should attack together, but B Company had lost most of its officers crossing the Rhine and never arrived. I got on the blower to the CO, Colonel De Winton who told me to go it alone, so I put a platoon and Co HQ Brens on the right flank to pour as much fire into the village as the could, then we went over the bund (*flood bank*) and into the village. We took Haffen and a large number of prisoners. I later saw an article in the *News of the World* reporting that we had taken Haffen, misquoting me, and saying soldiers had been rolling in the cellars cutting each others throats. That's not how it happened. We set the prisoners to walk back over open country to HQ – it was too much trouble to keep them – but B Company turned up and took them off our hands...and got the credit for capturing them.

Later we took a German general's HQ at Blarhousen where I found a brief case with a couple of NAAFI bottles of whisky and several tins of NAAFI cigarettes in it – marked HM Forces 'Tobruk'. I didn't smoke and I gave the whisky to the Mess.

Belsen in Microcosm

The Advance to the Elbe came next. Celle we took quickly, making camp at Ulzen. It was here that we came across the worst place I have ever seen. It was a small concentration camp, Belsen in microcosm, with a few hundred inmates, either dead or dying. It had been liberated a few hours before we arrived and there were no guards to be seen, they had either gone or been killed, just these poor, poor creatures with nowhere to go. As we passed, some of them came out through the gate, ragged scarecrows, all skin and bone, still in their striped prison uniforms. There was a dead horse lying in the ditch and they fell upon it, tearing at it to get something to eat. I've never forgotten the sight, or the smell. It was a horrible, horrible place. I felt so sad about it; it was the first we'd seen – we had heard stories, but we never realized just how bad it really was.

John Rennie's own 'C' Coy, 2nd Btn The Gordon Highlanders,
at the crossing of the Elbe in Germany.

The citizens of Celle said they knew nothing about it, but they were made to clear away the bodies and provide medical supplies and food for the survivors. Our medical people did what they could, but we couldn't stop, we had to push on.

We took a lot of prisoners, many very willing to surrender, particularly the young ones aged 15-17, but in some places the Germans hit back. The SS were more arrogant. As we moved up to the banks of the Elbe we saw the first German jets – Messerschmitts 262 – although we did not know what they were at the time, just thought they made a funny noise. They were attacking the airfields, not us.

At the Elbe the 15th Division was the only one to force a crossing, along with some Commandoes not in our area. The Germans were cleared out for a distance of about 10 miles back. My Company was right up against the flood banks and the Germans were still active on the other side. There was a civilian ferry operating for a while. At the village of Tespe we set up Company HQ to assess what was happening on the other side of the river. My batman and I also went to see what we could find: Richardson had been a gamekeeper – I've never seen anyone pluck a chicken as quickly as he could. The only way to move about without being shot was to wear civvies, so I put on a raincoat and a bargee's hat while Richardson found a top hat, and we set off. Suddenly we heard the shout 'Halt!' and a Belgian in British uniform appeared waving a revolver at us: he thought we were Germans. We were arrested and marched back to my own Company HQ to be identified...I dealt with myself very severely! We found a lot of looted goods abandoned by the Germans, including Worth scent - so much of it that everyone in the company got a box to send home...but in the end the postal service refused to take them because there were so many.

We crossed the Elbe at Artlenburg: we encountered heavier shelling than at the Rhine. Our job, along with D Company, was to sweep the banks, which were steep and forested, for about a kilometre. What we did not know until later was that the bank was a huge underground tank for V2 fuel. Gordon Campbell, who later became MP for Moray and Nairn, was our battery commander and was seriously wounded at the Elbe. We pressed on to Lubeck, a lovely city which had been bombed and badly damaged, where the Btn HQ was. I was at Gruthansdorf when the Germans surrendered and the war was over.

Meeting the Russians

The Germans were willing to do anything to help us. The Mayor asked to see me, and arrived wearing a top hat in a horse-drawn phaeton. He said he wanted to present me with a parachute he had found - it had obviously been looted (I sent the parachute back to the UK and it was used to made numerous garments including an end-of-the-war party dress for my daughter).

The Yalta conference, dividing Germany into zones, had now taken place and the River Trave was to be one of the boundaries, so we had to pull back to the west side. The Russians were raping German women, including children, and many were swimming across the river at night to escape. It was a deep, fast flowing river, and they risked their lives to cross it, which was a sign of their desperation. I came across one little girl of about 12 who had been raped. We had to try to contact the Russians to attempt to get it stopped. I was told exactly what to say in Russian when we greeted them, but they started shooting...not at us, but as a warning. A well-dressed Russian officer then came forward and said, in perfect English: "Welcome to our great British Allies. The Red Banner shall fly from shore to shore. Stalin!" I had an interpreter for the rest of the conversation, and through him I was told that the officer's men had to live off the land; from what I saw of them, most of them were Mongolian or at least of Eastern origin, although the officer was not.

I was extremely lucky throughout the war. I was posted to various units as an instructor, I was sent home from Singapore before it fell, and had three very happy years with The London Scottish where I never heard a shot fired, except on the rifle range. It was a smashing regiment to be with and I was very grateful to them for being commissioned. There were sad times, there were horrific times, but I wouldn't have missed it for the world.

The 2nd Btn The Gordon Highlanders with German
SS prisoners, somewhere in Normandy 1944.

Nan Howe

HAIRY TATTIES AND JUNKET

Living on a farm during the war didn't necessarily mean having plenty, as Nan Howe nee Fyffe (b. 1931), who lives in Elgin, remembers.

I WAS BROUGHT up at The Wards Farm in Elgin. I remember the Town Hall going on fire - the 6th Seaforths were billeted there and it was a Friday afternoon. I was going home with my friend Margaret Ralph but we were going to the mart first. Then a man opened a skylight and shouted that the Town Hall was on fire. I saw the reek, but thought I'd better go straight home so I didn't go to see the fire.

There were six of us at home and my mother spread the ration books round - I remember she had two of them at Simpsons in South Street. Sometimes she had a bit of meat that was just going off – no refrigerators in those days – but she'd wash it in vinegar and cook it and no one would know any difference. You didn't waste anything. We also had salt fish; I think it came from Iceland. It was cut into squares and hard as a board. You had to soak it for days. It was horrible. She used to make 'hairy tatties': mashed potatoes with the fish through it. It was no good for anything else. We also had junket – yern's milk – but I only liked it with sugar. My Aunt Nell made me a suit from a service blanket, probably an RAF one because I remember it was a blue colour. She trimmed it with green.

I can remember – it must have been during the scare of an invasion – an ack-ack gun in the yard. The crew of four or five slept in the barn; they didn't have beds, just blankets. I must have been about 12-ish, and Polish troops were stationed where the car park now is on Lossie Green. They were in wooden huts. We used to try to teach them English, but looking back their English was probably better than they let on. They disappeared for what I presume was D-Day.

One day my Dad took me and the Land Army girl to Hopeman to pick up two cows, the girl and I had to walk them home. We passed a farm with a horse trough and stopped to let the cattle drink, then a convoy went past – tanks, the lot. The cows were frightened by the noise of the tanks. There was a lot of whistling at us girls from the soldiers – I think we turned our backs as they passed, and I'm sure I had a red face.

West End School had been taken over by the military – I remember great heaps of coal piled outside to supply the camps. We had to go to East End School, but just half a day - a fortnight's schooling in the morning, then the next fortnight in the afternoon. That was until we got to the

Nan Howe.

'qually' – the last year before going to the Academy, then we went full time. First year at the Academy I was a member of the choir. It was the end of the war and we went to the High Church for a service of thanksgiving. We sang *Peace Lovely Peace*.

Peter Bruce

FAITH IN THE DESERT

*Peter Bruce (b.1919) was working in a draper's shop in Buckie in
1939. He went into the services as a Militiaman but was put into
the Medical Corp. He was wounded at El Alamein where he
received penetrating abdominal shrapnel wounds which should
have killed him, but made a miraculous recovery. He had another
lucky escape after D-Day when being bombed by a German plane:
a comrade jumped into his slit trench on top of him and took the
force of the blast. Peter received leg injuries and was unable to
walk for four days, but his comrade sustained a broken back.*

ONE SUNDAY MORNING I was listening to a visiting minister
preaching in the Buckie Methodist Church, telling the children that
Jesus still walks the earth today, bringing succour and solace to those
people who are so very sorely tried that they have lost all faith. This
instantly transported me out of the church in Buckie and back to a
bleak, lonely spot hundreds of miles away: to the empty, scorched,
burning wastes of the Western Desert in Libya, North Africa.

Our unit, the 174th Highland Field Ambulance, consisting of
about 250 men, was acting as the main dressing station of the 51st
Highland Division in some very heavy fighting against the
German Africa Corps and had a surgical team attached to the unit
for very seriously wounded casualties. The main dressing station
(MDS) consisted of a square of sandbags, about 30 feet square and
about nine feet high roofed over with tarpaulins salvaged from the
many vehicles knocked out during the heavy fighting.

The entrance to the station was an opening in one of the walls
and overhung by a rope with heavy blankets. The entrance was
open during the day unless closed for sand devils, – miniature
whirlwinds of sand about five or six feet high that danced
erratically over the desert floor, causing destruction wherever they
struck. The opening was closed at night in order to keep the light

from the hurricane lamps shining across the desert and being spotted by any marauding enemy patrols.

Our unit, together with the surgical unit, moved forward with the advancing Division and all casualties who were fit to travel were evacuated by ambulance convoy to the New Zealand Casualty Clearing Station, (CCS) which was some distance back down the line, leaving a corporal, six nursing orderlies and a cook to look after the post-operative casualties who were unfit to be moved. Thus we were left alone in the desert, with rations of food and water to last for a fortnight, with patients requiring intensive care attendance.

Peter Bruce.

Outside the main dressing station a huge Red Cross was firmly pegged to the ground and was strictly observed by the Luftwaffe when on strafing raids. During the day the sandbags kept out the heat when the entrance was open but when it was closed after dark the sandbagged walls that had kept out the heat during the day acted as huge storage heaters at night, giving out the heat that had been absorbed during the day. As there were no openings for windows the heat became unbearable, even though the desert is freezing at night. Added to this was the heat from the hurricane lamps, which also gave off the stench of burned paraffin oil. The MDS thus became a hellhole of heat and foul air.

We were supposed to work six-hour shifts with two nursing orderlies to a shift. The shift system was ignored during the day as there was too much intensive care work to be done and anyhow there was nowhere to go beyond the confines of the MDS. But with the seriously wounded being sedated at night the shift system came into effect and the lads off duty got what little rest to be had in the stifling heat.

Under such conditions we gradually began to lose our carefully nursed patients and the solitary, pathetic little wooden cross, made from a ration box and planted beyond the giant Red Cross, became two, then three and more. The air inside became full of expletives because of the misery of our suffering comrades and we cursed: "If there is a God in Heaven why don't you come down and relieve this hell hole on earth?"

Drums beating, pipes playing, the massed piped bands of the 51st Highland Division make a spectacular sight as they parade in the Western desert.

One day a truck from a Desert Sanitation Squad came to the MDS with their corporal who was very badly burned. The Desert Sanitation's job was to gather up all the after-battle rubbish in piles and burn it to try and cut down the millions of flies which were breeding in the debris. To do this they used liberal amounts of petrol and when setting fire to a pile of rubbish, the corporal was blinded by the flashback of the vaporising fuel and his head, face and hands were very badly burned. We dressed the burned flesh and by the time we were finished he looked like an Egyptian mummy with a hole in his facemask for feeding through. Being like this, he could do nothing for himself and we had to do all the menial personal hygiene tasks for him, and carefully feed him through his facemask.

We soon found out that he was a quiet, religious, and well-read man who came from the island of Mauritius and that his brother was a politician and well acquainted with Sir Stafford Cripps.

'Men of God'

To ease the monotony of his plight and silent suffering we took it in turns to walk with him in the area of the MDS. One day I was out walking with him, trying to be his eyes – pointing out the various features in our desert surroundings: a destroyed German 88 millimetre Backpack gun in the distance, the rusty barbed wire of a German mine field on the left with the sign 'Mien' hanging from a wire, and not far away in front of us a knocked-out German tank with a pathetic number of little wooden crosses of its crew, courtesy of the Desert Hygiene Squad. Here and there, too, I told him, there was an upturned rifle with the bayonet stuck firmly into the ground, marking the temporary resting place of its owner, with his helmet hanging by the strap from the butt.

Suddenly he cut across my conversation and said: "Truly you are men of God." I thought that I hadn't heard properly and asked him what he had said. He repeated: "Truly you are men of God." Us, who until he came had been cursing God to the high heavens! I asked him what on earth made him think that and he replied: "I am absolutely helpless with this bandaged face, arms, and hands and you do all the daily humble tasks for me so cheerfully: feeding me so carefully through the face mask and taking me to the latrine; undressing me and, when I am finished, cleaning me and re-dressing me; and to relieve my monotony you read to me from the Eighth Army News and The Crusader; and you take me for these walks and try to be my eyes for me. Truly you are men of God."

He then went on to tell me when the war would end. When I

asked him what gave him that opinion he said that it was all in the Bible, in the Book of Revelations, relating Hitler and his henchmen to the seven pillars in the Book of Revelations. Being very cynical and feeling anything but Godly at the time, I listened politely to what he was telling me but did not absorb what this corporal from the Desert Hygiene Unit was telling me. To this day I wish that I had paid more attention.

A moment to relax for men from the 174th Highland Field Ambulance, among them Eric Bruce (front, second left).

Eventually the CCS caught up with us and relieved us of our patients and I bade goodbye to my corporal friend. Looking back I realised that from the day that he came among us we lost no more patients, and strangely there was no more bad language.

After winding up in North Africa and then wading ashore under fire for the capture of Sicily, we were brought home to prepare for D-Day.

After being bombed in the beachhead in Normandy, we were acting as an MDS in a huge hangar just outside Caen. I was attending to a German POW with a very bad knee wound at the opposite end of the hangar to the entrance when all of a sudden there was a noise like thunder and the earth shook as though there was an earthquake. I looked up and saw all the walking wounded who had been waiting outside in the sunshine rush in and throw themselves down on the cement floor, irrespective of what kind of wound they had. Then I looked at the doors and my end of the hangar and saw white-hot shards of shrapnel slicing through the thick steel doors beside me as though they were paper and speeding along the concrete floor. Fortunately, they slowed down before they reached the prostrate personnel, or we would have had a lot of casualties.

We had been bombed by a group of American Flying Fortresses, and a second group of Fortresses was coming on in the distance to follow up the first numbing. A Spitfire pilot had seen what had happened and he weaved back and fore in front of the following lead Fortress to indicate they had picked the wrong target. When the American ignored the warning, the Spitfire just turned round and shot down the leading Fortress. When the Yanks saw their master bomb aimer shot down they realised a terrible mistake had been made and veered away.

More 'Friendly Fire'

There was another case of 'friendly fire' that ended tragically. The Polish Armoured Division was moving up the adjacent road to act as the 'cork in the bottle' and trap the entire German Army at Falaise.

The sad outcome for us was that two very young ambulance drivers had just joined us that morning at the MDS and were detailed to take two loads of 'walking' wounded down to the CCS, further back in the beachhead. As they had newly arrived and had no idea where to go, a senior RASC driver. 'Duke' Wellings, volunteered to go with them. Duke was a fearless John Wayne type of guy, hence the bye-name, and had just finished building an almost impregnable shelter of heavy railway sleepers on the lee side of a large steam railway engine from enemy artillery -- something he had never bothered about before.

The two ambulances had just gone out onto the nearby road and were going past the Polish division when they were caught up in heavy bombing by American Flying Fortresses. The whole brigade was wiped out, along with our three ambulance drivers and the two ambulances full of walking wounded, and the 'cork in the bottle' failed to complete the Falaise trap. This 'friendly' bombing by the Americans was never reported in the Press.

The armies were determined that the Falaise Gap be closed by

bombing the German transport and to be sure this was done they gave
the task to the RAF Pathfinders the following day. This elite group
was famous for accurately targeting their objective with fluorescent
flares, pinpointing the target for the following heavy bombers.

Running forward with the troops during an attack, members
of the Field Ambulance unit face the frontline unarmed, save
for their stretchers and medical kit.

The MDS had a sudden rush of all types of transport packed
with slightly wounded and unwounded Gordon Highlanders. I
spoke to a school acquaintance, Ian Maclean, who was a driver in
The Gordons (his father had a farm at Clochan, near Buckie) and
who arrived with a load of lightly wounded comrades. He told me
the reasons they were arriving at the MDS was that it was The
Gordon's transport that the Pathfinders had so accurately targeted.

Their Colonel, realising this, had told everyone who could drive
to grab a vehicle, load up and said: "Get the hell out of here before
the bombers arrive!" The Gordons got some of their vehicles away,
but the rest were well and truly bombed.

Thus the Falaise Gap was not properly closed and, despite heavy
losses, a portion of the Vermacht escaped to fight on in Germany.

There were lighter moments. Our unit was evacuating 51st
Highland Division wounded from a large villa on the outskirts of
a village called Ranville, about four miles from the beaches. In a

clearing in the middle of the wood behind the villa were situated the latrines, near a large hole, approximately 10 feet square by about 5 feet deep where all the blood-soaked uniforms and bits of limbs from the casualties were deposited. The latrines were just a long narrow box with six sittings and lids, which automatically fell as soon as they were vacated.

The location must have been under enemy observation because anytime the latrines were busy the Germans would sling over a few shells. The clap of the latrine lids could be heard clearly away down the wood as occupiers hastily dressed and scurried for the relative safety of their slit trenches.

This particular morning my slit trench mate dashed into the trench with eyes sticking out of his head like gob-stoppers. I asked him if he got a scare and he answered: "Aye, and I have just jumped the pit."

I said: "You are the unit long jump champion and 10 feet is nothing to you."

He replied: "Aye, bit I did it wi' mi troosers doon!"

In the desert, Padre Conlon offers comfort to a stretcher case at the advanced dressing station of the 174th Highland Field Ambulance.

Talk about fear lending you wings.

With the 51st Highland Division, our unit proceeded through France, Holland, Belgium and into Germany, eventually being billeted in a small village called Bremervoord not far from Bremerhaven

One evening there was a terrible noise of small arms fire, everything from Sten guns, Bren guns, rifles and revolvers, and we thought that the Germans were making a last final desperate attack. We learned, however, that it was a general from the 15th Panzer Division, which had fought the 51st Highland Division all the way from El Alamein to the heart of Germany, who wanted to surrender to none other than his worthy opponents.

Then it struck me like a bolt from the blue: the date was May 4, 1945. This was the date that the burned corporal from the Desert Hygiene Unit had said the war would end.

When I heard the minister tell the children that Jesus walks the earth today and comes unknown to all those who are so very sorely tried, and who have lost faith, I wondered. Did we go through that experience? 1 think we did.

Harry Bremner

WHAT WAR?

*Harry Bremner (b.1931) was brought up in Bishopmill, Elgin –
and is proud of it. For almost half a century he was a reporter with
"The Northern Scot"; in latter years Sports Editor and Local
Government Correspondent. He was in short trousers when the
war started... and still in short trousers when it ended.*

WAR? WHAT WAR? I spent the years 1939-45 blissfully
oblivious to the tremendous changes taking place all around, but
with hindsight I came to appreciate we were part of a grand scene
which brought in a whole new world; a whole new way of life.

At the time, Bishopmill consisted of fewer than 20 small
streets: a livewire community hemmed in by four landmarks – to
the south the bridge over the River Lossie, which distanced we
locals from those people from Elgin; to the north, the 'poorhouse',
(Craigmoray, later to be replaced by Bishopmill House for the
elderly, and now empty); to the east, that Mecca of winter joys
(sledging), Jock Wilson's brae; and the educational pride and joy
(though not to all its occupants) Bishopmill School to the west.

September 3, 1939 was like any other young boy's Sunday – not
enough hours to fit everything in. We waited and wondered. What
made an early impact were the new boxes containing the magic
gasmasks. Heaven knows what would have happened had we ever
had to wear them! Soon there was an invasion of strange creatures
from afar – evacuees – but in most cases they quickly settled down
and became part and parcel of everyday life. It must have been a
traumatic time for them.

But what of the locals? There was a great outcry when they
removed our front door iron railings in the name of helping the war
effort; First War memorabilia, old cannons, etc, went, too.
Strategically placed water tanks – real hazards they were – and
cleverly disguised pill boxes (which became favourite objects of

attention and were put to various uses!) spread like virulent rashes everywhere.

The war itself was scarcely noticeable, till one found that loved ones in distance places would not be coming back. Children could be unconsciously cruel: those serving their country who died of such afflictions as malaria or beriberi were harshly categorised as having 'just died', and thus could not be hailed as 'killed in action' in fantastic stories told by doting nephews. But the telegram boys brought many hearts to mouths as they delivered their sad news; their appearance in the street created panic.

Harry Bremner.

There was a near revolt at school when a grassed area was sacrificed in the Dig for Victory drive, but I welcomed it – I was regularly detailed to wheel barrow loads of leaf mould from nearby Braemorriston for the garden. No lessons! And what crops it produced.

The boys at school joined the girls in knitting patchwork quilts, miles of scarves, etc, for sailors on Arctic convoys. Lots of cottage industries sprang up, and the whole area was alive with backyard concerts and other fund raising activities.

Meanwhile, the womenfolk worked wonders daily, transforming all manner of garments into works of art, and used rations to produce menus that left you wondering. I remember one lunchtime being handed a plate of broth, which I was told, was special – it was rice broth, a real treat. I refused, as I hated rice. My granny, who ruled the roost, whipped it away but for the following couple of days it appeared in front of me, and nothing else. Sheer hunger forced me to capitulate in the end. But give granny her due, rice was never proffered to me again. The arrival of a box of Canadian apples in the town caused tremendous excitement; unprecedented queues; and the quickest sales in history.

Blackberry -picking and cone gathering, and countless other ploys ate up the time. Then there was the 'tuppenny rush' – the Saturday morning cinema – and the Cooper Park boats, where you could make a fortune in tips rowing elderly visitors around. And we made a proper nuisance of ourselves by interrupting the mock tactics of troops on exercise by giving away their positions, etc. How we loved using the dug-out trenches conveniently left for us by the army. I also have fond memories of exploring the 'dungeons' at Spynie Castle (not allowed today), and scaring the living daylights out of a crowd of Girl Guides being shown round by a none too sure leader.

And while all these happy boyhood escapades were taking place, life was changing, unnoticed by me. Worthies such as Big Johann and her like began to disappear; the scissors and knife grinders became a thing of the past.

The Old Bish'

I was transported back to the old Bish' one Sunday some years ago when I was stopped by a chap who asked if I knew Old Smokey

Joe's. Luckily I was able to take him there, and he regaled me with yarns of monster meals of bully beef, chips, bread and butter, all for (he thought) 9d during the war years. The food was, allegedly, 'acquired' by deals with regulars at Pinefield Camp… where those undergoing training got next to nothing.

Bishopmill was renowned for its community spirit, and VE-Day, when it came, was duly celebrated in style. Others will have vivid memories, but for me it was a strangely odd day. Along with a host of other loons and quines, I shared in the fun at the Caroline Street bonfire. The spirits were somewhat dampened when the 'bobbies' decreed that the heat generated threatened to seriously damage the road surface. This was an excuse for the site to be relocated on Morriston Road, and for a gang of the bigger loons to nip across to Elgin and 'acquire' some old tyres from P.S. Nicolson's garage yard.

But while practically everyone around was having a great time, my granny – who had lost an only son in Sicily – and my mother were going through a personal hell.

My dad, you see, was a member of the Forgotten Fourteenth, somewhere in Burma, who had not been heard of for quite a time. Though the final cessation of hostilities was obviously drawing nigh, VJ-Day was some months off, and the agonising wait, wondering if he had survived, must have been traumatic for them.

He did survive – as he had survived Dunkirk – but VJ-Day went practically unnoticed. When, very shortly afterwards, my father did arrive home, that was something else. For the first time, for instance, he saw his daughter, born while he was in India. One of many causes for rejoicing.

As a loon on the threshold of his 14th birthday, the burning ambition was to leave school behind (the leaving age was 14 at the time) and – a must for the majority of families – get earning. Soon I would be entering the real world where, for 17s 6d a week, I was master of all I surveyed.

Farewell to those carefree days of fishing into the wee sma' 'oors of double summertime and the fun of frolics out playing in the 'dark nichts' of the blackout. I had travelled through a wonderful boyhood, packed with wonderful memories. The war? What war?

Bill Ettles

LIGHTER MOMENTS

Retired English teacher and former Keith town councillor, Bill Ettles served in the Royal Navy as a Met officer, charting the weather for ships and operational bases in North Africa, Malta, Sicily and here at home. He kept a diary of the war years, and these are some of the more light-hearted incidents recorded in its pages.

AT THE START of the war I took to spending the weekends at home and operating in the Decontam HQ at Keith, which was run by my good friend and former teacher of English Mr David McCrae. At the gas station, built at Turner Memorial Hospital – it now houses the ambulances – I learnt a trick that was to give me some amusement later in life. One of my tasks was to set up, in an inner room, a concentration of tear gas which was designed to allow air raid wardens and the like to test their gas masks and to have confidence that they worked. Working with it frequently, I developed a considerable tolerance to the stuff, and could stand in a fairly lethal concentration with no mask and no tears either. After David's lecture, the students were invited to put on masks and to enter my room. There they were allowed to stay a short time, and then asked to slip a finger under the side of the mask and lift, allowing the gas to penetrate, usually with some unpleasant results. Worse, some noted that I was standing around with no mask, and simply removed theirs, with even more spectacular effects. Some time later, I attended a gas course at RNB Chatham, and found a Chief PO playing this trick. I still had my relative immunity, and shook him by removing my mask and continuing the conversation.

One part of the proceedings was a gunnery course at which I learnt the truth of the old Navy adage – 'Never Volunteer'. The chief gunner's mate asked: "Anyone here with a driving licence?" I raised my hand. "Ah," said he, "you must be a very careful chap.

Bill Ettles.

Carry this box of ammunition down to the range." And a very heavy box it was too!

Elbert (Nobby) Clarke and I were sent to RNAS Worthy Down, in Hampshire. The first surprise was that the senior Met officer was Instructor Commander Suthons, who had been part of the board that accepted me. This may have been meant as a lesson for him. The second was a pair of pilots who were better known in other circles. One was Laurence (later Lord) Olivier, and the other was Ralph (later Sir Ralph) Richardson. Both flew Proctors for training observers and air gunners. Since pilots were more plentiful than actors already on the verge of greatness, both were eventually returned to the stage and screen, as indeed was Michael Redgrave.

In North Africa the news of Rommel's forays in the desert were becoming more disturbing. Disaster was imminent. The first realisation of this for me was an order to go on an arms course. This was brief. I was sent to a firing range and supplied, by a Petty Officer, with a huge revolver and instructed to fire it. After around three attempts at a target, the Chief sadly took it away, suggesting that I would be safer without it as, he also suggested, would those immediately behind me, and those anywhere near.

My father had mentioned in a letter of the presence in Cairo of a friend of his, a former burgh surveyor with Keith Town Council. I looked him up and found Major George Stewart of the RASC, whose task in life was the importing of beer into Egypt. You can imagine the importance of the task and the individual who performed it. The only local beer available was Stella, allegedly brewed from onions. If you wanted beer, you had to know George Stewart. So an evening out with George was quite something.

His friendship gave me the freedom of the Gezira Club, and here I remember one of the happiest afternoons I ever spent. The club staged a cricket match, Egypt v British Forces. The players were all top-class, including a certain D. Compton, of England, and Peter Van der Byll of Rhodesia. (Test standard!). I was furnished with a deckchair and footrest, a table with sun umbrella, a swimming pool a few yards away, and every time I raised an arm, an Egyptian waiter brought fresh iced lager. With Rommel raging only a few miles away, this was a prime sample of the horrors of war in Egypt.

General Montgomery had just taken over command, and his first edict had been: 'No British serviceman is to be served liquor after 10 pm.' In a restaurant-cum-cinema, we were approached by a waiter who said: "What you want for rest of evening?" Sandy beamed upon him and said: "35 Drambuies." My state of mind was such that 36 would have been too many and 34 too few. Thirty-five, like Erasmic shaving soap, was 'just right'.

A Shortage of Cats

In Malta, the people were on the shortest of rations, but we always had something, partly due to the fast mine laying cruisers *Welshman* and *Manxman*, which ran from Gibraltar and Alexandria respectively with supplies largely for the Navy. These ran 'there and back' for some months without incident, but the first time they tried to go on from Malta to the other end of the Med, both were successfully attacked and damaged. Indeed the only time I recollect being concerned about the catering was a period when we were fed almost exclusively on rabbit – fried, stewed, pie, roast, under all guises. It finally struck us that there were no rabbits on Malta at that time, and that there was a remarkable dearth of pussycats. That apart, the Chief worked miracles.

One permanent memory remains of these early days. Two of my messmates, Johnnie Chew and Reg Walton, both Intelligence Officers, grabbed me one day with the request that I accompany them on a ploy, of which I knew nothing. They led me down Kingsway to the main square, and on to the roof of the library, over looking the square, where some sort of gathering seemed to be taking place. The square was crowded and the main theme seemed to be a mixture of military and civilian. The civilian in the centre was, I found out later, His Honour Sir George Borg, Malta's Chief Justice, and the Military headman the Governor, Field Marshall The Viscount Gort, VC.

Thanks to Johnnie and Reg, I was present at the handing over of the George Cross, presented to the People of Malta by His Majesty King George VI. A historic occasion indeed! When I visit Malta now, I look on the George Cross itself, and on one of the photos around the display, I can see myself – or at least three white shirts among the khaki, one of which is me – though it is a bit miniature. As memento of the occasion, I now have the George Cross 50th Anniversary Memorial Medal.

One of my less successful evenings was spent in the company of the Captain of St Angelo, Captain Crossley, who had with him a pleasant civilian gentleman whom he introduced as General Debrett. As we drank our beer, the General asked me what I though of Maltese Beer. I replied that the darker beer, Simonds Parsons, I liked but I found the Cisk was too light and gassy for my Scottish taste. "What a pity,"said the General. "I own the Cisk Brewery."

One incident from considerably later in my stay remains a fragrant memory. There is a theory that American Forces are rather lax in their dress codes. Not so the Navy! Our 'chummy ship', *USS Mayrant* a destroyer, was with us for a few days. As usual, the officers turned up at the club, and since among them was the navigator (who acted as Met officer for the ship) I was with them. Their First Lieutenant had gone ashore earlier in the day to liaise with the RAF on some matter of mutual interest. He was dressed in what they called a 'working rig' of khaki jacket and trousers, with rank markings on lapels. His hosts, the RAF pressed him to accompany them to the club as he was, pointing out that his kit was a deal smarter than what they had to wear. Reluctantly, he agreed. When he got there, his own officers refused to recognise him, as he was 'improperly dressed'. Only when he had returned to the ship and reappeared in white dress clothing did they greet him as: "Hello Franklin, nice to see you." Yes, he was Franklin D. Roosevelt Junior, eldest son of their President.

Clubs, too, did their bit in keeping us entertained. I remember a visit to Malta by the celebrated pianist, Solomon, when he played at the United Services Club, and I was able to get tickets for all the off-duty forecasters as thanks for all their help. Next day Solomon played at the British Institute, with a Maltese orchestra which did a noble job with *The Emperor*. Another highlight was a visit from Gracie Fields. As she was still convalescing from an operation, her manager warned us that she could only do a half-hour show. She sang for at least an hour and a half, to a packed and delighted audience. The Western Brothers came, but spent more time being entertained than entertaining.

Since I was static in Malta, various passing Keith people were directed to two of the 'residents'. The other resident was Willie Kelty, who had been in the island working with a bakery businessman, named Chalmers. By the time I arrived, Willie had become a sort of Minister of Food, running one of the lifelines of the Maltese people, the Victory Kitchens, where a daily meal could be obtained. What went in to the meals, Willie would never divulge, even years later when we were both members of Keith Town Council.

His 'Malta Experience', however, explains why Willie had such an interest in swimming, obvious in Keith when he chaired a committee which raised a considerable part of the cost of Keith's Swimming Pool. Willie was a little accident prone, and most of his accidents entailed falling in the harbour. One evening I remember we were invited on board a motor launch, moored alongside a creek. Access was along a floating catwalk to the after deck and wardroom. The Captain, Robin Bell from Auchterarder, led the way, pushing the catwalk a little away from the quay. I followed, pushing it a little further. Willie, in the rear, missed. His clothing was removed to the engine-room for drying. Much later, we found out that the ERA who organised the drying process came from Keith.

Perhaps I may have looked worse than the others, perhaps not but just before I got back to work I met the Captain of *St Angelo*, J.G. Crossley, who commented very kindly on my pallor. He suggested a remedy. Said he: "What about a trip on a hospital ship, from here to Algiers? Then you can see your Fleet Met officer, and fly back." Hospital ship conjured up the picture of pretty nurses and cool hands for fevered brows – and I fell for it. I'll never learn not to volunteer! Squaring things off at the office and with the Doc. I duly reported at the quay where the ship lay. I was met at the gangway by a very harassed-looking Lieutenant Commander RNVR, who asked who I was. When I replied, and he asked my job, his next comment was an odd one indeed. "Met." he said. "Maps – charts." Then he looked back to me. "You," he said, "are the navigator."Before I could protest that my knowledge of navigation consisted of two weeks in school class in Portsmouth, he had gone on to explain that the ship had been a German hospital ship, run by Greeks, and captured trying to evacuate secret papers from Tripoli to Sicily, along with unwounded men. It had been impounded as in breach of the Geneva Convention and was to go via Sousse to Algiers to become a ferry. He was on his way home, and had been appointed Captain. He added that we had on board a Merchant Navy crew who were experienced seamen. What he did not say was that they had no intention of helping as they were on an agreement only to take passage – with him, as parts of ship's company.

The first real shambles came during a middle watch, when the gallant navigator (me) was sharing the bridge with the Captain, whose hours had now become 24 on – stop on.

All Lit Up

Ahead of the pack as usual, we suddenly caught sight, looming out of the darkness, of what seemed like a flotilla of small ships, apparently landing crafts, and most probably ours. The Captain reacted with a shout to me: 'Get down to the chart room and switch on the navigation lights.' I dived down the ladder and found myself confronted by a bank of switches carefully labelled in German and Modern Greek! I had no German, and my Higher Greek was the language of Homer and Euripides, who had no knowledge of electrics. In desperation, I put on the lot. We had overall lighting with illuminated Red Crosses, and floodlights on the deck. The Commodore's subsequent signal made some derogatory remarks about Guy Fawkes – but they missed us!

In Sicily I was able first of all to take some of the officers on a drive round the 'left' side of Mount Etna, the towering mountain overshadowing Catania, which I had once seen from Malta on a very clear dawn. The road was a reasonable one, and I was happy to note frequent appearances of the sign HD which meant that the 51st (Highland) Division had travelled that way. En route, we visited Bronte, the Dukedom of which was once held by a celebrated sailor, Lord Horatio Nelson. In Bronte Village, we were able to purchase oranges at three lire per dozen. Helping ourselves was forbidden, not by the people, but by the notices 'Vorschacht Minen' which decorated the road.

The next ploy was to visit a new Naval rest house in the best-known resort of Sicily, Taormina. I was practically the first visitor, and found myself in the midst of an amazing coincidence. The staff being out shopping one morning, I answered a knock at the door to find outside a little lady in the habit of the Order of Franciscan Missionaries of Mary, the Grey Nuns. This I knew, because they had visited Keith frequently, and at times when the local convent was full, I had been evicted from my room to make accommodation for them. This particular lady had been one who had stayed with us in Keith. She explained that they ran an orphanage in Taormina, where they taught girls needlework which was then sold to pay for their keep. She was anxious that any unused food from the Naval rest house would not be thrown away. I promised to do my best to help – and did!

The flight to Naples was not the happiest I have had. It involved several stops, including Bari and Brindisi, and each one caused me some misgiving. The crew were South African, and had a curious technique of taking off, holding the tail on the ground till the last second and then going up like an express lift. But we got there and I reported as ordered to Navy House, an office block on the quayside, shared with the Americans. Even before I reached the Met office, the past had caught up with me. On the door of one office was the label 'US Navy Intelligence, – Lieut. Joachim Titolo, Junior, USNR.' Jo had been for a spell one of our Malta Staff and a good friend. He had been assistant District Attorney in New York City, with the famous Thomas E. Dewey, and had been seconded to Navy Intelligence because of his fluent, almost native Italian. Some time before the Sicilian Invasion, he had mysteriously disappeared and turned up on one of the beaches, disguised as a Sicilian peasant, with directions as to where the invaders were going to live.

I thought that on my way upstairs, I should look in on Jo, knocked, entered and said: 'Lieutenant Titolo around?' A young rating, still wearing his white hat at his desk, turned and replied: 'No Sir. He's in Rome!' I thanked him and closed the door before it struck me. We had not yet captured Rome. It was the case, though, and when we did, Jo had all the buildings arranged for messes, clubs and all.

I returned to London just in time for the attacks by the V1 and V2 weapons and found these not to my taste. The V1 was the more frightening, far worse than Malta, where time could be found between attack and shelter. These bombs could be heard, unmistakably, passing overhead, a most distinctive sound. Trouble came when they stopped! You then had seven seconds to wait for the bang. Seven seconds of terror, which could seem to be a lifetime. In comparison the V2 was less frightening, in that they gave no warning. The bang, if you heard it, meant that it had not hit you.

Communications were by teleprinters, oddly enough still run by the GPO and thus not to be interfered with by mere Naval officers. These were fed by automatic transmissions from Admiralty in Whitehall, who repeated Air Ministry Observations. The machines were really designed mainly for hand transmissions, and the constant pounding of the automatics was often too much for them. We had two, and usually they only broke down one at a time. We then phoned the GPO Engineers and someone came to repair the machine in situ.

Though I did not realise it at the time, a double breakdown put in my way what transpired to be the most decisive moment of my life – now or ever. It was a bad day, and observations were desperately needed. I knew they could be obtained by a radio broadcast from Air Ministry, in a code which we could handle. But we had no radio or operator. I wondered if Flying Control could help, and went along to ask. In their office was a Leading Wren wearing a Radio Operator's badge. She smiled and said: 'I'm not busy. I'll do that with pleasure.' I was then introduced to Leading Wren Helen Watson. I had just met my future wife!

Jane Mackenzie

DOING A MAN'S JOB

Women's contribution to Britain's engineering industries was vital during World War II and many were conscripted into working to keep guns, ammunition and other essential equipment flowing out of the factories. They often took on the traditional male occupations of forging, machining and other heavy manual work. Twenty-four hour production was commonplace, achieved by working shifts, and the work was often repetitive and even potentially dangerous. For Jane Mackenzie (b. 1923) from Burghead it was to mean not just her first trip away from home, but also her first outside Scotland.

I WORKED FOR the Forestry Commission at Newton and if I'd stayed there would have been OK, but I left that job and so was sent to Wolverhampton to work in an aircraft factory making planes. We were sent to Cannock first – it was just a street of houses then – for six week's training. I had to paint dope on sheets of metal to preserve it; then I was on the assembly line and had to learn how to do rivets for the wings. I did night shift, which was 12 hours' work, which I did not like.

It was my 21st birthday while I was there and all the English girls said we'd have to go out to celebrate with a drink. I was very small and slim, with long hair, and although I was the oldest of the girls, I didn't look it. They took me to a pub, but I didn't know what to ask for and they insisted I had something better than lemonade. But the landlord wouldn't serve me: he said I was under age and only looked 16, but he would serve the others, who were all younger than I was. We went to another pub and someone bought a jug of cider for us all.

I had to get digs in Wolverhampton. We were given a list of names of people willing to take workers, but the first house I went to the woman said she wouldn't take any more girls – the last one

185

had run away with her husband. I got digs with a Miss Marlow, a lovely person: I used to do her garden for her. She told me she was glad of my company: her brother had been lost on the *Royal Oak* at Scapa Flow. We couldn't get much because everything was rationed. She gave me watercress: I wrote home that I'd been given grass sandwiches to eat. I'd never seen watercress before. There was a canteen for people working in munitions and we used to have music for dancing and get tea and

Jane Mackenzie.

cakes. I was dancing with an airman one night and he said: "You come from Burghead!" He'd been stationed up here and recognised the accent.

Clothes were rationed, of course, but I remember buying a black dress with red sleeves, tight at the wrist, decorated with brass studs; very smart. Instead of wearing stockings, which were hard to come by, we painted our legs with stuff bought in a bottle at the chemist's and drew a line up the back for the seam. There was a boy in Burghead who used to do the line for us and made a lovely job of it. I remember him doing it for my sister and trying to get her to lift her skirts a bit higher, a bit higher, but she laughed and said she wouldn't.

Eventually I came home because my mother wasn't well. I remember the police came to check on me because my landlady hadn't reported where I'd gone.

Bill Mavor

THE MILK RUN TO CRETE

Bill Mavor (b. 1924), whose home is now in Elgin, joined the Royal Navy in November 1942 at the age of 18 and trained as a radio operator. After service in the North Atlantic and Denmark Straits, he was transferred to Light Coastal Forces which comprised of fast motor craft such as Motor Torpedo Boats (MTBs), Motor Gun Boats (MGBs) and Motor Launches (MLs). Early in 1944 he was posted to the Middle East and joined the 42nd ML Flotilla based in Alexandria as radio operator on ML 355, which operated from Tobruk supplying the Andartes – the Rebels - in Crete and also landing raiding parties of Commandos.

HEAVILY ARMED FOR its size, our ML 355 and its sister MUs usually left Tobruk early in the morning arriving at the dropping point around midnight. The last few kilometres were covered at slow speed whilst keeping a close watch for flashing lights, indicating that our Greek allies were in position to meet us. With their shallow draught, MLs were able to get within 100 metres of the coast, the transfer of men and supplies then being done by dinghy and raft. Supplies were mainly food, ammunition and arms, uniforms and cigarettes. The latter were most welcome to the tobacco starved Andartes who immediately lit up and started gabbling away – after we'd taken so much trouble to land secretly - causing some anxiety to the commander when the ship was lying so close to an enemy held shore.

After landing stores and troops, we embarked any passengers returning to Tobruk. As well as returning raiding parties, there were always a few German and Italian prisoners being taken back for interrogation, and also sometimes Greek civilians escaping from the unwelcome attention of the Gestapo. The departure from Crete was always at considerable speed, to get as far away as possible before daylight, usually arriving back in Tobruk by evening. These trips to and from Crete had become almost routine and we nicknamed them the 'milk-run' but they did emphasise the close co-operation of the British Forces and our Greek allies, both military and the irregular civilian Andartes.

Bill Mavor.

After some months on ML 355 I was transferred to ML 360, also of the 42nd Flotilla, but operating around the Aegean Islands. In the ensuing months I really got to know Greece and its people. At this time the islands were still under German occupation, consequently we operated from secret bases on the Turkish coast such as Derremen and Marmaris to which the Turks conveniently turned a blind eye.

Alexandria in Egypt was still our main base, but our visits there were only in cases of sheer necessity. Leaving Alexandria with full loads of ammunition, food and water, we steamed north to our first refuelling point which was the most easterly Greek island of Castelorozzo, after which we were constantly in German-held territory.

Shelling from the German gun positions in Cos and Symi was a normal occurrence as we sailed past but fortunately their aim was poor. By now we were well into our operating area. Selecting some remote coast we tied up to the rocks and covered the ML in camouflage nets during the day, casting off when darkness fell to start being as troublesome as possible to the enemy by patrolling against their supply ships or carrying out raids on their island ports. This was heavy on our fuel and every second day or so we required refuelling from Caiques crewed by Greek civilians. They never failed to be at the rendezvous on time. Refuelling was from 20-litre containers and was a long slow job calling for all hands. It was sweaty and uncomfortable, without even a hot cup of tea or coffee, or cigarettes, as the ship was full of petrol fumes and a potential firebomb. On fuelling being completed it was straight over the side for a welcome swim to rid ourselves of the dirt and sweat. Next to fuel, fresh water was always a matter of careful use as it was not easy to replenish. Our water tanks were used for drinking and cooking only. We carried a deck cargo of water cans for washing, each can being shared by three men. From time to time we were able to replenish the water cans from a suitable stream. Swimming was our favourite pastime, both for recreation and cleanliness.

Caiques were very much part of allied activity in the Aegean. The Levant Schooner Force is a story in itself, but in addition Caiques were our supply vessels. Also they were used for reconnaissance, being able to travel among the islands in their normal trading activities. Many were Greek crewed with a Royal Navy wireless operator who operated the hidden radio transmitter when necessary. A novel method of identification was introduced whereby friendly Caiques hung from their rigging articles of clothing such as shirts, trousers and jackets in a pre-arranged code, which was changed from time to time. To a curious German patrol boat this was simply passed off as the crew's laundry.

Feeding the Children

By now the Germans began to withdraw from some of the islands and the British Naval units were able to operate from Greek bases instead of the secret ones in Turkey. Chios was the first to be liberated and after a few days of reconnaissance we sailed into Chios harbour to the loud cheers and applause of the inhabitants. It was a great occasion for the ML crews as well, as we could now operate from an established port with its facilities as well as enjoy nights ashore. Ouzo and retsina were available in quantity and many a toast was drunk between sailor and islander. Food was very scarce and the civilian population was near to starving, especially the children. At meal times we were always careful to make extra which we shared out among the local children as best we could. They would come up with an empty syrup tin or the like and we'd give them a dollop of whatever we had: they would gobble it down; watching with their eyes to make sure no one took it from them. On the 50th anniversary of the Liberation of the Greek Islands in 1994 I went back. There was a great welcome for ex-servicemen's organisations – I was even on Greek TV. The next day I went into a gift shop and an old chap started rattling off. One of his sons could speak English and he told me his father wished to thank us for saving his life – he was one of the children we had fed. It was a wonderful experience.

But to return to the war; by now little was seen of the enemy though countless hours were spent patrolling the waters of the eastern Aegean by naval units. The situation was extremely fluid with neither side sure of where the other was located. A fact borne out by the German coaster Ems that entered Chios harbour under the impression the island was still German occupied. The British ML on guard duty swiftly came alongside and boarded her, capturing the vessel without a shot being fired. The crew and a number of German troops taking passage were then prisoners of war and landed on the quayside to the delight of the local population.

Samos was the next island to be liberated, the honour going to ML 360. As we sailed up the long approach to Vathi town firing broke out from the shore. Fearing the worst we went to action stations but it turned out to be the local Andartes giving us a rousing welcome. Island after island was vacated by the retreating German forces during the autumn months of 1944. Lesbos and Lemnos were then visited and subsequently Samothraki and Thasos until we reached Kavala on the mainland. At Lemnos, the custodian of the British 1914-18 war cemetery, where many of the dead from the Gallipoli campaign were buried, requested our commanding officer to inspect the cemetery which he had carefully tended throughout the enemy occupation.

To the south of Chios ML 360 called at Ikaria but no contact was made with the enemy until we reached Naxos. It should be mentioned that Italian troops were found on many of the islands but they were regarded as harmless and largely ignored, Italy having already capitulated. However, Naxos was still occupied by a strong German garrison, which had to be dealt with. Our skipper, Lieutenant John Ford, was in command of the naval force, which comprised of ML 354 and later ML 1385, in addition to our own ML 360. The MLs landed a company of the Greek Sacred Regiment some distance from Naxos town which were to mount a land attack on the enemy who occupied a large school and castle in the high part of the town. The naval units were to provide covering fire from the sea and consequently headed for a position close to the harbour mouth. This took place at dawn on October 13, 1944. As the light improved, a rowing boat was seen approaching from the harbour with two little boys and an older man at the oars. Sitting in the stern was a German soldier who turned out to be a senior non-commissioned officer and the garrison commander. He had mistakenly thought that the two MLs were German vessels sent to evacuate his troops and now found himself a prisoner. Shortly after the enemy realised their error and opened accurate fire on us with machine guns and mortars. From the sea we could witness the Greek troops advancing through the narrow streets of the town, exchanging fire with the enemy. At the same time the motor launches engaged the defenders with their 50mm and 20mm guns, which set the school roof on fire and also brought the flag pole with its German swastika ensign crashing down - a testimony to the accuracy of the naval gunnery. With the school on fire the Germans took up positions within the castle whose thick walls gave protection against the shelling from our guns. The situation became something of a stalemate. About this time two large German Domier floatplanes flew into Naxos Bay at a very low level. These came under heavy fire from the naval units and a number of hits were observed before they disappeared behind the neighbouring islands.

Beaufighters Arrive

Contact was made with the German troops in the hope that they would surrender, and the second in command and his interpreter rowed out to the MUs under a flag of truce. After some negotiations they were given until 11am to surrender, and at one minute past the ships opened fire again. Attacks on the castle continued throughout the day, but no progress could be made against the strong walls.

A fine trophy for the crew of ML 360 in the
Aegean after helping to liberate Greek islands
from the Germans.

The following day the Greek troops ashore were supplied with additional food and ammunition brought up by ML 1385, while ML 360 made a quick trip to Paros to pick up a Greek patrol, which had been checking that island. It was also decided that heavier firepower was needed to penetrate the castle, and air support was requested. A severe electrical storm broke over the islands which interrupted radio communication and it was the following day that more concerted action took place. Four Royal Air Force Beaufighters arrived overhead about 2.45pm and carried out rocket attacks on the enemy position with great effect. The Greek Sacred Regiment opened heavy mortar fire while at the same time the aircraft attacked with their cannons, their rockets having all been fitted. The attack continued until about 3.15pm. By now the Germans had realised that their position was hopeless and at 3.30pm word came of their surrender. They made one condition, that they be immediately taken off the island by the British ships, as they were terrified of reprisals by the Greek civilians. I later discovered why they feared reprisals: earlier in the war the Germans had blockaded a Greek village and all the inhabitants had starved to death. Consequently, that night we set sail for Chios, each ML with a deck load of subdued Germans. Thus was completed the liberation of Naxos and a successful Greek-British operation.

Lt Ford received the DSC and our ship was mentioned in dispatches; the crew cut cards to see who would get the honour.

About this time landings were made on the Greek mainland and in due course Athens was freed from the Nazi yoke and their unwelcome presence in Greece came to an end. A small pocket of German resistance remained around Rhodes and its nearby islands but forces operating from Beirut captured them, but this was outside my personal experiences.

With the war virtually over in the Aegean the British forces assisted in trying to bring life back to normal for the long suffering civilians. United Nations food and clothing supplies began to arrive and efforts were made to stabilize the economy. Under German rule inflation had made the drachma worthless, children played outside with large bundles of banknotes of huge denominations. For a short time British Military Authority money was circulated until new Greek banknotes could be printed and distributed. Politics also became an issue of national importance with something of a power struggle taking place. British MLs were pressed into service as peace keepers and many Greek personages of Church and Parliament were transported between the islands over the following months of 1944 and '45. NIL 360 continued journeying around the islands till the war in Europe ended. We celebrated VE-Day in Chios, very shortly after which I fell ill, spending seven weeks in hospital in Athens. On recovery I was sent back to Alexandria thus ending my war service in Greece.

Mr Mavor wrote the following poem recalling a poignant search by a shipmate for his brother's grave. The location they were based at was known as 'The Blue' - hence the title.

'THE BLUE'

*We were based in a Libyan harbour
A bomb-shattered dump in 'The Blue'
Where we cursed the dusty fly-ridden heat
And monotony of nothing to do*

*When Jock just happened to tell us
Of his brother being killed out this way
And how he would try and locate him
In the cemetery nearby, where he lay.*

*We thought we had better assist him,
For shipmates all help one another.
We went and we searched that grim burial ground
Until we finally came on Jock's brother*

*Just one of the many who had fallen;
Just one more mound in the sand;
A cross with his name and his number,
And the proud Gordons' badge 'Bydand'.*

*Just one amid hundreds of others,
Carefully placed in long orderly rows;
Their dirge the drone of cicadas,
Their wreath desert dust the wind blows.*

*Not only our own were war victims,
But Italians and Germans as well,
For as ours had to go, so they had to go
And suffer the bullet and shell.*

*We slowly walked back to the harbour,
Lighting our fags on the way,
Our thoughts with Jock and his brother;
But no-one knew quite what to say.*

For our shipmate was in great dilemma,
With a weight in his heart like a stone
For what do you write to your parents?
About a son who will never come home.

Well that is the end of my story.
It's not much of a tale, but it's true,.
Leaving me a memory I'll never forget
Of the lads who lie there in 'The Blue'.

James Douglas

BOMBS ON THE FARMS

James Douglas, Elgin, was at secondary school when the war started. He remembers listening to the declaration of war on September 3, 1939.

THAT AFTERNOON I went to Leuchars School where my father, air raid warden for the area, was handing out and fitting gas masks. The army occupied part of Elgin Academy, where I attended, and some other schools. The lower corridors were blocked up to form an air raid shelter. The air activity at Bogs of Mayne, seen through the big windows on the upper floor, was a distraction to lessons. The school arguments at this time were not about football, but more about aircraft recognition.

I lived on the farm of Sandyhillock, near Leuchars at this time, and it was there on the night of July 10, 1940, that the first high explosive bomb in Moray, one of four, was dropped in a field of barley. The house shook violently. There were also many incendiary bombs on the farms of Sandyhillock, Inchbroom and Bailiesland where, one went through the tiled roof of a cart shed and burned between the shafts of a farm cart. Spades and earth were used to put out the fires and little damage was done. It is not known why they were dropped here – about three miles from Lossiemouth aerodrome – but there could have been a nearer target. An army regiment evacuated from Dunkirk was regrouping and living in tents in the quarry at Coral Peel which was quite near. Polish soldiers also lived there for a time.

On the evening of Oct 26, 1940, three German planes flying in formation were seen at Calcots Bridge following the course of the River Lossie. Explosions were heard as they attacked Lossiemouth airfield. I was in Elgin waiting for a bus home and heard the loud explosions. The buildings shook and rattled and the noise echoed up the High Street. In a very short time the Plainstones were filled with servicemen, mostly airmen, assembling – presumably to be taken back to their camps.

Early in the war there was a dummy airfield at Cotts of Innes and Woodside, Leuchars. There were shelters at both places. Later Milltown airfield was built on the site. The buildings at Woodside were demolished and are now under the main runway. There was a bombing range at Innes Links. The triangular aiming point can still be seen in Lossie Forrest.

There were many buildings occupied by the army in Elgin. The old town hall (which was burned down); many church halls and Moss Street Church, with the air raid siren on top which could be heard for miles around.

Many houses in the country were also occupied. Innes House by the air force; Loch-Na-Bo by the army, where Nissan huts were also built. There were anti-invasion poles in all fields locally. Pill boxes were built at various places and big gun emplacements can still be seen at the Boar's Head.

Farmers were instructed what crops to grow. Besides ploughing up more grass to grow barley and oats, there were also allocations of wheat, potatoes and sugar beet. Farmers also had to apply for tractors and agricultural machinery.

In 1944 we moved to Nether Meft, Urquhart. There was much air activity around Milltown and at this time, Mosquitoes and Beaufighters, sometimes 20 or 30 at a time from Dallachy and Banff, accompanied by Mustangs, would rise and gather formation round Garmouth or Urquhart before setting off for Norway.

It was an interesting time to have lived through, occasionally frightening, but after nearly six years on May 8 the church bell rang out in Urquhart, and that night we celebrated in the local village hall.

Nina Simpson

TEN BOB AND TWO BATHS A WEEK

Nina Simpson (then Shand) was almost 16 years old when war was declared that Sunday in September 1939, and she remembers well her father coming into the house after speaking to a neighbour who had been listening to the news on the wireless. 'That's it then, we are now at war with Germany', he said. Nina, who now lives in Keith, had left Aberchirder Higher Grade School that year. She helped on the family farm until being offered a job in the North of Scotland Bank – now the Clydesdale – at Aberchirder.

MY SISTER MARY'S husband was killed at St Valery, France, and my brother was at Dunkirk (he was later to serve in North Africa and Italy and, wounded badly twice, was awarded the Military Medal).

My war started as the Government, with the country gripped ever tighter by anxiety, decided to recruit girls to the services – I joined the WAAF (Women's Auxiliary Air Force). We arrived in Wilmslow for training – late, tired and a bit lost. After a hot meal of some sort we were allocated a bed in a large Nissen hut. I remember well the first morning being rudely wakened at 6am with this loud tannoy right in my ear, to rise and shine. The ablutions (toilets and wash facilities) were outside. With 40 bodies in the hut it was essential to be up and about early to avoid queuing. There was no privacy but one had to get used to it.

There was then a mad rush to the cookhouse for breakfast. We were already issued with mug, tin plate and cutlery. For washing them, there was a big trough outside the door, with very hot water. We used to stab the knife into the ground before washing, to stop it rusting. It did work. Think of the hygiene… but we survived to tell the tale! Our hut had to be kept in immaculate condition; each person was responsible for their own bed space, inspected every morning by a WAAF officer. Our mattress was in three parts, called biscuits, placed at the bottom of the bed, folded blankets on top, all in line with the others. There was also kit inspection.

We had to spend every morning square bashing. Putting us through our paces was a male sergeant, who bawled at us. It certainly toughened us up. We had pay parade every week, receiving 10/- (50p).

I was sent to Blackpool on a wireless operator course. The RAF had commandeered guesthouses for their personnel and I shared a room with three others – wash hand basin in the room, cold water only. Twice a week we were marched to the Derby Baths for a shower or bath, a mark on the bath allowed only five inches of water. Food was very basic. The guesthouse couple were mean; they must have made a fortune. Breakfast was cornflakes, measured out, and one slice of bread. I can't actually remember our main course at dinner, but we had rice pudding all the time. Every Sunday evening we had a slice of cheese, sliced beetroot, bread and tea.

We moved on to Compton Bassett in Wiltshire to continue our training and had two different radios to master: a transmitter for which we used a Morse key to send messages, and a receiver with which we used a logbook to write down coded messages.

In the Nissen hut there was a wireless and sometimes we heard Lord Haw Haw (real name William Joyce) broadcasting propaganda: "Germany calling, Germany calling." All lies; it was amusing more than anything.

I was allocated a posting to No 19 OTU RAF Kinloss and took the train north from Paddington, London - the destruction from bombing in the city was unbelievable.

At Kinloss, I was driven to Seapark House, some distance from the aerodrome, a large old mansion in a wooded area. I shared a huge room with five others. No heating, shared bathroom (usual five inches marked in the bath).

It was quite exciting entering Signals Section and heading right up to the top to the control tower, where I was to work as a fully-fledged wireless operator, quickly getting into the routine of sending and receiving messages in Morse code to airborne planes.

During my time at Kinloss, the Air Sea Rescue was started. The men were so enthusiastic, going to meetings every day for practices. We often walked to Findhorn and all along the beach were huge cement bollards to halt any invaders. Winston Churchill was a hero and inspiration to all. He made broadcasts on the wireless; when we were at our lowest ebb he boosted everyone's spirits.

After almost three years at Kinloss I was promoted to LACW and posted to RAF Oakington, near Cambridge. For some obscure reason, wireless operators were made redundant and I was sent to RDF (Radio Direction Finding). This was a small hut in the middle of nowhere, completely isolated. We had equipment, charting where each kite (plane) was and logging every move. It was very intense work; it had to be so accurate. You were on duty alone, the door locked at all times. You needed a password to get in.

I was working on VE-Day, and on VJ-Day and missed out on the celebrations.

Ken Tuckwell

BOMBS IN BIRMINGHAM

Ken Tuckwell, Elgin (b. 1928) was 11 when war was declared and living in the suburbs of Birmingham. He was a construction engineer with the Hydro Board until his retirement.

I REMEMBER GATHERING round the wireless on the Sunday and listening to the announcement that we were at war. They delivered an Anderson shelter and we dug a hole in the garden. Some people went down just two feet, but ours was practically six feet down. We went in with neighbours and joined two Anderson shelters together to make it bigger and be more sociable I suppose.

The first time there was an air raid and we went into the shelter, I wet my pyjamas – I was so scared...I was really terrified. It was not nice down there at all, and not very warm. We had paraffin heaters, but they weren't very efficient and in such a confined space the smell was bad. We had candles to see by, and took a flask and sandwiches. For a while, we went into the shelter every night to sleep: going to bed meant going into the shelter. It was so cold that we started sleeping in our clothes.

Eventually, we got fed up with this. The centre of Birmingham was badly bombed, but the nearest they dropped bombs to us was two streets away – I think they must have dropped them on their way home –and we just stayed in bed when an air raid was on.

They threatened to close all the schools in Birmingham and so I was evacuated along with the other children. A charabanc took us to East Leake, Nottingham; we each wore labels with our names on them and carried gas masks. We were delivered to a hall and had to stand there while these people came in and picked out which child they would take. It was not very nice: I was just a little lad and wondered if anyone would pick me. I ended up with a butcher: I was expected to make sausages and do the deliveries – it was just cheap labour really. After 10 days many of us decided

Ken Tuckwell.

we couldn't stick it and came home – on the way back we all sang 'Rolling home, by the light of the silvery moon', we were so pleased to be coming home.

For a while after that we had to go to school in people's houses: different people, different houses each day, and the teachers came round to each group; there was probably half a dozen in my group. As you can imagine, we didn't get much schooling, just an hour or so a day – I feel I really missed out on an essential part of my schooling. After a time they realised that they would have to re-open the schools.

If you lived in the country you got extras, but we had to manage on the bare minimum when it came to food. We just got the rations and no more, but it didn't do us any harm. I don't remember really going without.

We went out to play a lot, which kids don't do these days – hide and seek, and the like. We never played in the Anderson shelter. Holidays away were non-existent during the war, but the year the war started we went to Butlins at Skegness. It had only opened in 1936 and one of my uncles was very keen on the idea. It was quite regimented, but I thought it was wonderful with several unusual rides. Most of the entertainment was provided by the Redcoats, who were people employed by Butlins to make sure everyone enjoyed themselves. (*By the following year, Butlins Skegness had been turned into HMS Royal Arthur and sailors occupied the chalets.*)

My father served in World War I, and was too old to be called up, but he became an air raid warden: he worked as an electrical fitter, building turbines for GEC, during the day, and then was up on the roofs night after night watching for the bombers. He never spoke much about it.

My mother was an usherette at the Theatre Royal in Birmingham, so it must have stayed open most of the war. I remember her saying how she had to pick her way to work through the rubble after a heavy night of bombing, and that she had seen unexploded bombs as big as cars lying in the street.

Despite my lack of education, when I left school at 14 I managed to pass the exam to get into Handsworth Technical School, where I went full time for the next two years. The war ended just before I finished the course.

Street parties were held up and down the country to mark the end of the war. This one was in Birmingham – Ken Tuckwell is the little boy on the right at the head of the table on the left, while his mother stands smiling at the back in the centre of the picture.

Norman Cameron

THE SURVIVOR

Some 24,000 members of the Merchant and Fishing Fleets died in World War II and have no known grave but the sea; a ratio of approximately 1 in 3 who served. All volunteers, they endured U-boat attacks, air attacks, mines, the might of the German fleet...and the perils of the sea itself. And if they were lucky to survive being sunk, their pay stopped immediately. Yet they performed an essential task: ensuring that Britain survived. Norman Cameron (b.1924), Elgin, was lucky to escape with his life on more than one occasion.

WE LEFT GLASGOW in ballast around March 13, 1942 on board The *Cape of Good Hope*, and sailed to New York. In New York we loaded aviation spirit in drums in No 1 Hold, in No 2 Hold we loaded grain and Holds No 3, 4, 5 were bombs and high explosives. On deck we had planes and light tanks. Leaving New York we were bound for South Africa and round the Cape and into the Persian Gulf.

We were only a few days out from New York in the South Atlantic when we were torpedoed. The torpedo struck No 2 Hold, which was a blessing. Along with the rest of the two watches who were below at the time, I was in my bunk asleep when we were struck. Of course everything in the fo'c'sle was in a shambles after the explosion and we felt that she was going down by the head.

The door to the fo'c'sle had jammed shut when we got hit, but fortunately one of the panels at the bottom had split so we were able to crawl out on our hands and knees. Seeing the ship was in a bad way we lowered the lifeboats and pushed off from the ship. The U-boat surfaced not far from us and started shelling the ship. Knowing what our cargo was we started rowing as hard as we could to get away as far as possible. The ship was taking a long time to settle, so the U-boat put another torpedo into her and this time it was like the Atom Bomb going up: there did not even appear to be any debris, just a massive explosion and a great mushroom cloud. The U-boat then came alongside us and in faultless English the commander asked if we required anything, provisions or anything. We said we did not require anything, so then he asked if anyone was injured and required attention. Our donkeyman had injured his leg but there was no way he was going on board the U-boat in case he was made prisoner. The commander then gave us a course to follow which he reckoned would take us to some of the islands in three or four days, and then left us to our devices.

The two lifeboats kept company for the next two or three days but as our compasses showed about a point of a difference it was difficult to follow a true course. On the third day an American plane flew over us and dropped a message to say that a rescue ship would be out that night or first thing in the morning – no such luck. The fourth day we decided to part company – the difference in the two compasses – as our lifeboat had a standing lug and jib rig whilst the other had a dipping lug. When there was any wind at all we seemed to be always pulling away from the other boat. After the decision to part was made a storm blew up, so it was a parting of the ways anyway.

Our daily rations were half a measure (1/2 gill) of water at daybreak and another measure at dusk, plus two hard tack biscuits. After so many days we could not eat the biscuits as we did not have enough saliva in our mouths to chew the hard tack. For the first few days we had the company of some sharks, but they must have decided there wasn't a meal after all so they left us. The engineers, whose quarters had not been so affected by the torpedoing, had managed to salvage some tins of tobacco, so the smokers were making up fags with bits of brown paper which was lying about the boat. As a non-smoker it was something I did not have to worry about.

A Dot on the Ocean

By this time we were all blistered by the sun, being watch below all I and my watch-mates had were a singlet and a pair of trousers. On three occasions we saw aircraft flying overhead but being such a small dot on the ocean it was highly improbable they would have seen us. During the long calm spells we took two-hour turns on the oars but as our strength was waning it seemed to be more a case of dipping the oars in and out of the water. We also took turns at getting a little shelter from the sail during the hottest part of the day.

There was great excitement one day when we spied what we thought was land, but after a spell of hard rowing it turned out to be a cloud which just melted away. Another day our hopes soared again: on the swell of the sea as it slipped past we saw slices of bread, some of the lads even declared it was buttered, and the cores of apples. We thought there must be a ship or land nearby. On the 14th day a bosun bird visited us just before noon, another cause for hope. The next day just about the same time we had a visit from a similar bird. On the 16th day it had a pal, and on the following day two more of them. They circled our mast for a time then flew away. On the 18th day, only one came and we thought we were drifting away from land again.

The donkeyman was sitting in the bows that morning when he exclaimed: 'Who's smoking?' Nobody was. 'Funny, I'm sure I smelled something burning... There is something smouldering.' We searched the boat but couldn't find anything smouldering but then the rest of us were getting this burning smell. We started rowing into the light breeze – following our noses – and then we saw land. It took several hours of hard rowing before we reached it. In fact, it was evening before we beached in a bay near a village in the Dominion Republic.

First thing we got was fresh water and then a feed of bananas - and we found out the burning smell we had picked up at sea was of smoke from burning canes on the sugar plantation. An army truck took us into the nearest town, Puirto Plata. The luxury of a hot bath and a thick steak at the hotel where we were billeted was next door to heaven. We were about four or five weeks in Puirto Plata and from there we were flown to Miami and thence by train to New York. After two or three weeks in New York we were then sent to Portland, Maine to pick up another ship to sail home.

I was the youngest in the lifeboat, celebrating my 18th birthday in Puirto Plata. The lifeboat was a whaler clinker built type of boat. Navigation was a hit or miss, as ships' lifeboats' compasses were not spot on. Our captain's name was James Hamilton from Glasgow. I would say that the man who carried the burden of sailing our lifeboat was a John MacLean from the Isle of Barra. The other lifeboat landed on San Juan Puerto Rica after being 12 days adrift. The *Cape of Good Hope* belonged to the Lyle Shipping Company of Glasgow. The *Ocean Traveller* which we joined in Portland also belonged to Lyle's.

I joined the troopship the *Duchess of York* in Glasgow on July 6, 1943, once more bound for South Africa and the Middle East. We were in convoy sailing through the Bay of Biscay when we were attached by German bombers. We were struck midship and set on fire which more or less divided the ship in two. Amazingly, out of the hundred of troops and crew who were on board we only lost 12 or 13 men. When the order came to abandon ship it was with great difficulty we managed to accommodate all the survivors on the remaining lifeboats - having been hit midship, we lost a lot of our boats. However after having safely got the survivors into the boats we were only an hour or two before our escort vessels picked us up and took us aboard. This time though it was our own ships that had to torpedo the *Duchess of York*, as it was afire from stem to stern.

The frigates which picked up took us to Casablanca where we were put into an American Army camp, under canvas, to await repatriation. This only took about two weeks this time. We were sunk on July 11 so I spent my 19th birthday again as a survivor.

In those days the minute you were torpedoed and sunk your pay stopped and your leave started.

After 18 days afloat in a lifeboat Merchant Seaman Norman Cameron (fifth left) and his fellow survivors show the strain of their ordeal as they land in the Dominican Republic.

George Chesworth

A SCHOOLBOY'S WAR

Air Vice-Marshal George Chesworth CB, OBE, DFC, (b.1930), Lord Lieutenant of Moray from 1994-2005, had a distinguished post-war career. He was station commander at RAF Kinloss from 1972-75, and was Chief of Staff, HQ 18 Group before his retirement in 1984. His interest in aircraft was kindled early in life, as reflected in his wartime memories.

ON 3rd SEPTEMBER 1939, aged 9 years, I listened with my mother, father and other relatives, at 11 o'clock, to Prime Minister Neville Chamberlain speaking on the wireless (as it was then known) telling the Nation that we were at war with Germany.

No sooner had he finished speaking than the silence, which descended on our family following this frightening announcement, was shattered by the wail of the air raid siren. We all rushed out to the garden to be informed, with absolute authority, by a 'know-all' neighbour that German aircraft were bombing nearby Croydon aerodrome!

We lived some 15 miles from Central London, and I was to hear those air raid warnings countless times over the next six years. My memories in the main are of the war in the air as, to me, it seemed always to be happening overhead the area in which I lived.

But I recollect that the first months were quiet while preparations for war on the Home Front were proceeding apace. The blackout, requiring no light to be showing, dictated all windows be covered by curtains, blinds, shutters or home made screens. The glass in the windows was criss-crossed with sticking tape to reduce the risk of injury from flying glass. I did not go to school until air raid shelters had been built in the school grounds. My father's wonderful garden was dug up to install our Anderson shelter. This corrugated steel structure was half buried in the ground and covered with earth. Bunk beds were fitted and the family slept in the shelter for many months. Other 'casualties' of the garden were the appearance of a large vegetable patch to be followed rapidly by chickens.

The quiet period, sometimes described as the phoney war, left no memories for me. But the Battle of Britain following the evacuation of our forces from Dunkirk certainly did. With the Fighter Command airfields of Biggin Hill, Kenley and Croydon fairly near, few days passed when the sky was not filled with 'dog fighting' RAF and German aircraft. When these combats were at high level our view was confined to watching the condensation trails of the aircraft as they criss-crossed the sky. Low level fights were much more exciting as the Spitfires, Hurricanes, Messerschmitts and other German aircraft were clearly visible. Sometimes, if the fighting was directly overhead, the used cartridge cases fell into our garden. These were much-prized trophies and became the first of the many spoils of war collected by schoolboys such as me.

The Battle of Britain was followed by the blitz on London. The principal target was the port of London in the East End of the city. The nightly raids resulted in huge fires clearly visible from my house. Even in daylight the glow could be seen on the horizon. From the comparative safety of our Anderson shelter we heard the bombers overhead on the way to, and from, their targets. The distant sound of exploding bombs and anti aircraft gunfire was regularly enhanced by the noise of local guns and stray bombs. This activity close to home usually enhanced my collection of souvenirs as shrapnel and bomb splinters were to be found on the ground in the surrounding area. Occasionally we boys were able to retrieve something from a crashed aircraft - hopefully German.

Skies Filled With Aircraft

School was regarded as the place for telling stories (boasting) of experiences and swapping memorabilia. I can't remember much else except that just about all the men teachers, other than the very elderly, went off to the Armed Forces. In due course some teachers came out of retirement to replace those who had left. These were very welcome to us boys as most were veterans of WW1 and had exciting stories to tell!

There followed a period when, I think, the skies were fairly quiet. But with the advent of the strategic bomber offensive against Germany and the occupied countries that all changed.

The daylight raids were mounted by the United States Army Air Force. In the mornings I remember hundreds of Flying Fortresses and Liberator aircraft in formations, still low as they climbed, stretching from horizon to horizon. Later they returned with many gaps in the formations and obviously badly damaged aircraft trailing smoke and with engines out of action.

George Chesworth.

Not long after the Americans had returned the skies were filled with the aircraft of Bomber Command flying out for their night attacks. It was not always possible to see the Lancasters, Halifaxes and other aircraft as they were always higher than the Americans and it was quite often dark. But one could always hear the sound of the many hundreds of Merlin engines.

1944 saw the preparations for the invasion of Europe dominating the news and then D Day, June 6, came the long awaited return to France. However, one week later the first V1 flying bomb - the 'Doodlebug' - flew over my home to remind us that the war was far from over. By then we were not sleeping in the air raid shelter, as there was, allegedly, no longer a danger from enemy bombers. On the first night we saw the very low flying V1 my father and I were looking out of a bedroom window in an attempt to identify the source of the, new to us, distinctive engine noise. The 'aircraft' appeared with long flames coming from the tail and father commented that 'we are shooting down a lot tonight'. We soon learned that as long as the Doodlebug could be heard it was unlikely to land near you. When the engine stopped it was time to take cover! I continued to go to school despite the V1, and later the V2 rocket, attacks.

But soon the war in Europe was won and, as was to be expected, the people went wild. Together with our neighbours, we lit a huge bonfire in the road and burned, among other things, the dreaded blackout screens. The crater left in the concrete surface by that fire took years to repair.

My lasting memory of the VE Day celebrations was being in the crowd witnessing the tremendous Victory Parade down London's Oxford Street. The road was filled with men and women of the armed forces, and civilian services, marching in company with the King and Queen in their open carriage. The watching thousands roared and cheered until they were hoarse - and my old, very staid, uncle threw his hat in the air!

Bill Barr Cochrane

SEWING TO SURVIVE

Bill Barr Cochrane (b.1915) Elgin, was working in his father's music shop when war broke out – little did he know that he would owe his life to a sewing machine.

I VOLUNTEERED IN March 1940. I had an uncle who was an engineer and responsible for the first automatic telephone exchange in Edinburgh and he suggested I went into the Signals because they always had sheets on the beds and tablecloths on the tables. I went into the 18th Divisional Signals and started training.

Much later I was told we were going abroad and was sent to Liverpool, by this time I was a corporal. We were being transported on ex-cruise ships – but it wasn't comfortable. I was in a cabin too near the waterline for my liking. The convoy consisted of some cargo ships and destroyers – the biggest war ships we had. Three or four days out we heard aircraft, went up on deck, and here was the American Navy to meet us.

We later went on board an American ship at Halifax, Nova Scotia – this was October 1941, before they had joined the war – it had been the *SS America*, but the name was changed to *Westpoint*. We had en suite cabins, but the en suite wasn't working, and there were 14 bunks in each cabin. We made our way to Trinidad to refuel then headed south for Cape Town. By that time we'd been at sea almost six weeks and we were allowed to go ashore.

The next day we heard about Pearl Harbour and all leave was cancelled. We immediately set sail from Cape Town, probably around 10,000 men in three ships, one of which peeled off at Mombasa. We went to Bombay with virtually no escort. I spent three weeks at a Hill Station as part of an advanced party for a signals unit. Then back to Bombay and set sail again. No one knew where we were going, and those that knew weren't telling. Two days out we were told it was to be Singapore. The crew was getting jittery at this point and on the look out for mines. They were throwing out terra planes (*floats*) to explode any mines just under the surface, but one went under the bows of the ship and we had to stop.

We docked in Singapore at 6am on January 27, 1942, 19 days prior to the collapse of Singapore. I have no proof, but I'm sure the Divisional Commander did his damndest to get the ship to turn round for Australia, but I think the authorities wanted the ship to take civilians and women and children off – they knew what was coming. It wasn't until 3pm that we got orders to move. That was a bad show; we were just sitting there waiting for the Japs to bomb us. We went up to a rubber plantation in the North-east of the Island and I had my first experience of being under fire when a shell came close. I was very lucky. We pulled back and were billeted in a bungalow, then a message came in I could not believe: it was for all organizations to 'please send by return' any boots needing repair. I wondered who was running the show.

Either just before or just after the capitulation, I was made up to Lance Sergeant to bring the section up to strength – I think I was replacing someone who realized it was all over and decided to make a dash for it. I said I would accept the rank if I got paid for it...but I never was. The CO came in and ordered us to lay down our arms. We took the bolts out of our rifles and threw them away. After a couple of days we were marched to Changi. I did not see any brutality at the time, but we learnt that the Japs had been going into hospitals and bayoneting patients and medical staff. I realized I had to hang onto as much gear as I could carry. Changi was a military camp so a reasonable billet.

On May 5 the opportunity came to go down to Singapore to unload cargo ships. The Japs we came into contact with were reasonable, and the facilities were quite good, if crude. Six months later we moved again, to River Valley Road in Singapore. It was Christmas and we were told we were going to Thailand. We left by train through Malaya to Chumphon where we discovered the monsoon had washed away part of the railway embankment and we had to rebuild it. There were no facilities for feeding us, but somehow, I managed to get a bunch of 17 small bananas. I ate the lot in one go; I couldn't stop once I'd started. Fortunately I suffered no adverse effects. What came to mind was my mother; she would never let me have a second banana because she said I'd be sick.

The Blood Railway

Eventually we got to Banpong, a dreadful camp, under water and alive with rats, this was where the railway joined the Bangkok railway. The Japs wanted 250 men to clear jungle, replacing POWs up north who were in such a state of health they were no use. They wanted fresh blood. All my pals were chosen, but not me, so I was left behind. Afterwards, when I heard what they went through, I realized how fortunate I was. At Nong Pladuk camp, a major base camp, I had the distinction of being in the party that laid the first rails for the Blood Railway. We had to be very careful we didn't get scratched by bamboo as we cleared a way, because the scratches could become ulcerated and turn to gangrene. After a couple of months my ankle had several ulcers – I still have the marks today.

A fellow POW drew this picture of Bill Barr
Cochrane while they were still in camp.

There was a sick hut looked after by a sergeant major in the King's Own Yorkshire Light Infantry who was quite a character. We had our own medics, but virtually no medicine. My legs were painted with blue stuff and I was told to lie up. During that time the sergeant major went down to the camp tailor's shop to get trousers repaired. But the fellow said he'd no needles or thread and threw them back at him. When he came back I said I'd have a go, I'd never sewed, but I was reasonably nimble with my fingers. I did the repair and he said it was marvellous. He later told me they were looking for tailors and he'd put my name in. I was shattered, for the simple reason that I hadn't a clue where I'd be going. But the next morning I presented myself at the parade ground with all the kit I had left and the next thing I knew I was at POW HQ in Banpong, Thailand, being given a Singer sewing machine that I didn't know how to thread, let alone operate! I realized that if I could bluff my way through, it might save my life.

A Japanese medical officer wearing a British 1914-18 medal was a reasonable type and cured my tropical ulcers. The Japs were not all bad, just some of the younger element.

The Japanese wore short-sleeved shirts with breast pockets. It was my job to make the white labels they wore with their rank, name, whatever. At one time I had about five assistants. We also did work for the POWs, but they'd expect the impossible – they'd come in with a couple of pockets and ask me to build trousers round them. We did our best. I was even asked to cut trousers out of a valise. There were no clothes dished out so it was all repairs.

I met a Japanese officer who gave a me a good price for a Parker pen and pencil with gold caps I'd bought while on board the *Westpoint* – I don't even know why I bought it – but I used the money to buy extra food like bananas and duck eggs – I never saw any hens. We had plenty of rice, but we had to eat it with the weevils still in it – the MO said if we washed it we'd remove all the goodness. Now and again we'd get a watery stew, and on special occasions we might get a pig – one pig to serve 2,000 men...you'd maybe get a faint aroma.

To be honest I never saw any real brutality, not like they experienced working on the railway: being a tailor saved my life. I never even saw the Bridge over the River Kwai, which was just along the road from our camp, until I went back in 1983 with Bill (the late Bill Gillan, Elgin, who was also a POW).

The Japs were supposed to have a voucher authorizing them to get sewing done. One day an officer's batman, they were called tobans, came with a satchel to be repaired, but he had no voucher and I refused. He started belting me, telling me to keep my hands to my side. I went straight to the administration officer, who could speak English and told him. The toban was belted...not for hitting me, but for not having a voucher. But there was some satisfaction in that.

One day I was beckoned by a toban and taken into the office of a Japanese major. He had put his knee through his breeches, and proceeded to take them off in front of me, fold them, and then hand them to me. I bowed and went off and repaired them, When I came back he was still sitting behind his desk in his underpants, and we went through the same ritual in reverse.

The Huntly Corner

Then there was the £10 corner. There were very few Scots, but one, Ian Aitken, a captain in the Royal Artillery, was from Aberdeen. He did the mail and used to come into HQ; we became lifelong friends. Later there was a lad McBeath whose father was a butcher in Lossiemouth. We'd been talking about the road between Aberdeen and Elgin: going home, I said, once you got to the Huntly corner and under the railway bridge you turned right; Ian said you turned left. We bet each other £10, to be paid when we were free and could check for ourselves. Any Scot who came into the camp would be asked whether it was right or left at the Huntly corner. As it happened we were both right, it goes one way, then the other. Rather than pay up the £10 I think in the end we had a drink on it.

At about this time the Thais broke in and stole the sewing machines, pinched the lot, but someone was looking after me because I was told to join a tailors' establishment at an officers' camp. It was very near the end of the war and we got an inkling of it. One Thai merchant risked his life to help prisoners – his bravery was recognized after the war - and he got news through. We knew when the war in Europe was over a while after it happened. We had a secret wireless in the camp. Sometimes news got to us in other ways: once a Gordon Highlander came into the camp from Chunkai. He handed me three strips of paper with current news on them. A Korean came flying round the corner and saw my hand going into my pocket and demanded to know what it was. I said I was feeling for a cigarette, and fortunately I had some Japanese issue. That was the nearest I got to being in real trouble.

Occasionally they would search the camp. I had a picture of myself in highland dress, which a Korean guard discovered. He indicated that he would like to have it and gave me one of himself. On one occasion when I had malaria, he searched the camp and found two tins of corned beef, which he brought for me. They searched their own people, and later when the Koreans were searched they came across my photo. I was sent for. I was quite frightened, but told them he'd asked me for it.

We were moved to an adjacent base supply camp, for which I was very grateful because the Yanks came over and tried to blow the HQ camp out of the ground. On August 16, 1945 Col Sugasawa marched into the camp and told us we were free. Sandy Lamont from Aberdeen and I walked up and down all night. I remember there was the biggest moon I'd ever seen. I was asked to make a Red Cross flag to mark a dropping station at a landing strip – it wasn't big enough for them to land. Stupidly I made a mistake and took the red cross right out to the border – I'd made an St George flag instead. I corrected my mistake.

In the early 1950s I was staying in Edinburgh with the £10 corner man and there was an ex-POW exhibition on in Stockbridge. We went in and there was my flag. There was a label saying it had been made by a soldier, name unknown. There was no mistaking it was my flag because of the mistake. I don't know what happened to it after that.

At the camp they dropped supplies to us and we started to walk out, eventually we were picked up by trucks and taken to Bangkok.

I saw a number of warehouses, jam-packed with handcuffs, which was significant. I think they had plans to handcuff us all and mow us all down. If the US hadn't dropped the atomic bomb, I don't think any of us would have survived.

We were billeted at the Thai university. Three British females came to visit us; one of them was Edwina Mountbatten. After some days Dakota aircraft flew in and we were flown out in groups of 25. It grew chilly on the aircraft and one of the crew came round with blankets. I asked if any of them had served at Kinloss or Lossiemouth – I was so anxious to have some contact with home – and it turned out two of them had been at Kinloss. 3, 000 feet above Thailand I actually made contact with someone who had gone into my father's shop in Elgin and bought records!

At Rangoon we went on board the *Worcestershire*. Our first meal was rice –there was almost a mutiny. At Ceylon they said only the officers were allowed ashore – no one had a clue what we'd been through – but they eventually agreed we could go as well and we had a pleasant afternoon meeting WRENS and ATS. At Liverpool there was just one person to greet us, the father of a Jewish furniture maker from Glasgow – he'd managed to get a message to him. In Liverpool at transit camp we got paid and I went to my brother in Nottingham, I wasn't fit to struggle all the way up to Elgin. I weighed 8 stone, but some POWs lost a lot more weight: one was down to five-and-a-half stone. I had two kit bags, but couldn't lift them up on the train. I asked a soldier for help, but you've never heard such language.

I don't have any hatred for the Japanese. My philosophy has always been, you cannot live with hate.

The Korean guard who exchanged photographs with POW Bill Barr Cochrane.

Helen Barr Cochrane

ABERDEEN BOMBED

Helen Barr Cochrane, Elgin, spent most of the war years as a student in Aberdeen, a city which did not escape its share of the bombing.

I WAS AT the Central School in Aberdeen for the first year of the war and then a student at the Aberdeen Domestic Science School – Central School was used to house old people from Woodend Hospital which became a military hospital. We did a shift system with the Grammar School. If the siren went we had to go to the air raid shelter, if the exam was less that half way through we had to take it again, if more than half way through we were OK.

Aberdeen was bombed, the worst night was April 1943. I was a student by this time and heard the siren. I was on duty at one of the forces clubs on a voluntary basis, cooking, cleaning, and office work. I said I must get home; I stayed with elderly aunts and an uncle. Half way up Union Street I saw a Heinkel coming down letting off tracer bullets. A chap pushed me to the ground. When I got up there were shells all over the place. I wasn't terrified, I was 20 and it happened to everyone. I started walking, but someone yelled there was another wave coming and we went into a basement. When we came up I was told the Tartan Kirkie, the Episcopal church in Carden Place had been bombed, but I walked past and could see nothing. It had been bombed at the back, the front was still standing.

Because of my domestic science training I remember the food well. We had dried eggs: we'd put a bit of baking powder in with them, reconstitute with water and pour into egg cups, then steam them and serve with lettuces and radishes and make a salad. Dried milk wasn't bad for making cocoa, but it was sweetened with saccharine. There was the national loaf, made with potato flour, very stodgy and grey.

We had to queue everywhere for food. Luckily my uncle was a

fish curer and we had fish two or three times a week, although I didn't appreciate it at the time and got fed up of it. We got very little meat. My grandmother used to get a bit of hough, boil it up with home-grown vegetables and have it as soup with boiled tatties, all piled into a soup plate. We did a lot of fruit bottling, raspberries, gooseberries, apples, using kilner jars; sometimes they were just bottled in water because sugar was kept for making jam. There were a lot of sausages – I wouldn't like to know what went into them. Everyone made 'banana' sandwiches – boiled and mashed parsnips flavoured with banana essence. We didn't taste real bananas for years.

At Do' school I had to bake a cake and the family saved their dried fruit for me; I felt responsible for making sure it turned out well. Marzipan was made from soya flour with almond essence and a little sugar. We preserved eggs when they were plentiful in isinglass.

Bill (*Japanese POW Bill Barr Cochrane*) was missing 18 months before his parents knew he was alive. I was staying in Elgin with friends and was asked by a friend to deliver a parcel to them. I was invited in, but I'd not met Bill. The first news they had of him was a postcard with 'I am well' on it.

In 1945 I was teaching in Edinburgh and visited my friends in Elgin again. I went into the shop to say hello to the Barr Cochranes and met this very thin fellow with yellow skin – Bill. I was introduced and he invited me out. We married in April 1948.

Jock Mackenzie

THE ONE THAT GOT AWAY

A family tradition saw Jock Mackenzie (b 1921), now living in Burghead, volunteer for the army. He joined the 6th Seaforth Territorials in 1936 at the age of 15 and two years later signed on as a regular. Both his father and grandfather, from Bishopmill, Elgin, were in the Seaforths. He was at Fort George when the war started and was transferred to the 5th Seaforths, then to the 2nd Seaforths in 1941. He was sent to Egypt in June 1942; saw action at El Alamein and other desert battles, then on to Sicily.

OUR FIRST BATTLE was at Francofonte. There were bullets coming from all directions and the first person to be killed was a Sergeant Ross from Elgin. I was going up a hill when I saw Frank Fraser, also from Elgin, coming back down the other way on a stretcher. Three days later we were going up a hill at night; what we didn't know was that most of our officers had been ambushed and captured. In the morning we were told to dig in, but it was just hard rock so we couldn't. We were also near a cliff – my platoon was nearest.

It was a very hot day, July 19, 1943, and we were bombarded the whole time by mortar shells. Then at about 6pm the Germans set fire to the grass at the back of us and we saw these German paratroopers. They had automatic rifles, we just had rifles, so there was nothing we could do and they captured us. They put us in trucks and took us away. We were taken to tents to be interrogated by three officers sitting at a table. I told them my name, rank and number and one of the officers said: 'You are from Elgin?' He had been at Gordonstoun School and recognised the dialect! We were put back into wagons; by this time we'd had nothing to eat for three or four days. There were grapes growing beside the road so I asked if there was any chance of getting some. The guard got off with me. I threw some grapes into the back of the wagon and climbed in, but the wagon started off, leaving the guard behind. He handed me his machine gun to hold while he caught up and clambered back on – and I handed it back. It was like a farce.

We crossed the Messina Straits and they took us into a wood with barbed wire going from tree to tree and gave us tattie soup – the best soup I've ever tasted, it seemed at the time. Then we were put on a train and taken to a POW camp near Naples – on the way the train was machine-gunned and bombed. Reaching Camp Centramiento PG66, one of the first people I saw was a bloke with a beard; it was Hugh Kemp from Elgin, who'd been captured in Africa.

It was not very good at the camp; there were maybe 3,000-4,000 prisoners. The Americans were bombing ammunition trains at a station a couple of miles away: there was an explosion and some of the huts in the camp collapsed with the blast. An English bloke found a Pears soap tin; he got some white clay, rubbed it with a bit of soap to make it smell right, put it in the tin and used it to barter with – the Italians couldn't get soap. He spent about half a hour haggling with the Italian guards across the wire and eventually he threw the soap over to them and they threw back a loaf of bread...only we discovered they'd eaten the inside of it. The Italian guards were worse than the Jerries.

Everyone had dysentery: the latrines were just trenches with two poles to sit on, and when you went down in the morning you'd find three or four blokes sitting on them, dead.

The British were advancing and we were moved to another camp near Florence; everyone was in it, and there was nothing to eat. At night I crawled under the trip wire and grabbed handfuls of chickweed, which we boiled up and ate. When the Italians surrendered, the Germans took over the camp and took us away to Germany in rail trucks. They took the Italian guards away, too, but they didn't put them with us: they knew better than that. We were in the trucks for about a week, stopping and starting. It was terrible: by the time we got to Spittle in Austria we were up to our ankles in slime – so many of us had dysentery – and you couldn't sit down.

Jewish Bodies

We came out of the trucks and the first thing we saw was this big black and red German flag with the swastika on it. There was another train that had been full of Jews, men, women and children, and we had to empty out the dead bodies and put them in a pile at the side of the road. A couple of days later we were shifted to Torgu, Stalag IVB. We had to stay in a queue, which moved about three yards an hour. There were two Russian women; one ran horse clippers over our hair to shave us to the skin, the other had a needle which she jammed into our arms – the same needle was being used over and over again, no sterilisation. She turned round as I stepped forward and so missed me.

We were in tents with wood shavings on the floor to sleep on; nae blankets, and were so packed in that if you were in the middle you couldn't get out. About 50 of us were taken to a sugar factory at Lutsen to work. I had to empty wagons of coal from 6am to 6pm, no breaks, and all I got was a bowl of soup and a bit of bread. Then I emptied loads of sugar beet. That lasted for about two months, and then I was sent to Halle to work on the tramlines. We worked with iron bars, but had no gloves so our hands stuck to them in the cold. We made our own shoes – wood clogs – and instead of socks had squares of canvas wrapped round our feet.

I did various jobs, but finished up working with a Jerry who'd been a POW in Aberdeen during the First World War, so we got on quite well. We were working in a square in the city when the bombing started. I was choking and felt someone pull me into a shelter in the middle of the square. A woman in there started giving me hell for the bombing but I told her they were American planes. When I came out I thought I'd better make for the camp – the other fellow had disappeared, I suppose he'd been killed. There was a German policeman lying with his leg off who shouted at me, and when I didn't stop, he fired at me, but I kept going. There were buildings falling down all over the place, and when I got back to the camp I found it had been flattened – I never saw any of the other POWs again.

I decided to take off and head west. I met up with a South African and a Londoner – I never did ask their names. The Londoner was good at breaking into places and stealing food. He went into a shop one day and the woman in there got wise to us so he cracked her over the head with a loaf and we got away. We were wearing our uniforms all this time, with a red diamond on the sleeve to show we were prisoners. We didn't want to take the uniforms off because we could be shot as spies. We stole horses and rode horseback for a while. This went on for 19 days.

We'd taken shelter in a barn; it was about 4am and I said: "Let's go," but the others had blisters and said they'd had enough, so I went on my own. It was about 10am when I heard a plane and dived into a shed full of tatties. I looked up, and there was this British sailor hiding in the rafters. Things quietened down and we heard tanks coming up the road – it was the Americans. They had a lot of German prisoners and were stealing watches off them – the Germans did the same to us.

I was interrogated so that they could make sure I was who I said I was, and I told them I'd left two others up the road. The Americans took me up in a jeep: it had taken me three or four hours to walk the distance, but just minutes to drive back. I went into the barn and found the others had been shot dead. The American officer went over to the farmhouse to find out what had happened and the farmer pointed to another building. A few minutes later I heard shots and the Americans pulled the body of a lad out of the building. He was about 13 or 14, and wore the Hitler Youth uniform.

Travelling in an American truck, I was taken to an American plane and put on board. The crew were playing cards, so I asked who was flying the plane...they said 'George'. I didn't know they meant the automatic pilot. I asked where we were going. They said they hadn't got a clue, and to ask the navigator. We landed in Belgium, and I was able to shower and was kitted out with a uniform, then put on a train for Brussels to be handed over to the British Army and flown back to the UK. We landed at Blackbush in England: everything looked so bonnie and green. We went into a hangar where WAAF girls had tea laid out on card tables. I hadn't had contact with a woman for nearly two years. One of the girls asked where I was from – she was from Lossiemouth.

We were put on a train for Scotland. There was a young lad with me from Forres. At Aberdeen the WRVS had laid on soup for us. I asked the lad to go for a pint, but he said he wasn't feeling so well. So I went for a haircut. I was sitting reading a book; waiting my turn, when I noticed the bloke sitting opposite looking at me...it was my brother. He was in the Navy and I'd never seen him in uniform before. He asked for some extra day's leave so that he could come home with me, and our father met us at the station in Elgin.

It was a sad homecoming for me. Before I'd gone abroad I'd had a letter saying my mother was ill: I'd wanted to visit her, but the captain said I wasn't needed at home. I was on a boat, looking into the water, when something told me she had died, but there was so little in the way of communications that it wasn't until I was in the desert that Sergeant Harvey came to me with a letter, and in it was a picture of my mother's grave.

On the train to Elgin were Sergeant Jamie McKenzie and George Geddes, and we'd agreed to meet in the Stag Bar in Elgin on the Saturday night. But when I got there I was told that the young lad from Forres had dropped dead when he reached home. We all went to the funeral.

I met Jane from Burghead just after. She took me home to meet her mother, and there on the mantelpiece was a picture of George Geddes – he was her brother. We were married in 1946.

Jock Mackenzie and his bride Jane.

Ken Ward

PLAYING TRUANT

Ken Ward, now living in Burghead, was brought up in Oldham, Lancashire, and went to Limeside School. He remembers the famous speech of Neville Chamberlain on the Sunday before his 7th birthday.

DURING THE EARLY days nothing much seemed to be happening other than the local Oldham Chronicle producing silhouette images of various German aircraft so we would be able to recognise them. My father cut these out and pasted them on the inside of the kitchenette door so we could refer to them. We were all issued with gas masks and had to take them everywhere with us; this once got me in trouble. Kenny Smith, Stinker Johnson and myself decided one afternoon, realising we were late for school and would get the strap, it would be better to play truant. We wandered to a local beauty spot called Crime Lake, which had a few penny slot machines we could play on and rowing boats. We didn't have much money between us so we decided on putting a penny in the machine entitled 'What the butler saw'. We had to stand on tiptoes and share the looks until the penny ran out. We had a good time that afternoon and we were about halfway home when I discovered we had all left our gas masks back at the slot machines. We returned to retrieve them and on the way home again we agreed we had all had a good time and it was much better than going to school. We then decided that was going to be the life for us, we were never going to school again.

We were about two hours late arriving home, so that took some explaining. Next morning we all met and Stinker Johnson chickened out, he went to school and told the teacher what Kenny Smith and I were doing. At lunchtime I was enjoying my meal when I suddenly heard crying coming down our path and quickly approaching our back door. In stepped Mrs. Smith holding Kenny's left ear, she thrust him into our kitchen and demanded he told my mother what we had been up to.

In the afternoon Mrs Smith and my mother escorted us to school, demanded to see the head- master and then related what we had been up to. The headmaster punished us with the strap giving us both two strokes each and saying our names would be entered in the punishment book. This did not satisfy my mother, she asked the headmaster to give us some more but he wouldn't. She then informed the headmaster and myself that I would be in for some more when I got home. I had trouble sitting down for a week.

Ken Ward.

As the war progressed we started to experience air raids which were usually at night. At first we were able to go into the Anderson shelter which the council had erected in our back garden, but later it just became full of water and a haven for frogs. Then we stayed in the house during air raids hoping the stairs would shelter us. We never suffered a direct hit but we had our windows blown out twice with bomb blast. It was during one of these air raids that our headmaster's house was hit. The whole house was flattened but the wooden garage was left standing undamaged.

Fortunately the headmaster wasn't at home, but unfortunately his wife was and her life was lost. I felt very sorry for Mr Scott our headmaster, because he was a fair man and didn't deserve such a dreadful experience. He continued teaching us and I was glad he did because I learned a lot from him.

The bomb craters used to fill with water and became useful for sailing our model boats, which were often not much more than a piece of wood. As the war progressed we experienced daylight raids. I remember one day hearing the planes and machine guns - the Germans were attacking A.V. Roes at Chadderton, makers of the Manchester and Lancaster bombers.

Towards the end of the war we heard the V1 and V2 flying bombs. When the engines cut out there would be a few seconds of silence and then the bang which shook the earth. During those few seconds of silence one hoped it wasn't going to be you. I remember one Christmas Eve a wedding was being celebrated in a terrace house on Abbeyhills Road, Oldham, when one of these dropped. Everyone in the house had been killed.

We went to see the damage and a whole row of terraced houses had been flattened.

Finally the end of the war came and the celebrations began. For a number of years the parties were repeated annually on the anniversary of the end of the war.

Edna Wilmot

A FAMILY VC

The Victoria Cross is Britain's highest award for gallantry in the face of the enemy. Only 182 were awarded in World War II: one of them went to a relative of Edna Wilmot (b. 1924), who now lives in Forres.

I WAS LIVING in Hatfield Woodhouse, near Doncaster, when war broke out. It was a quiet village, but we were just three miles from Lindholme airfield, where they had Hampden bombers and later Lancasters and Wellingtons.

We used to hear the planes going over our house, and run out to watch them coming in. One day we saw a German plane following one of our own aircraft in; they were always trying to find the airfield, but it was in a big dip and well hidden. The German plane had used all its bombs and only had incendiaries left, so it dropped them on the airfield, causing a lot of fires but not a lot of damage.

We listened to the wireless a lot, especially Lord Haw Haw – he used to amuse us. He said they were looking for Lindholme, but after the German plane he never said they'd found it, and the Germans never came back.

I had three uncles in the army, but two of them were called back to work in the peat works – they'd been called up but later the authorities realised they needed peat. The third, Fred, I looked on as my brother. We used to wait for letters from him: they were little photographed copies of the original. He couldn't say much on them, and we didn't really know what he was doing or where he was, but we were always waiting for the post to know he was fine.

Fred went right through the war, but my mother's cousin John Harper was killed.

He was 28 years old, and a corporal in the 4th Btn the York and Lancaster Regiment, and was awarded the VC. We were very proud of him. (*It happened in 1944 in Belgium. The citation said:*

Corporal Harper led his section across 300 yards of completely exposed ground, with utter disregard for the hail of mortar bombs and small arms fire from the enemy. He was killed in the action, but the subsequent capture of the position was largely due to his self-sacrifice.)

I went to work on a farm when I left school, so I continued to work there when the war started. We had to walk past the aerodrome to reach the farm, and had to have a pass to go so near to it. We could see how many aircraft had not made it back by the gaps in the lines of planes, and that would upset us.

Edna Wilmot with her husband-to-be Leonard.

There was one big air raid shelter for the whole village. The first week of the war, as soon as the siren went everyone rushed down to the shelter with our gas masks, etc. It was fitted out with all facilities for making tea, but after the first week most of us didn't bother going. There were never any bombs.

I married Leonard in 1943. He was a miner, and so in a reserved occupation. We just had a quiet wedding; there weren't coupons for a wedding dress so I wore a suit with a spray of flowers on it. There was no wedding cake because of rationing. I don't know how we managed on the rations, but we did and thrived. One day they'd tell you bread was good for you, the next time it would be potatoes…it depended what there was a shortage of. Because my husband was a miner, we had plenty of coal: we got a ton a month, so we could sometimes barter coal for things we were short of, like butter and sugar.

My mother was in the Women's Institute and they had a house practically next door where they would make food for the troops, like beans on toast. There was also a room where they could write letters home. The house was very useful for the lads and a bit of comfort for them.

There wasn't a great deal to do. The buses stopped running to the village at 7pm, so if you wanted to go to the town to the pictures you either had to go in the afternoon, or face a walk, which we did a time or two

People didn't go on holiday: there was no point in going to the seaside because you couldn't get onto the beach: it was all wired up.

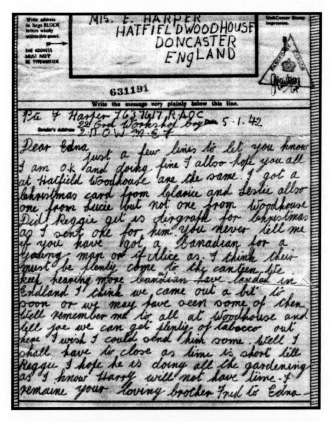

A compressed and photocopied letter home to
Edna Wilmot from her brother Fred.

William Colvin

WITH THE PARAS AT ARNHEM

With World War II in the final stages, and the Germans believed to be on the verge of collapse, Field Marshal Montgomery's ambitious plan to capture key bridges, including the bridge over the Rhine at Arnhem, involved the largest airborne assault in the history of warfare. William Colvin (b.1924 d.1995), the son of a Lossiemouth solicitor, was one of 35,000 paratroopers dropped during Operation Market Garden. He had been called up in December 1942, and was in the Seaforth Highlanders training at Fort George before volunteering for the Parachute Regiment. Later he served in the Far East. After the war he resumed a banking career, worked in Africa, where he enlisted with the Kenya Police fighting the Mau-Mau, and trained as an accountant. On retirement he returned to Moray, living at Lossiemouth and then Burghead. He left three diaries covering the war years. They are now in the possession of his daughter, Lyn Colvin, Nottingham, who has allowed us to use these extracts.

WE CROSSED THE Rhine just after 1400 hrs on September 18, 1944: on the second lift of the 1st Airborne Division on its way to Arnhem to capture the bridge and hold it for 24hrs.

Flak had been crashing against our plane for some time, but as we approached the drop zone it intensified to a regular tattoo on the fuselage; small arms fire was also coming up and several rounds pierced the framework without much damage. Suddenly someone shouted; we all lumbered to our feet laden with equipment; several minutes elapsed; it seemed like hours; then everyone dragged himself to the door and fell out. For one sickening moment I felt as if I must crash down with all this weight. The next moment I almost wished I had: small arms fire was pouring up; anti aircraft shells were bursting above and below on the heather-covered drop zone; small puffs of smoke indicated the fire of mortars.

My precision rifle, carried in a valise, had slipped out and I could see it far below, twisting and turning till it disappeared. A few seconds later I was on the ground tearing desperately at my equipment. At last, I flung off my harness and, having collected my kit, I strolled off as everyone was doing, despite the heavy fire, towards the rendezvous, slinging away the accessories for my rifle, now useless.

William Colvin.

Halfway there I came upon someone lying very still and in the hope of obtaining arms, I turned him over. Christ! I had never seen a dead man, but here under my very nose was my best pal, blood gushing from a gaping wound in his throat; his pulse was still. I turned again to the rendezvous with no thought of collecting the Sten gun, which I knew he carried.

By this time one of the companies had disposed of Jerry and peace reigned for a little while. We collected our depleted forces and set out for Arnhem following a path along the railway. Night came as we stumbled along, resting now and again our aching backs. At one halt we commandeered a horse and cart and put our packs on it, this was the last time we saw these packs and the precious box of rations inside; we never missed our washing and shaving kits.

Rumours were coming back now that there was a German strong-point ahead, but confidence in our force and ignorance of the enemy strength made us push on even more eagerly. We were approaching a thick wood when all hell broke loose. The Germans had waited to the last moment to open up on us then they gave us everything they had: flares lit up the area like daylight, tracers zipped well overhead while unseen shells screamed, tore and thumped all around us. Worst of all was the larger gun, some quick-firing weapon, which sowed its shells at a terrific rate all along, backwards, and forwards of our bewildered, stunned ranks. I had never been so close to mother earth in my life, my hands were gripping the soft earth as I waited for the one to grind into my back and blow me to kingdom come.

Someone dug me in the ribs and ordered me to follow him. I removed the rifle from the body of the next man to me and crept silently forward. Straight into the wood we went, hardly breathing as we followed the officer in front. I stepped on something which gave a loud pop; I screamed out 'mine' and was lying in the ditch when the explosion echoed and re-echoed among the trees. Someone was shouting "Get back and take cover quickly". I needed no second heeding but was close on the officer's heels and as we ran. I counted all eight of us, so no one had been hit.

Scarcely had we taken up cover when two machine guns opened up. Immediately we engaged the nearest one – firing at the flashes from the gun and the sound of excited foreign voices. It stopped firing almost immediately, but the other one kept hammering away incessantly.

"Retreat," said the officer, "leave it till daylight"; so we retraced our steps to the battalion which had now withdrawn from the wood and was awaiting the dawn. As soon as daylight broke we lined up in sections facing the wood and advanced steadily towards it. A terrific burst of firing and we all went to ground, returning the fire with equal ferocity. One man had dashed forward in a hopeless effort but he did not get 10 yards. Our medium machine guns and mortars then had their turn. We rose as a man and charged straight into the wood.

Silence greeted us as we moved under the trees – spent shell cases, deserted fox-holes told their story: the birds had flown, except for the one or two unfortunates. Positions were taken up immediately; one man jumped in a vacant foxhole and immediately disappeared in a terrific flash, explosion and a cloud of smoke. We filled in the foxhole. Now warned, we carefully examined each hole before entering it. Patrols were sent out: one officer, one sergeant and six privates (myself included) to hold a railway bridge about a mile away.

Along the friendly embankments we marched, and finally reached our destination, a small station with a bridge overhead. Someone was there before us: a swish, a crack and another one of our men crumpled up without a sound, a hole burned through his temple. Into the station we tumbled and peered from the windows; nothing could be seen, but slightly back from the embankment stood two trees with thick foliage. The light machine gun opened up on them with a long burst, ripping the leaves off the trees to shreds; a slight movement and all our rifles joined in.

A Near Shave

Bursts of fire were now coming from behind us, and we investigated. Crawling up to the top of the embankment we peered over cautiously and there was the gun poking from the upstairs window of a house about a hundred yards away. Immediately we opened fire and the gun disappeared; we were just getting up to go forward and investigate when we heard the roar of a powerful engine, and bounding towards us was an armoured car. I got my head down quick, and two of the lads rolled down to the bottom and crouched there. I was just thinking of joining them when the car reached the top, swerved hard left and tore away, but not before two stick grenades swirled over my head and exploded almost on top of the two at the bottom: one was dead, the other died within five minutes.

We took up positions each side of the bridge and for a hour or so we had peace, then over came six fighter planes and strafed all along the railway, riddled the station and searched along the embankment, but left without scratching any of us lying very still among the grass.

Later that day, I had the nearest shave I ever had in those nine days. Having heard no shots very close for sometime, I was walking carelessly among the allotments eating green tomatoes. Something red-hot whistled through the left-hand pocket of my smock burning my chest, and then the crack came startlingly close – the sniper must have been too eager. I dropped flat and rolled down the embankment, wasting no time getting back to the station.

Firing was coming from all sides now, a big attack was starting. The officer decided to withdraw to the rest of the battalion, where we discovered everyone moving off to a new position on the edge of the wood. We reached our new position and began digging in like hell. The sharp crack of ack-ack fire was heard, then aircraft: Stirlings and Dakotas flying majestically, a mere 300 feet up, disdaining the flak which poured up at them. Two Dakotas and one Stirling burst into flames, but they carried on till all the supplies were floating downwards before their noses tilted, and they crashed to earth, bursting into flames almost immediately.

Later we took up new positions on top of the railway. No sooner had we got there than field grey figures poured from our wood. Our gun started firing immediately. They soon took cover and halted, but there were some maniacs among them with mortars who immediately mounted them and popped bombs into the barrel as fast as possible – almost the first one blew our gunner sky-high. These mortar-men were dead accurate; they laid their bombs right across the top of the bank and kept our heads down. Then came the most hideous noise I have ever heard – the roar, whine, then the scream of long-range artillery getting their range. They were not far off to start with. The OC wasted no time, but withdrew us into the wood behind, pursued and harassed by mortars and artillery. Every path in that wood was covered: as soon as anyone showed a finger on even the most deserted-looking path, a hail of lead greeted them.

The remains of 11 Platoon stuck together and we made several attacks on small gun-posts – but one proved a bit stronger than the rest. It was a bungalow in the middle of a lovely garden. With the help of a projectile infantry anti-tank bomb, we cleared the house and chased the Jerries into the garden. It was a trap: the sergeant fell wounded and two Poles (who had reinforced us) dropped dead from the murderous crossfire of two machine guns. Back we crawled to the house. The officer then tried by himself: with a 36 grenade (pin out) and a Sten gun, he crept carefully forward while we drew fire. But Jerry was well organized: a short burst and we saw the officer fall on his knees; a few seconds, and the grenade burst in his hand.

Then they attacked. About five of us, all that remained, withdrew, firing as we went, and shortly joined up with a much diminished battalion who were being shelled, machine-gunned and sniped. A tank was hiding nearby. It dashed out as we came up, spitting death all around. One chap charged it with his rifle (God knows why) then off it went, careering madly along the path.

The OC stood up among all the shrapnel and waved us on; up we rose and moved forward at a walk first, bayonets fixed, then we charged, screaming like mad-men, shooting, stabbing and bayoneting. Three men I accounted for with my bayonet, and a fourth with a knife who came at me before I could pull my rifle out of the third one. Suddenly the enemy guns stopped firing, everything was quiet: our main body had consolidated in a hollow in the wood, I joined them, amazed at finding myself unhurt except for a few small cuts and bruises. There were about 70 of us there, including the Brigadier, looking as filthy and tired as the rest of us.

Only a few moments peace: Jerry had the map reference of that position, and started laying it down thick with his 'moaning minnies'. He killed quite a few of the Germans we had just taken prisoner! Now their infantry came in close, firing from the thick trees with submachine guns at a range of about 20 yards, right into our hollow. This went on for hours and we had several casualties. One time they came forward with a white flag, the Brigadier rose to take them, but they were shouting for us to surrender and the Brigadier wasted no time but loosed off a couple of shots at them with his pistol, yelling to us to give them hell!

Things were getting a bit too hot though, so the Brigadier ordered to break out, flinging a few phosphorous smoke bombs in front. We charged out straight through the amazed Germans (who thought, we were ready to give in), and made a dash for the sound of a Vickers gun in the distance. There was an open field right in front; across it we dashed, a terrific barrage of mortar fire ripping up the ground all around us. Very few of us arrived safely behind the comforting fire of the King's Own Scottish Borderer's Vickers. But we were needed again: a crossroads had to be guarded, a weak point in the Division's defences.

At The Crossroads

The remains of our brigade now took up a position around the crossroads near Oosterbeck. Six of us occupied a bake house right on the crossroads and dug slit trenches in the garden for protection. In the cellar we unearthed some bottles of wine, which we got cracking on.

Jerry scouts soon found us: the crossroads had been ranged by them beforehand, and in a very short time the usual 'pop' in the distance and the terrific explosion nearby started again. Smack on their target. We could do nothing but get down in the trenches and stay down until it was over. After 15 minutes, continuous pounding, there was a short lull, one bomb had landed almost on top of me and covered me up in sand and bricks. When I managed to extricate myself, I crawled out and had a look around in the other trenches. Only one man was in the trench - a bomb had scored a direct hit - the rest were across the road, digging in another garden. I whipped across the road, bullets kicking up at my heels, and joined them, tearing at the hard earth with bare hands, continually pestered by a sniper.

Their infantry was coming again now, six of us could do nothing against them, so we made our way back to a position nearer the centre of our perimeter. No rest for us, we were sent back to our old position again: the crossroads must now be defended at all costs. There were two officers there now, and several other lads getting organized. I was stationed at the front window of one of the houses, with a corporal covering a road. Three Germans tried to cross the road and mount a machine gun, but the corporal was too quick for them. I put a few rounds into the bodies huddled in the middle of the road just to make sure.

Later I was sent to the rear of the house with two others, one just in front and the other beside me, sitting on chairs keeping a watch through a broken part of the wall. A few minutes later the sound of a heavy armoured vehicle came to our ears: there was a flash, clouds of smoke and an ear-splitting explosion directly in front of us. I was blown right back against the wall which saved me a worse injury. Dazed and almost senseless, I stumbled to my feet, picking up a rifle, less its magazine. Everything was dark, only very faintly could I see with my left eye. We cleared out across the road and into the gardens where the OC decided to make a last stand. There was no protection, their mortars opened up again. One sergeant attempted to retreat, but the OC warned him with a light machine gun, which he had now taken possession of. The Germans were singing as they marched along the now undefended road. They brought loudspeakers up, playing some of the latest English song-hits, followed by an announcement asking us to consider our wives, sweethearts etc. and surrender; we would be well treated etc, etc.

Blood was trickling from a wound on my face, and my right eye was completely blind; only very dimly could I see with my left. The OC ordered me to get to a hospital, giving me rough directions as no one could be spared to lead me there. Eventually I reached the hospital: a huge pile of our dead lay outside in a bloody, ghastly heap, and inside were the horribly wounded. My eyes and the shrapnel wounds on my face were dressed: one piece had just grazed my nose, and very luckily for me had missed my eye. I stayed there for a day, then rumours came through that the Division had been ordered to retreat across the river so I got out of there quick and hunted around for my battalion.

Like so many others during the war, the family of
William Colvin received official notification that he
had been wounded.

The OC welcomed me back and told me the Division was moving out that night. I followed everyone's example and tied some pieces of curtain around my feet so as to make as little noise as possible when we moved out. We crept across the road then off we moved in single file through the woods. 25 pounders from across the river were laying down screen on either side of us as we moved. Several times we ran into trouble but managed to deal with it; I was worse than useless with my poor sight. Halfway there someone in front lost the column in front of him and, as we could not shout, we just had to hunt around till we met another column moving towards the river. They were a bit more organised: each man held on to the tail of the Airborne smock of the man in front, and thus we reached the river – or rather the end of a huge line of soaked, hungry, filthy men, standing stretched across the open ground beside the river, waiting for one of the two boats to take them across. For hours we were content to lie there waiting in the drenching rain, constantly sniped at and occasionally mortared, although no one took much notice of them – except those who were hit.

William Colvin arrived in Malaya two days
after the Japanese surrender.

It would have been suicide to wait there till dawn, exposed to our enemy, so one or two of us who could swim made our way to the river. It looked black, and very swift, but there was little choice. Stripping off, and with our boots and smocks round our necks, we waded in. The ice-cold water freshened me up and gave me the necessary energy to cross safely.

Exhausted, I dragged myself out on the opposite bank, scrambled over the slippery riverside and reached the road – joining on the end of another queue, this time for a ration of rum.

I managed to get a lift on an overcrowded jeep, and then we were taken by Ducks to Njmegen where an MO put me in hospital.

During my few days there, the 2nd Battalion lost and retook the Njmegen to Eindhoven strip, which they had raced across in a desperate final effort to relieve us. Our 1st Brigade and our Air-landing had held the bridge for much longer than they should have, but as no relieving forces had arrived they had to withdraw, completely outnumbered. From Njmegen I was taken by ambulance to Eindhoven, passing by many of our tanks knocked out in their desperate bid to get to us. From Eindhoven we were flown to Brussels, and after a few days stay I was flown back to England. A month in hospital and I was back home on leave as right as rain.

The Parachute Division left behind nearly 1,500 and 6,500 prisoners at Arnhem. Exactly a year after their epic parachute landing, William Colvin was among other survivors who took part in another landing, this time at Morib, Malaya. The action on this occasion was unopposed – two days earlier the Japanese had signed the terms of surrender on those same beaches.

Men of the 1st Airborne Division, somewhere in England - but not for long. William Colvin is pictured at the rear, second right.

Hannie van der Ham

A CHILD AT ARNHEM

Hannie van der Ham (b. 1940) grew up in Arnhem, Holland, and although only a small child during the war, has vivid memories of the occupation by the Germans, and subsequent liberation by the Allies. She is a frequent visitor to Moray – she fell in love with the area after seeing a film on television about the Search and Rescue service at RAF Lossiemouth. Hannie had a child's eye view of the Allied Airborne Invasion at the Battle of Arnhem.

I WAS BORN just 10 days before Holland was mobilised. My father worked at KEMA Dutch Quality Control Institute for electrical materials and appliances in Arnhem. We lived on a rural estate, Den Brink, where the company was established. My father worked for many years with English and Scottish people: they called him Mr Kingshop because our surname was Rexwinkel (rex = king; winkel = shop).

It was relatively quiet for three to three-and-a-half years; then our lives changed.

It started one day when the air was full of aeroplanes on their way to Germany to bomb cities. The regulations came that my parents had a duty to take German soldiers in their house – we lived near a railway bridge and the Germans had to guard the bridge. The Jerries, as we called them (and still do in 2005) were a disorderly bunch, with their commander, Herr Tiedke. I see him in front of me as if it was yesterday.

One soldier was different, his name was August. August was a young father of two and missed his children terribly. Every free minute he took the chance to walk with me and called me 'Hannoesch'. My mother didn't like that and forbade him to walk with me.

Most of the soldiers were Hitlerjugena (Hitler Youth); they were about 17-18 years old, and very fanatical and dangerous. In our

Hannie van der Ham.

living room stood a couch. Every night, before I went to bed, I put all my bears and dolls tidy, next to each other, against the wall. One morning, when I came downstairs, all my bears and dolls lay on the floor – a Jerry did it in a drunken fit. Later, my mother told me I was so angry that I said: "That Jerry is a jerk!" I had learnt a lot of bad words from the Germans because some of them spoke Dutch. I did not know that it was dangerous to call them Jerries.

My father had homing-pigeons and was a real pigeon flyer, but homing-pigeons could deliver messages and it was forbidden to keep them. If you were caught by a Jerry, you got the bullet immediately. At the risk of his life, my father had several times taken a pigeon, hidden in the inside pocket of his jacket, on his bike to his friends in Oosterbeck (a village near Arnhem Airborne Cemetery).

In August 1944, my younger sister was born. The situation was deteriorating perceptively. During an air raid alert, complete strangers rang at the front door and asked the maternity nurse for shelter in our house, and everybody went into the cellar. My mother had a difficult delivery and could not walk, but the strangers looked after her and the baby.

On September 17, 1944, my parents got the order to evacuate. (*This was the first day of Operation Market Garden, the Battle of Arnhem, when 500 gliders and 1,500 aircraft dropped British and American parachutists; their goal was to capture the bridges that spanned the network of canals and rivers on the Dutch/German border. They met unexpectedly fierce resistance from the Germans*). My father took my doll's cot with us for my baby sister to sleep in and we went from building to building. My parents decided we would make for our neighbour's house, 15 minutes further: first my mother and the baby, then an hour later, my father and I. But on our way to the neighbour's house my father and I met a couple of British soldiers and they told us to stay where we were: it was too dangerous to go any further. My father and I went back into the building, separated from my mother and sister.

We were there for three days; the only food we had was sugar, one spoonful a day. I remember it very well; the pain in my stomach from the hunger was horrible. Finally, we joined my mother and sister. We sat in a cellar with three families. We heard shooting: at the back of the house British soldiers sat in the trees and, at the front side of the house, German soldiers sat in the trees – and shot straight across the house at each other. No one knew we were there, but when the soldiers found us they said we must leave immediately. My parents decided to go to my mother's friend who lived in the northern part of Arnhem. There I saw how the airborne troops landed on the Ginkelsehei (a big heather field). My father and I looked out of the attic window and saw the aeroplanes dropping many, many soldiers. To my child's eyes, they looked like dolls gliding to earth. Often, very often, I saw the 'dolls' shaken – they were all targets for the German bullets and had no chance.

Father in Hiding

A day later, we left Arnhem. We walked to a village east of Arnhem, where my father's parents lived. On the way I remember a lot of soldiers, tanks, the thunder of cannon, shooting, and grenades – even now I am still scared in a thunderstorm. After many hours walking – poor Mum! – we arrived at my grandparents' house. In the meantime, my mother's parents had arrived, too. All we had were the clothes we wore at that moment. There were eight adults and two children in a small house with three bedrooms; it was not comfortable. My sister slept in my doll's cradle. My grandfather had dug an air-raid shelter in the back of the garden, and during air raid alerts we plunged into that hole.

My father and his father went into hiding, but for my other grandpa it was too late and he had to work for the Germans in their kitchen: he was a confectioner. In the kitchen stood baskets with bottles of Dutch gin. Every day my grandpa took some gin, put it in a small bottle, and topped the big bottles up with water. The Dutch gin he took served as a means of exchange for flour and butter. Once my grandfather came home with a cow's head under his arm; stolen from the Germans. My mother boiled sugar beet and used the syrup to make sandwiches. Electricity was not allowed, so we used an oil lamp – filled with petrol and a spoonful of salt, it gave a very bright light. I still have this old oil lamp in my living room.

The Battle of Arnhem is over, and Hannie van der Ham's father returns to find their home destroyed.

My memories are also of the night when we knew the Germans would start to bomb. We could hear the noise kilometres away. They used very often the V1: as long as you could hear the sound of a V1 it was OK, but if it stopped you knew that it was possible it would fall down very close. By day, I also remember seeing many planes fallen down, brought down by German Messerschmitt and Focke-Wulf.

After the liberation, my father had to go back to his work as soon as possible, but our house was destroyed. My mother's parents' house was still intact and we went back to Arnhem on a horse and cart. After a few months living with them, we got another house. They only things my parents found in the ruins of our old house were a half-torn picture and the electric cooker, upside down between the trees – my mother used the cooker until 1972, when she bought a new one.

For the first few months, we had mica instead of glass in the windows, and corrugated iron on the floor. A lot of trees were damaged, but were filled up with cement and are still there. My father made a vase from pieces of shrapnel and it is still in use.

I don't remember everything from that time, but some things I remember very well. The antipathy towards the Jerries is still there.

My sister died in January 1969, 24-years-old, of acute leukaemia; my father died in September 1969, 61-years-old, cardiac arrest; my mother died in October 2001, 91-years-old, of old age. They rebuilt our old house, exactly the same but a mirror image, and it is now used as a kind of office; the garden is now what they call a bush garden: the ashes of my parents and sister rest underneath the rhododendron still growing there. Sometimes I go to the estate for a walk; it makes me very sad when I see that the house has changed.

Norman Mackenzie

A HUNGRY BOY

Hunger is an abiding memory of the war years for former Bishopmill loon Norman Mackenzie, whose home is now in Inverness.

I HAD JUST reached the age of 10 when war was declared. The things that I remember were that food was scarce; I always seemed to be hungry. There was frozen mutton from Australia, and tins of dried powdered eggs, they tasted a bit like an omelette; occasionally we had a real egg. There were no refrigerators in those days, eggs were kept in a dark cool cupboard and preserved in a bucket of white plaster-type substance, they tasted all right and were better than the dried stuff.

We listened to the wireless nearly every day to hear the latest news. I had the job of taking the wet batteries over to Elgin to have them recharged; they were heavy things to carry. The wireless also had a large dry battery but it lasted much longer.

In 1939 a battalion of the Highland Light Infantry came to Elgin and were billeted all over the town. The Commanding Officer took over our front bedroom; he had a batman-cum-driver, his car was often parked outside our house. On a few occasions the driver would give my brother, sister and myself a lift to school – boy, did we feel 'Archie' as the other kids stood with their mouths open watching us get out of this lovely, big, Rover car.

At weekends we used to go over to the hall to make friends with the soldiers, who let us play with their rifles (unloaded of course) and try on their equipment. But the best part was when they would take us to the kitchen and give us a plate of custard and peaches or pineapple – that was a real treat as we had never tasted peaches or pineapples before.

While I was in the Boys' Brigade, at weekends I used to go to a church hall (near Yeadon's book shop) which was turned into a sort of 'Tearoom for the Troops'. A few of us helped with collecting used cups and plates and returned them to the kitchen. It was a very friendly place and sometimes we got a tip.

When I was old enough, I joined the Army Cadets: there was always a large company of us in the Drill Hall. Our Sergeant Major was a George Grassick; he was always smartly dressed and kept us on our toes. I joined the cadet pipe band as a drummer and on VE night marched up and down the High Street.

Near the time of the D-Day landings, Elgin was a busy place with many troops and all kinds of transport. I remember

Norman Mackenzie.

the playing field at the old Bishopmill School in Balmoral Crescent being full of military vehicles, including Bren gun carriers. I never liked the look of them, especially after one of them had a bad accident in Elgin which I saw happen.

It was a wet day. Bren gun carriers and wet cobblestones do not go together and most of the streets in Elgin were laid with these cobblestones. There was a convoy of these Bren gun carriers. They came up Lossie Wynd, turned onto the High Street, then another quick turn in the opposite direction and up Commerce Street. Most of them made it with a bit of difficulty except one poor fellow, he crashed into the corner at the bottom of Commerce Street (it was a bank at that time). Unfortunately, a young girl of about 18 or 20 years old was standing there; I can't remember her name but I think she came from the east end of the town. She was killed. I think of her every time I pass that corner.

Eric Phelp

THE AUSTRALIAN FLYER

Hundreds of thousands of men from the Commonwealth trained in Canada during World War II under what was known as 'The Plan' – Canada was chosen because of its climate and distance from the dangers of enemy activity. Australian Flt Lt Eric Phelp (b. 1918) was one of them. He now lives at Meadowlark Residential Home, Forres, with his wife, June, but comes originally from Ballina, New South Wales.

I WAS WORKING in a furniture factory at the beginning of the war. I was called up in 1942 and spent three months with the 1st Btn City of Sydney Regiment. My mate said we should be pilots so we went down to the recruiting train and said we wanted to be aircrew. We passed the tests, and then I said, the trouble was that I was already in the City Regiment, so the bloke said, well, get yourself down there immediately and get yourself out of it. So I did.

I did my initial training, and then I was posted to Canada on the Empire Training Scheme and got my Wings in Ontario. I got lost once in a snowstorm – it was the worst winter they'd had for 50 years. I came out of the storm, but didn't know where the hell I was, everything was white. Then I saw this black track far below, a railway line in the middle of nowhere, and I followed it until I came to a station, and then flew low to see the name of the station. Once I knew that, I could check where I was on the map and get back to base.

I was sent to England on a banana boat in a convoy of about fifty ships – it was 1943 by this time. The voyage took two weeks, but I only spent the first two nights in my bunk. The hooter would sound the alarm that we were under attack and that was the end of sleep. We lost five ships during the voyage, all sunk by subs. There were depth charges being dropped all around us, and I'd never been so frightened in my life. The convoy couldn't stop to pick anyone up from the boats that had been hit; I think the Navy boats did that. I just don't know.

At Peterborough in England I did my advanced pilot's course, and was then sent to Cairo. We sailed from Gourock in a convoy of five big ships, all over 30,000 tonnes. We lost one entering the Med. We ended up in Cairo, where I met the girl who was to become my wife. June was originally from London and with ENSA.

Monte Cassino

I was with 450 Squadron, 239 Wing Royal Australian Air Force, flying Kittyhawks fighter aircraft: they were well-armed, carrying three bombs: a 1,000lb bomb under the belly and a 500lb bomb under each wing, and six 0.5 inch guns. We were giving close air support to Monty's Desert Force as they were going into Italy after the Anzio landing in 1944, and took part in the biggest battle of the war at Monte Cassino, where 22,000 men were lost. The Germans had an observation point on top of the mountain from which they directed artillery fire, and the first job I had with the RAAF was to try to silence their machine guns so that the army could get up there.

Day after day we were under fire, and my aircraft was hit on several occasions – I lost four, maybe five aircraft, but they were just replaced and I was back up there again next day. I'd come in at about 7,000ft in a 70° angle dive; I'd get down to about 2,000ft, let the bombs go and pull up. I pulled up one day and the Germans hit me with an explosive bullet in the left wing, making a big hole. I thought I was going to have to bail out, but I managed to get back to base flying with the control column at an angle. They gave me a replacement and I was back up the next day. You just didn't stop – there were times when I flew three sorties a day, and that went on for 10 months.

Then I was given a whole squadron to take out on raids, dive bombing and strafing. I walked into the mess one day and the CO asked me what I'd been doing, I told him. He had a cap with 'operational tour expired' on it and he put it on my head... and that was the end of my fighting days.

After Italy I was sent to Palestine to fly Hurricanes in fighter affiliation with Wellington bombers. My job was to simulate attack on the bombers while it was being filmed. In the meantime June was posted to Beirut, and I told my CO I'd like to see her. He said I could do an 'oil and petroleum consumption test' by flying up to Beirut, so off I went and spent the whole day with her.

We were married in All Saints Cathedral, Cairo in 1945 by the padre Bob Davies, who later became Bishop of Hobart, but we both had to return to our respective countries to be demobbed. June later went out to Australia to join me on a Brides' Ship – there were many such War Brides – the *Stirling Castle*. We eventually moved back to England.

Eric Phelp in the cockpit of his aeroplane.

Our elder daughter Sandra married an RAF serviceman who was stationed at Kinloss and we came up to Moray several times on holiday. When I retired we decided to move here permanently.

In the 1990s, an Italian, Gastone Mazzanti, was writing a book about the Battle of Monte Cassino. He wrote to 450 Squadron's association in Sydney asking if any surviving pilots could help him with his research and was put in touch with me. The result was a place of honour in the book and an invitation to go out to Italy with another former pilot, now living in London.

We were given a very warm welcome in Italy. They said we had liberated them from the Germans. Gastone took me to a farm where the family had been kicked out by the Germans and the farmer came out to meet us. He said we had given them their home back and kept repeating the word *Grazia, Grazia.*

Gillian Tuckwell

GI GLAMOUR

Gillian Tuckwell (b. 1931), Elgin, lived in Taunton, Somerset, as a child and has vivid memories of the American soldiers stationed near her home. They appeared very glamorous to a young girl.

I WAS ON holiday in a caravan with my family at Blue Anchor when war was declared. I remember everyone in the caravans and tents coming out and gathering in the middle of the field to discuss the situation, and to tell others the news if they hadn't heard.

My father didn't go away to war: perhaps he was too old, but my mother said it was because he had an important job. I was at primary school and when the air raid siren went we had to prop our chairs against the desks and climb under a desk. Even when the siren didn't go, we had to have regular practices, and we had to practise putting our gas masks on. Gas masks went everywhere with us, and we used to hit each other with them when there was a fight.

There wasn't much bombing around us. Bristol was bombed, and sometimes the planes would shed surplus bombs near us – we had one in the brickyard chimney, which was about halfway between my home and the school. It didn't explode and I think they left it there for the rest of the war.

Because we were in a fairly safe zone they built an American hospital near our house. There used to be men on guard at the gate and when the siren went they left their posts and ran, while we didn't make much of it. There was a park opposite our house where they used to go and sit, and they were very good at giving things to children. They really did get asked: 'Give us some gum, chum!' And they always did.

My mother used to invite the GIs in for coffee and some of them became good friends. A lot of them were killed; we'd hear about it from their friends and be very sad. One was a particular favourite. We called him Big Bill; we thought he was a cowboy, but I don't

Gillian Tuckwell.

suppose he really was. When he was killed we were quite a bit upset.

There were some black GIs. The local people treated them the same as anyone else; some of the girls went out with them and there were a few black babies born; some of the girls married them. But for the Americans it was different. They had a white night and a black night when GIs could go into town: they couldn't have black and white serviceman mixing. This was long before the Civil Rights Movement, of course.

The American soldiers gave us lots of things we couldn't get because of the war, like Christmas cake at Christmas, and sweets, but because we lived in the country we could grow our own vegetables, so we didn't really go short. When mother suspected the war was coming she'd stocked the loft with things she thought we might need; she remembered what her mother was short of in the First World War, and so we had goods we could barter with. We ate rabbit a lot… sometimes there would be a bit of shot when you went to bite.

We went to the pictures often. We were under-age for 'A' films, so we'd ask an adult to take us in. A friend's sister was an usherette, so sometimes we'd get in free. The 'movies' were very popular with the GIs as well.

I hoped the war would go on until I'd grown up so that I could marry a GI, go to America, and become a film star; but it ended when I was still only 13.

Donald Cargill

THE GREAT ESCAPER

I interviewed Donald 'Cocker' Cargill in 1995 at the time of the 50th anniversary of VE-Day. Even in old age, he was a remarkable character, and he had a remarkable story to tell. Cocker has since died, but his family has kindly given me permission to retell the tale, with additional material he recorded before his death. Born 1918, Cocker was brought up in Elgin by his granny Elsie Mathieson; was a well-known footballer in his youth; married Millie in 1938; and with little steady work available, and encouraged by the bounty offered and the chance to travel, joined the Territorial Army. So when war broke out in 1939 he was among the first to volunteer for service.

I ENLISTED IN the Seaforth Highlanders Territorial Unit, 6th Battalion. We were stationed at the Drill Hall, which was beside the Cooper Park (*now part of Elgin Library*) and did our training in the park in readiness to go to France. We went first to Aldershot and then to France in early January 1940. Our task was to defend a gap in the Maginot line, a long stretch of fortress-like defences erected specially to protect France and Belgium against German invasion, but we were ill-equipped. We only had about 60 rounds of ammunition, an old rifle from the first war, and two Bren gun carriers for the whole regiment. We were sitting ducks, no doubt about it. We'd about as much chance of stopping the Germans advancing as the Salvation Army would have! While many made for mass evacuation at Dunkirk, my friend Lance Corporal Jim McCulloch and I were among the unlucky ones chosen to stay behind and defend the position. We were the boys that should have got all the praise - not them that escaped in boats. Every day we were fighting rearguard action. We had been holding defensive positions for quite a while when the Germans broke through. There had been a big push in May 1940 so they went through us like a dose of salts.

255

We lost a lot of boys. My best mate was killed just beside me. I aye mind him turning round to Millie in the High Street, before we left, saying, "Dinna you worry, I'll look after him."

I was taken prisoner on May 30, 1940 – and didn't see my family again for five years. We were marched for several days, and then the Germans herded us into a railway truck for the journey across Germany into Poland. At Berlin we halted briefly so the Germans could show us off to jubilant crowds, then once in Poland we were taken to a Prisoner Of War camp called Stalag XXA near Marienberg.

The German's took this propaganda photograph of POWs in Stalag XXA, 1943, to show how well they were being treated: as the prisoners worked in the camp laundry they could wash their uniforms after work, and so looked reasonably smart. Donald 'Cocker' Cargill (centre, back row) was already planning to escape.

It was bad there, but it could have been a helluva lot worse. Within the huts we all maintained our ranks. The Sergeant Major was still in charge and it was up to us ourselves to keep the accommodation as clean and orderly as possible. There were 40-50 men to a hut and we slept in bunks, in rows of three. There was little food. Once a day we'd queue up for a bowl of barley soup and a slice of bread. It wasn't very good, but anything tastes good when you're starving. We had a little loaf between 5-6 of us. As the bread got scarcer, more had to share. There was a lot of childishness - the boy that was cutting it took his life in his hands if he didn't cut it equally! Polish winters are hard. Sometimes it was 20 degrees below zero. But there were bright spots: we had football games among the different nationalities in the camp – I had a medal to show for it. There was also a concert hall.

In the winter of 1942, after I'd learned a bit of the language, we made our first attempt to escape – the first of five for me! And it was a bit of a disaster. Eight of us made up a working party in a laundry. We were locked in a room at night, second floor up, with bars on the windows, but we discovered we could get out through the bars. Me and an English POW called Mark Northmore escaped through the window one night by tying blankets together. It was winter and we thought the rivers would be frozen over, making it easy to cross. But it was bitterly cold and the first ditch we came to, my mate fell through the ice. A run and a jump and he landed in the middle! I said: "We can't go on further, it's freezing. I'll go back with you." So we crept back in the same way we'd got out. But we'd had six hours of freedom, the Jerries were none the wiser, and we'd learned a lesson... not to go in the dark for a start!

Escape number two, a few months later, was better planned. We were still working in the camp laundry and amused ourselves by taking a razor blade to the seams of the German uniforms, nicking the stitches so they'd fall apart within a short time. The uniforms had come from Russia and were often very dirty, so the boss of the laundry thought it was too much soda in the laundry to blame - he used to keep telling us not to put so much in. The Germans were usually easily fooled. I must say we were streets ahead of them as far as using our loaf was concerned. This time, we didn't just nobble the uniforms: we filched them, bit by bit – a jacket here, a pair of trousers there, and a belt – till we were both fully kitted out. We thought this was a good enough idea, so we could travel through the day, as long as no-one asked to see our papers.

Heil Hitler

I was dressed as a Private but the uniform my mate had got was a Lance Corporal's, and that stopped a lot of lower ranking soldiers from checking us out. We got a supply of food together and just walked out; nobody challenged us. We decided we'd make for

Warsaw, 400-500 kilometres away and try to meet up with the Polish partisans. We walked all the time, but we used to keep ourselves smart so as to avoid attracting attention ... brushed our boots and shaved and all that sort of thing, and we saluted 'Heil Hitler' when we thought we should. We would listen at windows to see if the occupants were speaking Polish or German. If they were Polish we would go to the door and explain we were British Tommies and ask if they had any food to spare, or cigarettes. We tried not to endanger them more than we could help. They just left food out for us. They aye had plenty of eggs. We lived on boiled eggs and slices of bread. Sometimes we would come across two or three British boys – other POWs – working in a field. They'd had Red Cross parcels. We'd shout across to them and they'd tell us where the food was left unguarded at night when all the men were locked up.

Once we found a garden full of beautiful apples. Rather than steal them, we thought we'd do the honourable thing and offer to buy some with loose change we'd found in pockets while doing the laundry. When we went to the door it turned out to be the Burgermeister – the sort of mayor! He said: "Heil Hitler!" My mate asked, could you sell us some apples? He said: "Certainly, for the sons of the Fatherland! Take what you want, for free!" That stripe on his uniform was coming in affa' handy.

In the two to three weeks we were on the run, we covered a fair distance: 300-400km, but our luck was running out. We had gone to this house to ask for food and a young Polish loon came to the door and said come in. And when we got in, two German soldiers were in there. We tried to bluff it out, and they didn't say anything, but we had an idea they knew there was something not right. They never challenged us like, but they smelled a rat and reported it to the authorities in the town we were headed for. The next day we were walking along and all of a sudden German soldiers with rifles were right across the road. This boy, an officer, came up on his horse and asked us for our papers and of course we didn't have any. He said: "Who are you?" We said: "We're just having a wee walk round, a bit of a holiday from the POW camp." He listened and laughed and then he said: "I was a POW in the last war, in Edinburgh, and they were good to me. So I will be good to you." I said I came from Edinburgh and he was delighted. I said to my mate: "You come from Edinburgh too." He was a bloody Londoner! That officer was right good to us though. He gave us soup, bread and fags. He kept us there for two-to-three days and said: "Feeling fit now?" He sent for someone to escort us back to camp.

It was an SS boy that came and I mind there was a post with a sign on it, he fired a couple of bullets into it. He couldn't speak English, so that was his way of warning us that if we were going to run he wouldn't miss! He took us on the train. There were a lot of Germans on leave and they were delighted at seeing two Tommies captured. They thought we would get shot when we got back. Still in our stolen German uniforms, eventually we arrived at a special punishment camp where the officer in charge looked us over and said: "Well, you look a damn sight smarter than my bloody shower!"

We were sent back to Stalag XXA for court martial. We said we'd 'borrowed' the uniforms and were given the maximum 21 days solitary confinement with only bread and water and a plate of soup every third day. They had a queer system where you got 21 days for your first escape, I think; 10 days for your second and 7 for your third. After your third you started at 21 again. It was something to do with the Geneva Convention.

The Germans had a grudging respect for Tommies whose records showed they'd demonstrated courage and cleverness in trying to escape. Each time an escapee was court martialled he'd offer up the expected response: "It's a soldier's duty to escape Sir!" and it was accepted that it was. Most of them were trying to escape. It was always the same boys. None of us thought of ourselves as heroes particularly and our fellow prisoners didn't treat us as such.

Our third escape was on Christmas Eve. We were in a working party in a sugar beet factory and it was bloody hard graft; twelve hours at a time. After about two weeks I said: "Bugger this. I'm not staying here to do this. I'm getting out for Christmas." It was night time and the factory wasn't wired off or anything, and there were maybe four guards to 50 blokes. So we just walked out. I knew we would get captured but it was a lot easier loafing about in solitary than bloody knocking your pan in. We got into the town (Riesenberg), still in our British uniforms, and sat in the square smoking a fag. We got some funny looks like, but nobody challenged us. We made no attempt to hide. After two or three days in the cold without much to eat, we were nearly on the point of giving ourselves up when someone twigged. Two SS boys came and asked us for papers. We said we are just out here because it's Christmas. We were only about 7-8km away from where we'd started and one German soldier was told to escort us back. The boy was in a right rage. You're not supposed to tie anybody up but we did get tied up. It didn't strike us till later the poor bugger was missing his leave or something like that. Christmas, and here he was escorting two Tommies into the nick.

The Russians Were Coming

I had a marvellous escape after that. All the prisoners were being taken back into Germany from Poland and so on. They marched for weeks and weeks. They had a helluva time of it.

Well I escaped about two days into the march – me and about half a dozen boys. When we came to trees we asked the guard if we could go for a piddle and we just never came back. There was nothing they could do about it – there were thousands of boys and only 50-60 guards. We went back to the village where there were still some POWs in a compound. I mind there was a boy from Elgin there, a butcher by name of Mackay: he killed a couple of pigs and cut them up. There was also a Gordon Highlander from Buckie called Craig Gordon. We thought of staying put and waiting for the Russians, but the Russians were inclined to shoot first and ask questions after.

Unfortunately the retreating Germans caught up with us. They came all round the compound, and the German officer said: 'You will be going back to London and we will be going to Moscow'. They knew the war was over. This German officer – a decent bloke – said they had a train of wounded coming through any day now and he could get us onto that if we liked and that would get us further into Germany. We were on the train for about a week with little water and even less food. I don't even know how we existed. One time we stopped and there was a trainload of neeps nearby so we went and helped ourselves. The guard let us.

I suspected, though I can't be sure, that Russians who had been taken prisoner and were also on that train had been killed at some point and their bodies dumped in a mass grave; the Germans didn't have the resources to keep them.

The train took us right into Fallenborstal, a big POW camp.

After a couple of weeks there, me and the boy Craig from Buckie got out under the wire during an air raid when the search lights were switched off, and into the wood and escaped. We were afraid the Germans might kill us all before the Allies arrived, and most of the POWs were going to hide under the floorboards. It was my fifth and last escape.

We spent the night in the woods, and the next day heard the rumble of tanks - British Army tanks. I gave myself up to them and I was such a sight – I had khaki trousers on and only a vest. I had a helluva job to try and identify myself, I had no papers, nothing. The officer said: "Where do you come from?" I said: "I don't suppose you know Elgin? It's a small town between Inverness and Aberdeen." But one of the crew remembered they'd got an Elgin boy in their platoon, and the brought him up. I was quite confident the boy would recognize me. But he was looking at me, not knowing me, and I says to him: "I see a family resemblance here – if I'm not mistaken you are a King, and your family stay near the college. You have a sister, Maisie." He said: "That's right."

This was the boy who was supposed to be identifying ME and instead I was identifying HIM!

The British forces were on their way to liberate the Fallenborstal camp. Two or three days after that I found himself on one of their lorries, then on an airfield and finally landing in High Wycombe in England. I'd a few days in which to be checked over, spruced up and kitted out in a new clean uniform before being allowed home to Elgin on leave.

When I landed in England, I'd sent Millie a pre-printed telegram announcing when I'd arrive. Only me and one other soldier, a Jackie Wilson, were expected.

I just stepped off the train and there was a wee crowdie. I didn't realize it was me they were looking for. The bloody streets were lined.

Cokers' 'distinguished service' had been mentioned in dispatches – a great honour – and news of his remarkable exploits had spread. His wife Millie was there to greet him with son Donnie, who by now was six or seven. Coker's daughter Margaret, who was born just nine months later, recounts a story that when her brother first saw the heroic figure he could only remember hearing about, his first reaction was: 'Is that wee mannie my DAD?'

Coker's leave lasted about six weeks. He served out the remainder of the war in Derby. Of his experiences as a POW, he said it was: 'A nice long holiday at the Government's expense.' But there was also a personal cost: 'I lost my best friends; my pals. One who was in the RAF, Adam King from Keith, was my mate for years. I met him when I was home on leave and that's the last time I ever saw him. He said he was going out on reconnaissance and that it was a dangerous job. He was killed somewhere over the North Sea.

'I just say I'm lucky. I never used to look on the black side of anything. I just used to think to myself, here's me playing football and other poor buggers are getting killed.

We were lucky being prisoners. At least we would see Blighty again.'

Robert Grigor

BABY SHOES AT BELSEN

Robert Grigor, 5 Pringle Road, Bishopmill, was in a reserved occupation when war was declared, working in the telephone exchange; and with a widowed mother at home, felt unable to volunteer along with his friends.

WHEN WAR BROKE out there was just one man working in the telephone exchange in Elgin after midnight, and if there was an air raid alert code red, he had to phone the police, hospital, fire brigade and coastguard. It was all done manually. When the all clear came, he'd have to phone them all again. It was as if this one operator was on guard...and woe betide him if he fell asleep. Later in the war they had four men on at night.

I was called up in August 1940 and, after training at Catterick, was posted to Glasgow.

In 1942 I went to North Africa, sailing in a convoy of ships. I didn't know it at the time, but my future wife, Emma Kean, nee Noble, from Lhanbryde, whose first husband was killed early in the war, was on board one of the other vessels – one which was torpedoed.

She was a Queen Alexandra Nurse, and she and four colleagues went into the water. She said she'd never forget the men on the boat singing 'We'll meet again' as they floated away. They were in the water for seven hours before being picked up. One of the nurses had a little silver whistle, given to her by her boyfriend, which was heard by someone on the destroyer sent out to look for them. They were taken onboard – they were in their night attire, – and were given blankets while their clothes were dried in the engine room, a mug of cocoa and a big bully-beef sandwich. They were put ashore at Algiers and issued with men's kit – there were no women's clothes available. She found the khaki trousers itchy, but later an American patient gave her a pair of their pants, which were made of finer material.

Emma Grigor.

They later discovered that the ship hadn't sunk, but was beached at Casablanca, so they could have stayed on board.

There was another occasion in the war when our paths crossed: I was told there was a nurse who came from the same neck of the woods as I did, but I was busy and didn't have time to see her. We finally met in 1946 back home in Moray, became engaged within the week, and married two years later. We had a daughter, the light of our lives, and were very happy until my wife died 11 years ago.

I served as a sergeant in the Royal Signals Corps attached to the London Corps of Signals in North Africa, Italy, Germany and Austria. In 1944 I had the opportunity to visit the Vatican, and although I am not a Catholic, it was a memorable experience. I spoke to a Swiss Guard in halting French, and he replied in perfect English. He told me where to stand if I wanted to see the Pope and said that the Pope might even speak to me. And so I presented myself...and the Pope did come over to speak to me. He said: "You are English?" and I said I was Scottish. He noticed I had a rosary and asked if I would like him to bless it, and if I would like a blessing. He said: "I am sure in my own mind you will

Robert Grigor.

survive this terrible war and be reunited with your family."

When the war ended, I was near Belsen Concentration Camp and my CO said he thought I should go and see it. It was a horrible place. It had been liberated, and all the prisoners had gone, but there was this great heap of shoes – the size of St Giles Church in the centre of Elgin, but maybe not quite as high. There were shoes of every size, right down to little baby shoes. As a soldier you are not supposed to cry, but I cried for all those who had been exterminated. There was a silence about Belsen...no birds sang... there was just this great silence. I have never forgotten it.

Helen Ettles

A WREN IN A WIGWAM

*When war broke out, Helen Ettles, now living in Keith, was 17 and
home was with her family in the Fens of Lincolnshire. They were
farming folk and had no connection with the sea.*

I DID 'WAR WORK' – a turn at the report centre, at the service
canteen and in the knitting circle, where we knitted socks for
soldiers. Here my forte was turning the heels, grafting the toes.

By the time I was 18, the Wrens (WRNS) were recruiting
wireless operators. I had been a Girl Guide and knew the Morse
code, so I applied and was accepted. I was told to report to Dundee,
to Mather's Temperance Hotel. The hotel equipment and furnishings
had been stripped and there wasn't even a cooker left. Our first
meals were corned beef, bread and cornflakes. We slept on the floor
on mattresses, three to a room, and were kitted out in serge uniforms
bearing labels 'Hector Powe' and 'Beau Brummel'.

In addition to "the Morse", we learned naval procedures and how
to maintain our wireless sets. We had the use of 'Confidential Books'
which we had to collect and sign for at the beginning of the lesson and
return at the end. The books were bound with lead covers in case of
disaster at sea when they would sink to the bottom and not float so that
the enemy could recover them. My copy of Signalling Instructions
was stamped *HMS Thetis* – an ill-fated submarine which had sunk
during its acceptance trials off Liverpool some time earlier.

Next, I was sent to the Isle of Man with three other girls. At the
beginning of the war, there were girls who lived in port areas who
were allowed to live at home and would never have been sent
anywhere else; they were known as 'Immobile Wrens'. We were
the first 'Mobile Wrens'; always seen in uniform and a great
curiosity. Our duty was to communicate with 'Search and Rescue'
and to transmit and receive messages from Liverpool. These
messages were intended for shipping in the area which had to

maintain W/T silence for fear of revealing their whereabouts.

Then it was on to Shropshire to an embryo naval air station. My billet was a farm house at the end of a dark lane which proved to have no electricity, no running water and an outside 'loo'. On my first day, I discovered that I was the only girl on the station – no wireless sets, no flying control – but they did have aircraft. I spent my first days attending to the Captain's correspondence.

Helen Ettles.

The Captain had been a pre-war pilot and he was set to devise procedures for getting the aircraft back safely when weather conditions turned nasty. I was thrilled to have a part in this and we spent many hours practising and trying out schemes. Eventually a Direction Finding set was installed and we could do the QGH (Homing) procedure for real. The Direction Finding had to be placed in the middle of a field far away from any metal objects. It was housed in a wooden wigwam, the doors and walls of which were of double thickness with pebbles in between – to defeat enemy machine-gun bullets!

Each week, a course of Navy pilots came to what we termed 'Blind Flying Training' – real title 'Advanced Instrument

Training'. They flew with instructors in all weathers. If the weather was too good, they had to wear 'blinkers' so that they could only see their instruments. In my four years there, we lost only one aircraft and that on a beautiful sunny day and due to mechanical failure.

As Wrens were outnumbered by men by some 600%, our social life was very agreeable, even the least attractive girls having plenty of dates. We had dances, discussions, musical evenings and, later, even a camp cinema. Having witnessed many heartbreaks, I decided not to date anyone I might have to work with – lots of friends, but I could always wave a cheerful goodbye when they left the station.

VE-Day came and went without much celebration. We still had to send our aircrews to the Far East, so the training went on. VJ-Day was announced in the late evening when most of us had gone to bed. Apart from a few devout prayers of thanksgiving, nothing changed for me. I was on duty next morning, and, as I had no instructions to the contrary, was well through the day before anyone thought of me in my wigwam across the field.

Meantime, everybody else had been celebrating! There was a dance in the evening. A certain young officer asked me to dance and in the course of the dance said: "Why don't you and I get married?" Thinking he would never remember the next day, I said: "What a good idea." Two years later we were.

Walter and Jean Childs

A WARTIME ROMANCE

Wartime romances were usually swift: with uncertain futures, young couples wasted no time in declaring their intentions. Walter and Jean Childs, Anvil House, Dyke, had known each other for just four weeks when they married in the spring of 1945. Mr Childs, a retired police inspector with the West Midlands Police Force, was a Paratrooper when he met the pretty ATS girl from Port Glasgow.

MR CHILDS: I come originally from Leominister in Hertfordshire, and I worked in an insurance office for 12 months after leaving school, then moved to a Birmingham small arms factory, which had just been bombed when I arrived. I joined the Home Guard and went on fire watch duties – Birmingham was heavily bombed. I tried to join the Fleet Air Arm, but was told I had an eye defect; I tried the RAF, but was rejected for the same reason. In Birmingham I was considered to be in a reserved occupation, and couldn't leave, and so I stayed there until I was 21 when I became eligible for military service.

I did my training in 1944 with the South Staffordshire Regiment then volunteered for the Parachute Regiment – the 3rd Battalion. I was interested in sport and the pay was better. We did our training drops at what is now Manchester Airport, then advanced training, then jungle training. One of my friends in the Paratroops at that time was William Franklyn, who later became famous as the man in the Schweppes advertisement on TV.

MRS CHILDS: I had been working in the accounts department at the Co-op: I had wanted to join the Wrens, but my father wouldn't let me go; I tried to join the WRAF, but my boss refused to let me go. However, when I reached the age of 21 I was conscripted into the ATS – and had to go.

It was a terrible time, but it was also a happy time because everyone was so friendly. You were here today, but everyone knew you might not be here tomorrow.

After training I was sent to London, this was June 1944 and the Germans were sending over doodlebugs during the daytime – if we heard one coming we'd get under the table, there was no time to reach the shelters. London was full of British and American soldiers heading for D-Day. We were near Hyde Park and there was always something going on.

There were tea dances: so many people worked at night that having dances in the afternoon was the only way to cope. There would be a three-piece band, and they really did serve tea and cakes.

MR CHILDS: We met at a dance, but within weeks Jean heard she was being posted to France. I decided the one way to stop the posting was to propose, and Jean accepted. I got a special licence – which cost 11s 6d (a normal marriage licence at the time was 7s 6d), and we were married at Birmingham Registry Office.

MRS CHILDS: I'd have liked a wedding in church, but there just wasn't time. I was married in my uniform – most girls did at that time – and I didn't have flowers.

MR CHILDS: I could only buy a standard issue 9k gold wedding ring, I think it cost about £4, but I did give Jean pearls as well.

Later my battalion was posted to Burma. We set sail from Southampton, but while at sea, VE- Day was announced and our destination was switched to Palestine where we arrived equipped for the jungle! Various terrorist organisations were fighting each other, and it was a hectic time. Even off duty we had to carry our weapons with us. At one time we were billeted in a civilian house on Mount Carmel. It was a luxury mansion with a steep climb up to it. The Jewish terrorists filled a milestone with explosives and blew it up by remote control as one of our trucks was passing. It blew the truck sideways down the hill.

At St David's Hotel in Jerusalem, they disguised themselves as Arabs delivering milk, but filled the churns with explosives and blew up the wing being used by military intelligence. It was all very frustrating, and at times I felt we should just leave the Arabs and Jews to get on with it.

Jews were pouring out of Europe, mainly through Italy, and

hiring anything that could float, and cramming themselves in to get to Palestine. The Navy would incept the boats and we had to evacuate them to prison camps, then they were sent to Cyprus. They were mainly young men, women and children and I felt very sorry for them.

Phyllis Whitson

THE CLYDESIDE BLITZ

Up until 1941 most German bombing raids had been against Coventry, Liverpool and London. But in March that year improved weather conditions, and extended range, gave the Luftwaffe the opportunity to target Scotland. Retired architect Phyllis Whitson, Elgin, had the misfortune to be in the city when the bombers arrived.

MY MOTHER AND I were living in Kirkmichael, Tomintoul, where she was a teacher, and both my father and brother were in the army. My aunts in Glasgow asked my mother if I could go down to stay with them.

One of my aunts worked in the Censor's office. This was where mail going abroad was checked for information that might help the enemy. She worked on the mail to Southern Ireland – now called Eire – a neutral country. I think the censors were mostly retired people, sitting in a former car-showroom, cold and draughty, cutting bits out of letters. They were sworn to secrecy about what they did, but she did tell me that sometimes the letters looked like lace when they had finished.

Her sister, who kept house, had been ill, and I was needed to run errands, stand in the long queues, and generally cheer her up. No one thought of bombs, so that is how I came to be in Glasgow during the Clydebank raid.

There was no air-raid shelter, so when we heard the siren we took chairs into the entrance hall of the flat away from the windows. We were south of the river, so we could hear the heavy drone of the laden bombers going over above us. The air aid warden came by, and my aunt went out to speak to him, leaving the door ajar. Something made the door rattle, with a noise like machine-gun fire. These two noises are what I remember. For the rest of the war, if the siren went, I would be listening for that sound.

Someone told me later that the German bombers had been sent to bomb the docks, but saw the road through Clydebank shining in the rain and thought it was the river, so they bombed the houses on either side. One family had a fruit and veg business: we got to know later that the father and the grown-up daughters went to a pantomime, but the mother didn't want to go – when they came home there was no house, no business, and no mother.

My father, Walter Kennedy Whitson, had served in World War I in the Highland Light Infantry and later the Machine Gun Corps. He was largely at the front, and was awarded the MC and commissioned in the field. He received a head wound, but came through it.

He was really too old to serve in World War II – he was in his 50s – but had always been certain another war was coming and had joined the Officers' Reserve. He had advised my brother Donald that as there was going to be a war he should make sure he was in something that interested him, so Donald joined the TA in the Signals – the day after war was declared he was in the Army.

I was on my way to school one day when I saw the postman coming with a yellow envelope. My brother at this time was with the 52nd Lowland Division, Royal Corps of Signals, and had gone over to Cherbourg along with the Canadian Army. This was after Dunkirk, and we had heard nothing from him. When I saw the yellow envelope I thought the worst... it was one of those times when you grow up rather quickly. However, it turned out to contain my father's calling up papers. A week or so later a field postcard came telling us my brother was all right. I remember sitting in the classroom and thinking no one else had a father and a brother in the army.

My father went into the Duke of Wellingtons, but because of his poor eyesight and his age he was put in charge of the Pioneer Corps, and then in charge of those Italians who had been born in Britain, but were not allowed to fight – if captured they would have been shot as traitors. My father enjoyed that because some generations back we have Italian blood.

Having a husband and son in the army and a daughter being bombed in Glasgow was too much for my poor mother and, as my aunt was better by this time, I went home to Kirkmichael.

Archie Gill

WRONG NUMBER?

Retired Hydro-Electric engineer Archie Gill (b. 1922), of New Elgin, was in Cologne when the war ended, as a sergeant in No 3 Company of 1 Corps District Signals, and has two abiding memories of the final days of the conflict.

IN THE DAYS between the end of the fighting and VE-Day, when all of the German commanders on the mainland had accepted that their war was over, the commander on Jersey was still refusing to accept defeat.

His brother, who was also a fairly senior officer, by this time in captivity, volunteered to convince him of the hopelessness of his situation if he was given the opportunity to speak to him.

When it was realised that a submarine telephone cable would probably exist between Jersey and a convenient landfall on the nearest point of the French coast, on the west side of the Cherbourg peninsula, the French telephone authorities were approached and a concrete pill-box type of termination housing was eventually located.

Tests indicated that the cable was healthy, and my unit was instructed to try to make contact with Jersey at 15-minute intervals, and given basic guidance in French and German on suitable responses if anybody should answer.

Since it was lovely May weather and we had a super bit of beach to ourselves, the duty was a very pleasant one, but unfortunately nobody on Jersey ever did answer the phone, and it was a few more days before the German surrender on the Channel Islands.

I have often wondered what might have happened if we had made contact. A colleague who was on holiday on Jersey about ten years ago came across a paperback in a bookshop about wartime in Jersey which referred to this attempt at contact, but I'm still waiting for Hollywood to phone and offer me a part in the film of the story!

Archie Gill.

Just a few days later, I found myself in Paris, as part of a bigger story – the celebrations marking the end of the war in Europe. Paris showed mercifully few signs of war damage, and I felt very fortunate to be there on that historic day and to see and take part in some unforgettable scenes.

The background was the magnificent wide Avenue des Champs Elysees. The straight section, about one and a half miles long, between the Place de la Concorde and the Arc de Triomphe, was just one huge mass of humanity celebrating the end of the war.

Although wildly demonstrative French civilians made up most of the crowd, many thousands of servicemen from the Allied Forces were also there. We saw General Charles de Gaulle, later to become President of France, marching proudly at the head of the Free French detachment, and Spitfires and other aircraft roaring at low level over the crowds along the length of the Champs Elysees and over the Arc de Triomphe. It felt as if this great thoroughfare had been specially designed just for the occasion.

One particular incident I still recall was seeing Sir Duff Cooper, the British ambassador to France, and his wife, Lady Diana, being driven from their residence just off the Champs Elysees in a highly polished open-topped limousine. Within seconds the whole car had been engulfed by a squad of exuberant American GIs.

I remember feeling sorry for the chauffeur, who must have spent many hours polishing his beloved car, only to see it disappear under numerous American hob-nailed boots.

Sir Duff Cooper, obviously a diplomat, smiled serenely through it all, but it must have been a testing time for the 'Special Relationship', if it existed then!

James MacBeath

FROM WORLD WAR TO COLD WAR

The family of James MacBeath (b. 1926) moved from Lossiemouth to Lancashire just before the war. Now living in Elgin, he recalls that he was in his final year at school when war was declared.

I REMEMBER YOUNG men in the area getting their call-up papers to join the armed forces. A nearby holiday camp was being converted into a POW camp, but this was halted to accommodate troops being evacuated from Dunkirk. I went along to see them arriving by coach, lorry and train; there I met a Seaforth Highlander who I took home to meet my parents for a cup of tea. To their great surprise, he turned out to be Charlie McKenzie, a next door neighbour from Drainie, where I was born, and he and his parents were well remembered by mine.

My older brother Alasdair joined the Border Regiment and then went into the 4th Lincolnshires. He was sent overseas to India and later lost his life in the Burma Campaign. My father became a member of the Home Guard and did other Civil Defence duties, firewatching, etc, while my two sisters joined the NAAFI and were posted to Army camps.

There was not a great deal of air activity in the Morecambe area. There were a few raids by aircraft presumed to be looking for a nearby oil refinery and local harbour, with some bombs falling less than 100 yards from our house, with the resulting casualties and damage. I later discovered that my Sunday school teacher had died in the raid.

There were several youth organisations involved in pre-military service training and I had joined the Sea Cadet Corps, from where I was recruited into the Police Messenger Service where a knowledge of semaphore and ownership of a bicycle were essential. This involved signalling and carrying messages in the event of the breakdown of communications after an air raid, and you got to march with the police in the numerous parades that were held with the other forces. Morecambe and the local area were used as a training area for the Army and the RAF and many of the boarding houses were used as billets.

James MacBeath.

Later, when I went to register for military service my friend, who had accompanied me, was marked down to be a Bevan Boy in the coalmines while I, with fingers crossed and a feeling of relief, was recruited for the Royal Navy, where I had general training in North Wales, and further training as a radar operator in Glasgow.

After training I joined a rescue ship for duty in North Atlantic convoys. The convoys were generally escorted half way across the Atlantic by the Royal Navy then picked up by escorts from the Royal Canadian Navy. The purpose of these rescue ships was to pick up seamen from stricken ships and give medical aid. Each rescue ship had a doctor, sick berth attendants and a small operating theatre; they would also attend to severe accidents and sickness throughout the convoy. Although during my crossings no ships were lost, this was due mostly to the speed of the convoy and the vigilance of the escorts. We had some near fatal accidents in the convoy, such as one seaman being crushed in a hydraulic door, and transfers had to be made by a small launch, sometimes in mountainous seas and gale force winds. Not the ideal doctor's practice!

The war in Europe ended when I was in Halifax, Nova Scotia, where the local council had decided on a 'dry' celebration. The locals thought otherwise and they forced open a government-run liquor store. After much parading and celebrating we returned home to the Clyde.

Radar sets had been put on such ships as Troopers and fast Merchantmen that could travel at faster speeds than convoys would allow. These sets were the property of the Admiralty and were still considered to be secret and could therefore only be operated by naval personnel. On returning to the Clyde, and after a short period, I joined a merchant ship bound for the South Atlantic and spent five or six months cruising up and down the South American coast where lights were bright, shops were full, steaks were large and there was no rationing. Football matches were arranged against such teams as Santos (no Pele), which was to become major players in Brazilian football. A fitting end to my war I thought.

Following this I was posted to a Polish destroyer which had managed to escape from Poland to Britain at the beginning of the war. At the end of the war the original crew chose to stay in the west, but the Polish Navy wished to have the ship returned and sent an inspection team, which included a political Commissar. We were warned of this man's presence and told to keep personal lockers locked. However, while the crew were on the upper deck, he slipped below decks and opened some of the lockers – he was looking for information on the Polish crew and where they had dispersed to.

I was eventually demobbed in 1947.

David Thomson

A SMALL BOY'S MEMORY

In May 1945, just days after VE-Day, an RAF Wellington on a test flight crashed into four houses in Church Street, Lossiemouth, killing eight civilians, including a young mother and her four sons, and the crew of three. Although only a small boy at the time, David Thomson, now living in Duffus, remembers the day.

I WAS STILL only four years of age, but recall clearly walking down to the crash site early that afternoon, with my father and older brother. The firemen had just begun to take bodies out of the burning building. I remember the gasps and cries of women onlookers as the charred bodies were carried out on stretchers.

Horrified crowds turned out to see the tragic scene at Lossiemouth when bombs were dropped on neighbouring houses.
The Northern Scot.

Five family members and three RAF crewmen were killed in the resulting fire. A plaque now marks the spot, and one of the family member survivors recently visited the town to pay her respects.

The picture shown in *The Northern Scot*, (*reprinted here*) may have been taken the following day. My reasons for thinking that are that the roof has totally gone, and there is no sign of the aircraft. When we arrived at the scene, much of the roof was still intact, and the tail of the aeroplane was sticking up out of the roof where it had plunged into the house.

THE MORAY SPIFIRE

WHAT ELSE WERE Moray people up to during the war?

In 1940 communities throughout the Britain were asked to contribute towards the purchase of extra Spitfires for the RAF, and Moray rallied to the cause with many fund raising activities in the autumn of 1940.

They produced the necessary £5,000 for one of the famous fighters and, in recognition of the county's efforts a Spitfire was named 'Moray' and a plaque commemorating the event still hangs in the editor's office of *The Northern Scot*.

The Mk VB Spitfire W3773 took the name when it left the factory at Castle Bromwich on August 22, 1941. On September 7, it was flown to Hornchurch where it joined 54 Squadron. Ten days later it saw action for the first – and last - time.

The pilot was Sqd Ldr 'Fanny' Orton, who already had at least 17 kills to his credit.

The operation was one of the 'Circus' type where the Spitfires protected Blenheims attacking factories at Lens and Bethune in France.

During the attack the British planes were set upon by ME 109s and in the confused fighting which followed Sqd Ldr Orton was shot down. No trace of the pilot or plane has ever been found but another pilot saw a ME109 being shot down by the Squadron Leader.

'Moray's' life was short – a mere nine flying hours – but even that brief life was sufficient to strike a blow against the enemy and the people of the county of Moray could be justly proud of their very own Spitfire.

ADDENDUM

Jim Hughes

PER ARDUA AD ASTRA IN MORAY

IN THE LATE 1930s, the Government decided that many more airfields would have to be built to accommodate the increasing air force.

Flat land fit for flying was at a premium around the North-east coast of Scotland – except in Moray which also had an exceptional fog free climate. Government inspectors viewing the area in 1937 decided that two large airfields could be built at Kinloss and Lossiemouth, with provision for smaller airfields at Bogs of Mayne and Balnageith (Forres). The January 29, 1938 edition of *The Northern Scot* claims that four fighting squadrons would be based at Kinloss, but by March 1938 the same paper was stating that only landing strips would be constructed. Obviously a lack of official information started these rumours.

The survey work was completed at the end of 1937 and 375 acres, bounded by the Kinloss/Burghead and Kinloss/Findhorn roads, were earmarked for an airfield. Four farms were involved: Kinloss Home Farm, Easter Langcot, Doon Park and Muirton. On January 21, 1938, the owners and tenants of these farms received written notice to leave.

As the Kinloss area was supposed to be one of the best barley growing areas in Scotland, the farmers would not have been too pleased when ordered to move out. Yet there are no records of any protests or petitions, and the farmers appear to have left their homes with little objection. We do not know what compensation these people got but, with the run down state of farming in the '30s, moving out was probably the best option.

The farms on the actual airfield site at Kinloss were mostly thatched cottages with huddles of outbuildings which were soon demolished; along with the boundaries around the fields which were mostly wire fencing. Traction engines appeared along with strange earth moving equipment, but a lot of the work at that period would have been done by labourers.

Some of the larger houses were retained by the RAF for their own use. These included Kinloss House, which was owned by Cardhu Distillery, and Langcot House belonging to a Mr Matheson. Apparently Langcot House (now the CO's residence) was first occupied by Borstal boys enlisted in the army who were supposed to have done a lot of damage to the building.

After the area was cleared and drains constructed, the workmen of the Aberdeen firm involved were paid off until contracts were concluded for the actual buildings. Kinloss had originally been planned on the standard permanent building plans of most RAF stations of that period. However, with war approaching, plans were changed. Permanent hangars were erected but the rest of the accommodation was to consist of wooden huts which, though supposedly of only a temporary nature, were still in use 30 years later.

The first wooden huts were constructed by the firm of Coulsons (Glasgow), while Whites (Edinburgh) built the hangars. The blister hangars on the North side of the airfield were covered by grass turf as camouflage but this was a problem due to the sandy soil. Part of the roof of one of these hangars collapsed during its erection.

Satellite Airfields

While Kinloss station was being constructed the same preparations were being carried out at Lossiemouth. 550 acres were appropriated from the farms at Newlands, Coulard Bank, Greens, Smithfield, and Kinneddar. The area was more sandy and bare than Kinloss so less disruption was caused to the occupiers. Also during this period, land at Balnageith (Forres) and Bogs of Mayne was being prepared for what would be satellite airfields for Kinloss and Lossiemouth. Farther afield an airfield was laid out at Brackla' Distillery in Nairnshire.

14 Flying Training School (FTS) Kinloss opened officially on April 1, 1939, with a strength of 38 officers, 53 airmen and 13 civilians, plus a pupil population of 62 officers and 34 airmen. A

month later, on May 1, RAF Lossiemouth was opened as 15 Flying Training School FTS. The Commanding Officer Gpt Capt Maitland met his first four officers in the Steamboat Hotel and was supposed to have commented that his new command was a bit top heavy. However by June he had 16 officers and 122 other ranks. The first aircraft, 13 Oxfords and 5 Harts, also arrived though there seems to be no record of the actual first landing.

RAF Kinloss from the air – a picture taken by the Luftwaffe.

The first landing at Kinloss was recorded as Oxford N 4584, piloted by Flt Lt Widdowson, which touched down on May 9, 1939. Other different aircraft were to be added to the strength of both stations during the next year. As well as Oxfords and Harts these included Harvards, notorious for their rasping engine sound - even worse than present day Tucanos.

The attitudes of the residents of Forres, Elgin and the surrounding area to the influx of first civilian workers, and then what was to be thousands of airmen, was generally favourable. After years of depression and unemployment the prospect of new jobs was very welcome and new customers were a godsend to the local shops and hotels.

What were the reactions of the many airmen who were now based in Moray? A posting to Scotland must have been seen as a voyage to outer space. Expecting snow and gales, the balmy spring of Moray in 1939 would have been a welcome surprise.

The majority of the airmen would have travelled up from London by train; changing at Aviemore in the early hours for the trip over the Dava Moor to Forres, and then a further trip to the railway station of Kinloss. If they were lucky they would have been met by trucks, but often it was a case of hitching up one's kitbag and staggering down to the camp main gate.

The Lossiemouth airmen may have come by Aberdeen, stopping at Elgin for the train to Lossiemouth. The last mile would likely be a foot slog. If they were lucky, some airmen would have been allocated new huts but often they ended up in old huts, left filthy and damaged by former occupants. Accommodation seems to have been a problem right from the start and various hotels and houses in the vicinity were commandeered for billets. These included Burgie Distillery where the prospects of the odd dram probably made up for the many rats and mice - plus the cold water washing facilities.

In October 1939, 32 WAAFS arrived at Kinloss and this number was increased to 85 in February 1940. In those days before female emancipation, billeting the girls as far as possible from the men appeared to be the aim of the RAF authorities. With this in mind, they were housed in Culbin Sands Hotel. However after reports of wild parties in this establishment, the WAAFS were all moved to Seapark House in Kinloss where a WAAF camp was established and remained for the rest of the war.

Due to the chaos in 1940, the RAF seemed to be in a constant state of flux. Almost overnight the flying training schools at Kinloss and Lossiemouth were moved down south and replaced by 19 Operational Training Unit flying Whitleys from Kinloss, and 20 OTU flying Wellingtons from Lossiemouth.

At the same time large Maintenance Units for receiving, servicing and dispatching aircraft, were established at Kinloss and Lossiemouth. The MUs processed many different aircraft types and very soon space for parking became a problem. More local fields were commandeered, but apparently the Ministry of Agriculture objected strongly to this use of good agricultural land. Eventually satellite landing grounds for aircraft storage were established at Leanach, (Culloden), Blackstand (Black Isle) and Dornoch and Kirkton on the Dornoch Firth.

Dragons' Teeth

1940 saw a huge build up of aircraft and manpower at Kinloss, Lossiemouth, Bogs of Mayne and Forres. With the threat of invasion during the summer, defence of the airfields became of extreme importance. Barbed wire, defence posts and anti-aircraft guns surrounded the camps. A lot of these defences were manned by army personnel, but the RAF were now being trained in ground defence; a skill they sadly lacked during the retreat from France earlier in the year. These defence duties combined with aircraft work proved an excessive work load for the ordinary airman, only partly alleviated by the formation of the RAF Regiment in 1941.

During the invasion trees were cut down and embedded in concrete on the Findhorn beaches. Briggs contractors built concrete 'dragons' teeth' which had to be increased in height by nine inches when they were found to be too low for the tide. Most of these concrete blocks are still in existence. Poles for stopping gliders were erected in open fields and some of these were sawn down for timber by local salmon fishermen.

A lot of the work on these defences was done by local labour but many more workers from all over the UK and Ireland arrived for what were well-paid jobs. Civilian tradesmen were employed on the MUs which also had detachments of the Air Transport Auxiliary for transporting aircraft to and from the squadrons. This added to the huge mixture from all parts of the Commonwealth which on the face of it seemed a recipe for conflict with the locals. Strangely enough little friction between incomers and locals has been reported. Fights did occur between the RAF and the many army regiments stationed in the local area. To solve this problem an RAF SNCO and six airmen would patrol Forres and Elgin on Saturday nights to ensure airmen returned to their camps safely.

In those early days of the war airmen had little time for recreation and at Kinloss spare time was mostly spent at the NAAFI, or a well-loved Church of Scotland canteen situated on the Kinloss/Burghead road. When a rare 36-hour pass (Sat 12:00 to Sun 23:59) was granted, some airmen might venture as far as Inverness, but Elgin and Forres were their favourite haunts.

Cinemas, dance halls, pubs and hotels did a roaring trade despite the archaic Scottish licensing hours. The Sunday 'bona fide' travelling rule meant crowds of airmen wending their way between the two towns. The many 'chippies' had huge queues of all ranks for this popular fare when the pubs shut at 9:30pm. At the end of the evening the Moray roads would be packed with returning airmen. The lucky ones might hitch a lift in a lorry but most walked, staggered, or used station bikes often 'stolen' and usually without lights. The road casualties were still smaller than the present day.

Food has always come high in the priorities of fighting men. The RAF mess food depended largely on the skill of the cooks and was often awful and usually mediocre. Fortunately this could be augmented in the many local cafes with egg and chips for about the equivalent of 6p. Rationing in a rural area like Moray was never as drastic as further south. Many lonely airmen were invited to local homes where they got acquainted with the famous Scots high teas.

An Embarrassing Incident

The strength of the RAF in Moray built up throughout the war. Milltown was constructed from a Q site and operated Liberators from 1943. Airfields were opened at Banff and Dallachy in 1943. After a year of flying training they became Strike Wings flying Mosquitoes from Banff and Beaufighters from Dallachy on anti-shipping strikes in Norwegian waters. There were also smaller units operating wireless and radar at various places throughout the area.

Perhaps the oddest was the Oakwood Tea Rooms outside Elgin: used as a billet for aircrew in 1941 and referred to as RAF Oakwood by P/O Hodgson in his book, *Letters from a Bomber Pilot*.

With the building of concrete runways at Lossiemouth and Kinloss in 1942, both airfields became important as forward bases for bombing attacks on Norway and boltholes for returning bombers when their home bases down south were fogbound.

RAF Lossiemouth, a picture taken from the air by the Luftwaffe.

Unfortunately aircraft crashes became the major source of casualties in Moray throughout the war. A combination of worn out aircraft, inexperienced crews, mountainous terrain and bad weather was a recipe for disaster. Many of these aircraft simply disappeared over the sea but most crashed in inaccessible spots in the Highlands where bodies and debris were often salvaged in terrible conditions by the salvage crews from 56 MU RAF Longman Inverness.

Only three crashes were recorded in urban areas. A Whitley crashed, killing all the crew, in Forres in November, 1940; and just after the war in May, 1945, a Wellington crashed in Seatown,

Lossiemouth, killing its crew. The worst wartime crash occurred a week later when a Wellington crashed into buildings in Lossiemouth killing three crew and eight civilians.

One crash which has since become famous was a Wellington from Lossiemouth which on New Year's Eve 1940 ended up in Loch Ness. In 1985 this plane was salvaged in remarkably good condition and now resides in the Brooklands Museum. In April 1942 Halifax W1048 flying from Kinloss on a bombing raid on the Tirpitz crash landed on a frozen lake in Norway. When the ice thawed the plane sank to the bottom of the lake, but in 1973 it was salvaged by an RAF team and is now part of a display in the RAF Museum at Hendon.

A more embarrassing incident happened in October 1943 when an Anson landed on the top of a Whitley taking off from Forres. The only casualty was the crew's pride.

Most of the debris was removed from the crash sites but local youngsters were able to liberate many small items and a steady trade of swapping souvenirs soon started. Probably some of these souvenirs still exist in local garden sheds.

Moray was to play host to airmen from many different countries. Aircrew from Canada, Australia and New Zealand were trained at the OTUs. There were Canadian, Australian and New Zealand squadrons at Dallachy, and Banff had a Norwegian squadron. In 1944 Free French airmen trained at Lossiemouth.

On May 7, 1945, it was announced that the war in Europe had ended. On May 8 all the RAF stations ceased flying and held parades, sports and parties, some of which lasted all night. The OTU at Kinloss was disbanded with any remaining trainees finishing at Lossiemouth, which closed later. Personnel got ready to move down south and it is reported that the CO at Kinloss signed over aircraft, buildings, equipment and a chest full of money to his replacement, all on a Saturday afternoon before having a huge farewell party. Milltown, Dallachy, Banff, Elgin and Forres were soon closed but Kinloss and Lossiemouth carried on under new management to become, in 40 years, two of the largest RAF airfields in the UK. Kinloss was supposed to be taken over by the Navy but this move was changed to Lossiemouth. One can only wonder what difference the original decision would have made.

The war years had seen Moray evolve from a small farming and fishing community to the thriving area it is today. Men and women from many nationalities, through their service locally in the RAF, grew so fond of the community that they settled here.

Jim Hughes

GERMAN AIR ACTIVITY OVER MORAY

THE SIX RAF airfields in Moray did not receive much attention from German aircraft in World War II, despite the fact that these were large training stations which were also used extensively as forward bases for air attacks on Norway.

In the early years of the war most large RAF bases built dummy landing strips outside the main airfields. These camps, fitted with landing lights, were supposed to attract enemy aircraft away from the main bases. How effective this deception was has never really been proved. Early in the war one of these Q sites was developed for Kinloss at Roseisle and one for Lossiemouth at Milltown. There are no reports of enemy aircraft attacking either site and the one at Roseisle was soon abandoned while that at Milltown was developed into a proper airfield.

The Kinloss Operation Record Book contains eight references to enemy activity in the area between 1941 and 1944, while Lossiemouth mentioned six incidents. Some of these reports mention the type of aircraft but that is unlikely to be accurate considering the height they flew at and unreliable recognition. Since the end of the war captured German archives contain aerial photos of the area, which show that some activity had not been noticed by the RAF as the dates do not coincide with the relevant ORBs.

One of these photos has quite an astonishing history. During the chaos of the German retreat in France in late 1944 a young RAF airman found a batch of aerial photos in a burned out German bunker. Seeing they were of Scottish airfields they were 'liberated' and brought back to Scotland. A copy now hangs in the Kinloss Officers' Mess.

One photo taken in Sept 1942 shows an airfield under construction. This is Milltown airfield which the Germans referred to as Stonewells, which is the name of an adjoining farm.

On September 10, 1940, enemy aircraft were reported to have dropped bombs on waste ground two miles from Lossiemouth. On October 11, 1940, Sgt Jeff Pryor was the trainee rear gunner on a Wellington flying out from Lossiemouth. He saw what he first thought of as a Blenheim approaching his aircraft from the rear, but suddenly, realizing it was a Junkers 88, he opened fire and the enemy aircraft dived into the sea. This is supposed to be the only record of an enemy aircraft being destroyed by a gunner under training. Sgt Prior later gained his commission but sadly was killed in action over Germany later in the war.

A few weeks later on the evening of October 26, 1940, Lossiemouth airfield had its first and only air raid. At that time Blenheims of 21 and 57 Squadrons were operating out of Lossiemouth attacking Norwegian bases. Their aircraft were lined up being serviced and refuelled when at 18:27 three Heinkel llls attacked at low level with bombs and machine guns. One Heinkil crashed, either shot down by anti-aircraft fire or blown up by its own bomb. Two Blenheims were destroyed and three damaged. Damage was also done to two Magisters, two Moths and a Hurricane. Damage to hangars is still visible over 60 years later. Unfortunately one officer and two airmen were killed and others injured, but as an air raid it was not a great success. No Moray airfields were ever attacked again.

Throughout the war the whole of the North-east of Scotland suffered from nuisance air attacks when single enemy aircraft nipped in quickly over the coast and dropped bombs at random. On July 12, 1941, one of these nuisance raiders dropped four bombs on the town of Lossiemouth, killing four and injuring eight civilians. Some of the casualties had moved to Lossiemouth to escape the bombing down south.

The last incident of German air activity over Moray occurred on the night of June 21, 1944, when a Junkers 188 crashed near Rothes killing all four crew. As the aircraft did not burn it is believed some important radar equipment was salvaged from the wreckage.

On the whole the Moray airfields escaped lightly from German air activity. Its airfields were able to produce thousands of trained aircrew in comparatively peaceful air space, and they were also invaluable as forward bases for attacks on German occupied Norway.